MARY S. PALMER

GEORGE WALLACE: AN ENIGMA

*THE COMPLEX LIFE OF ALABAMA'S MOST
DIVISIVE AND CONTROVERSIAL GOVERNOR*

MARY S. PALMER

MARY S. PALMER

An Intellect Publishing Book

Copyright 2016 Mary S. Palmer

ISBN: 978-1-945190-02-5

Cover design and artwork by Michael Ilacqua
www.cyber-theorist.com

Proofreader
Ellie Lockett

Logo Design:
Anne Kent Rush

Cover Artwork
Michael Ilacqua

First Edition: 2016
V37PDF

Visit the website: **www.GeorgeWallaceBook.com**

Intellect Publishing, LLC
6581 County Road 32, Suite 1744
Point Clear, AL 36564
www.IntellectPublishing.com
Inquiries to: info@IntellectPublishing.com

DEDICATION

*To my husband, Buddy Palmer,
who patiently proofread this book
over and over and over.*

ACKNOWLEDGEMENTS

Many thanks to all the people who helped make this book a reality, especially Dr. Dan McDonald, James White, Dr. James Dorrill, Jimmy Faulkner, Catherine McLain, Betty Smilie, C. Terry Cline, Jr., Pat Guidry, Ellie Lockett, Meredith McDonough, Carol Ellis, Jack Schluter, Judge William McDermott, TJL and any others who contributed.

FROM THE PUBLISHER

This was a difficult decision to make: should I publish this book or not?

The question is complex and important. To many people, Wallace represents all that is criticized about the American South, including isolationism and racism. Even today, some idolize Wallace and use his demagoguery as a rallying point to perpetrate stereotyped, negative relations between whites and people of color.

Author Palmer's account, extensively researched and footnoted, paints a multi-dimensional portrait of this infamous man -- one that documents his politics of rage, while simultaneously presenting behind the scenes accounts of Wallace facing the divisiveness and darkness he created.

In today's inflammatory political discourse, many point to Wallace as the source for their prejudices and actions. This biography reveals that those who continue to embrace his early stance as an ideal, as a confirmation of their misguided beliefs, are basing their idolization on a phantom; for George C. Wallace, after an assassination attempt, came to realize that the ideas he espoused, and the vitriolic discourse that ensued from it, were wrong, and even un-Christian. Although this recognition does not balance out the negative he was responsible for, it does show that in his later years, he came to personal realizations that will surprise many.

For these reasons, I have chosen to publish this book, in the hopes that friends and enemies alike come to understand that Wallace is not the leader of those who espouse hatred and racism -- that the views they hold, and Wallace once held, he ultimately rejected.

It is further hoped that Wallace's journey into more enlightened beliefs could ultimately encourage people to be less xenophobic and more inclusive in their thoughts and deeds; that Wallace's spiritual transformation confirms that even the most hostile and divisive of us can evolve. Rather than bow down to divisiveness, we may stand tall, open our hearts, and seek to heal our communities.

John O'Melveny Woods

Publisher

AUTHOR INTRODUCTION

If books received awards for the amount of time they took to write, this book would get one.

It was begun in 1973 and underwent revisions, though not continuously, until 2015.

In *As You Like It*, William Shakespeare made reference to the seven ages of man. This biography also went through ages—ages of progress, ages of setbacks. Often, it seemed as if it had a life of its own and would only be finished when it wanted to be.

In the first place, even the way it began was different. I never had any intention of writing a biography. What happened was that, as a newspaper reporter, I covered Hurricane Camille. When it missed my hometown of Mobile, Alabama, and plowed into the Mississippi Gulf Coast on August 17, 1969, I went with a team of reporters to survey the damage. What I saw and experienced led me to attempt to fulfill a lifelong dream and write a mystery novel, centering it around the storm.

In an effort to get that mystery story published, I found a publishing house in New Orleans and made an appointment to show the editor my work. After a short two-and-a-half hour drive, I marched into his office, confident that I had a chance of becoming a published author.

He glanced at my work, said, "You can write," and shoved my year's labor aside. "Would you be interested in doing a biography on George Wallace?" he asked.

I was caught off guard, but a "Yes" popped out of my mouth. I was interested in writing any book that could be publishable.

They gave me a tape recorder, two-thousand sheets of typing paper and credit to charge other supplies.

I began, not really realizing how much work would be involved. But if I was going to do it, I was going to do it right. I immediately made contacts to set up interviews with Wallace supporters and staff, plus his adversaries, moving in a radius from Mobile to Montgomery, from local people to members of Wallace's cabinet to members of his family and his opponents. I wanted my biography to be objective. I managed to get materials that were primary sources and only one of a kind, such as letters and other first-hand information, and a collection of photographs. Soon, I was sending the publisher lists of everything I'd gathered and copies of interviews—at first monthly, then weekly. He liked what he received and was elated at my progress.

Six months into my research, though, the walls of security of publication crashed. The publishing company that gave me the assignment went out of business. What to do? *Stop* wasn't on my agenda. So, I just kept writing, and interviewing, and praying. As one contact led to another, I found myself in Mississippi, Florida, North Carolina, and even in Silver Spring, Maryland, where I talked to Dr. Joseph Schanno, Wallace's doctor in Holy Cross Hospital after the assassination attempt.

I had some help with my writing, too. Catherine McLain, a Doubleday author from Camp Hill, Alabama, edited my work by mail. She taught me a lot. I was discontented with my use of material, though, so I made contact with Professor John Craig Stewart at the University of South Alabama, thinking his creative writing courses might be helpful. His response didn't encourage me much. "It'll take a year of courses," he said. I wasn't sure, but I think he meant "to get this in shape." So, I didn't pursue writing courses—not then.

Instead, I found another publishing company in New Orleans and the editor showed a great interest in my biography. After six months, however, I couldn't get a definite answer regarding their acceptance. I finally found out what the problem was—the editor and the publisher were brothers—but while the editor wanted my book, the publisher didn't—stalemate. Worse yet, when I asked for return of the manuscript, I got only half of it, and not all of the hundred and ten photographs I'd accumulated. It took a couple of phone calls and mild threats, but I finally recovered everything.

Obsessed with getting this biography published, I took another course of action. I asked a local author, Terry Cline, to recommend me to his agent. He did and J. Garon-Brook was interested. Another bite. Fate wasn't on my side, though. Three weeks after I mailed my manuscript to him, he telephoned me saying that he had editors waiting to read it, but he hadn't received it. Although it was clearly addressed "To" and "From" in the proper places, it was returned to me. Garon-Brook finally got it, liked it, and tried to market it. Somehow, though, it just didn't sell. Timing may, or may not, have been a factor, but I guess I'll always believe that it was.

Next, in the fall of 1978, I decided to take the year Stewart said would be necessary and study writing. Funny thing, though, when I returned to college at the University of South Alabama, I almost completed my B.A. in English before I made any effort to take creative writing courses. In fact, in two and a half years, I hadn't even seen Mr. Stewart.

Two quarters before I completed my undergraduate degree, I signed up for Stewart's course. The first day I attended his class, I was ready to read my thriller entitled *Mascot*. I was convinced that he'd like it because a New York agent, Harvey Klinger, had thought it worthy enough to submit to ABC for a TV movie. Mr. Stewart didn't like it at all. In fact, his criticism was so harsh that another student followed me into the hall, saying, "Don't be discouraged."

Actually, I wasn't. I have a tough skin—a requirement for writers. Anyway, one month later Mr. Stewart told me I'd improved greatly. Six months later, I got approval to do my Wallace biography as an M.A thesis. The help I got then was fantastic! Dr. James Dorrill, Dr. Dan McDonald, and James White (Stewart's replacement when he retired) all spent months editing my work.

After my thesis was finished, approved, and on the University of South Alabama's library shelves, my work still wasn't done. In order to turn it into a popular biography, I revised the entire manuscript one more time.

Then, with a five-sentence query letter, I got a new agent, Mitch Douglas of International Creative Management. He didn't sell my book either; yet, it did stir some interest. A Putnam editor had a bittersweet reply. "I really like Mary S. Palmer's writing," she wrote. "I just wish she'd chosen another topic."

In 1976, I traveled to North Carolina with a group campaigning for Wallace in his last presidential bid. Wallace was in his last term as governor and he still had support, but he wasn't hot news. The timing for this book just wasn't right.

In 1984, when an M.A. in English with a concentration in creative writing was offered at the University of South Alabama, I was the first person to receive that particular degree. I didn't intend to, but the following year, in 1985, I went to work at Faulkner State Junior College (now Faulkner State Community College) as an English instructor. I liked being a member of the adjunct faculty; it gave me more inspiration to write. I co-authored and published a book entitled *MemoraMOBILEia: Alabama Gulf Coast Potpourri* with Elizabeth Coffman, Ph.D., taught English courses including creative writing, and put George C. Wallace aside.

Early in 1995, I saw a news report on the newly established Lurleen Wallace Foundation and decided that the time might be right to interview George Wallace again, update my book, and get publication of *Keep On Keeping On: The Story of George Wallace*. Like George Wallace, despite discouragements, I followed the advice of that title and kept on keeping on.

Since March, 1995, I have made numerous trips to Montgomery, conducting research with over fifty hours of interviews with Wallace and his aides, plus members of the museum staff. Adding three chapters and an Afterword, I brought the book up to present time.

Whether this book gets any awards is really unimportant. It wasn't written for that reason. Hopefully, though, the research material—photographs, tapes of interviews, memorabilia, and information unavailable elsewhere—will be preserved for posterity and readers will make their own appraisals of this man who was an enigma.

Then, this long labor of love will be justified.

Mary S. Palmer
Mobile, Alabama, 2016

CONTENTS

FROM THE PUBLISHER:
AUTHOR INTRODUCTION:

CHAPTERS:

1.	Clio	3
2.	One of Them	17
3.	Spinal Meningitis and Army Service	25
4.	A Handshake and a Smile	39
5.	The Fighting Little Judge	51
6.	"Park Your Car in the Back, George"	61
7.	"Segregation Now, Segregation Tomorrow, and Segregation Forever"	69
8.	A King, Not a Kingmaker	91
9.	Fifty Long Miles	107
10.	A Wonderful Woman	115
11.	The Dollar Bill Campaign	131
12.	A Day Off	161
13.	The Man Who Is	165
14.	The Second Mrs. Wallace	171
15.	The Thrill of the Chase	175
16	"George, Hey George! Look Over Here"	181
17.	Blood-Splattered Asphalt	191
18.	From Montgomery to Montgomery	199
19.	A Step Back	205
20.	Respect for the Presidency	221
21.	Style and Philosophy	225
22.	Running up the Fifty Capitol Steps	231
23.	Still the Same George C.	237

24. Making More Marks.................................. 245
25. Hitting the Road Again............................. 255
26. Once More 'Round the Block.................... 261
27. A Tip of the Scales.................................... 267
28. A Dime's Worth of Difference.................. 271
29. The Last Hurrah... 279
30. Keep On... 293
31. Keeping On.. 303

LAST WORD FROM WALLACE 315
THE AUTHOR - 319
REFERENCES 321

MARY S. PALMER

GEORGE WALLACE:
AN ENIGMA

*THE COMPLEX LIFE OF ALABAMA'S MOST
DIVISIVE AND CONTROVERSIAL GOVERNOR*

MARY S. PALMER

CHAPTER ONE

CLIO

On the southwest side of Montgomery is a house that George Wallace bought for Lurleen. It is a modest one-story red brick home with a small but neatly kept lawn. When the Wallace family lived there, neighbors knew that garbage cans put out on Tuesdays and Fridays might be full of cigar wrappers, but there would not be any empty whiskey bottles in them. George did not spend money on liquor. Nor did he care for a fancy home.

This house has neither an entrance gate nor a swimming pool. And, it is not on an acre of ground. In fact, the distance from Farrar Street to its front door is less than forty feet. The houses on the block-long street are comfortable, middle-class dwellings in a quiet but unpretentious neighborhood. Most people would never expect one of them to belong to a governor. However, Wallace's friends and associates are not surprised that George once lived here. At any rate, he didn't buy another house to impress anyone; his current home on Fitzgerald Street is no more pretentious than the Farrar Street one was. A roof over his head seemed to satisfy George Wallace.

But George never intended to live in the little cottage on Farrar Street long. Chances are, if Lurleen had not pushed him, George would not have bought a house of any size. Why did he need one? He planned to, and did, occupy the governor's

3

mansion a long, long time.

In the governor's office across town, when George Wallace gave an interview, he became intense. Though some facts he elaborated on differed from time to time, the oft-repeated scene is vivid.

His brown-leather executive chair has been shoved aside to make room for his wheelchair. A highly polished mahogany table reflects his furrowed brow as he thinks back to his childhood. He taps the ashes from a cigar held between the first two fingers of his right hand into an octangular ashtray. And slipping his left hand under the right side of his coat, he presses under his ribs. Leaning forward, he reminisces about a big wish he had when he was a boy. One lip curls slightly upward, exposing a few straight teeth. His widely spaced brown eyes sparkle as he pushes a strand of slicked-back hair, worn in the same style since he was a schoolboy, off his forehead. He shifts to the left in his chair. His enthusiasm seems to melt away the years. The Southern accent becomes more pronounced as he says, "I have seen the times when I would look in the Sears-Roebuck catalog and be unable to get something I wanted very badly."

He begins to tell about a cowboy suit that he wanted when he was four years old. He and his brothers had a make-believe ranch where they played cowboys and Indians by the pecan grove near their home in Clio (pronounced Kly-o), Alabama. At night, George would pull out the Sears catalog, put it down on the floor and turn to item number 40L3374 which showed a boy wearing a "complete cowboy outfit." The advertisement stated that it was made of "Good Weight Khaki Material" and "Includes hat, shirt and long pants, bandana handkerchief, belt, toy pistol, holster and lasso. Nickel plated spangles." It was listed at a dollar and eighty-nine cents, too expensive for the Wallaces.

There were two other boys in the Wallace family: Gerald, two years old and Jack, one. His father, George, Sr., owned four hundred acres of farmland outside of Clio. He suffered from Brill's Fever and never pushed a plow—all his farming was done by sharecroppers. But it was difficult for his tenants to raise enough corn, cotton and peanuts to make the venture profitable for themselves and their landlord. So, Mozelle, George's mother, taught neighborhood children piano to supplement the family income. Whatever money they had needed to be handled wisely. The cowboy suit was one of the non-essentials out of reach.

George was born in Clio, a sleepy town tucked away in the wiregrass section of Southeast Alabama. Older and newer homes faced Highway 29 with back roads jutting off into the farmland. Today, the route to town has a few abandoned stores, but the population has not changed. It stays right around a thousand.

It was a big event when George Corley Wallace was born in the early morning hours of August 25, 1919. A neighbor, Lucy French, who had introduced Mozelle to George Wallace, was there as an observer. She remembered taking the newborn into her arms and cuddling him. When he became famous, it pleased her to brag that she was the first person to kiss George Wallace.

Ella Hartzog, a white maid, was hired to help George's mother Mozelle. Soon, though, Mozelle had other help with George. His grandfather, Dr. George Oscar Wallace, lived next door and had his office in the front room of his house. From the time George was about three years old, on cold winter mornings, Mozelle would bundle him up in a sweater and his only jacket and he would sit on the front steps waiting for his grandfather. The old man would lift the little boy into his buggy, give the horses a lick and off they would go. "C'mon,

Dr. Franpa," George would say, "Let's go see the sick folks."

Before long, everywhere Dr. Wallace went, the little boy trailed along. From the age of five, George became exposed to patients who were seriously ill—from adults with chronic bronchitis to children with terminal leukemia. Everyone in Clio knew "little George C."

Living in a small town, where everyone knows his neighbor's business and secrets are hard to keep, helped George develop a sense of reality about people that most city-bred youngsters never understand. The protective shield of aloofness prevalent in urban areas reduces the chances of such close personal relationships. George C. didn't have those barriers. He may not have known a large number of people but those he knew, he knew intimately.

The Wallace home was modest, but comfortable. As governor, when George talked of his early life, he spoke with great sincerity. His eyes always brightened and often were fixed on the American Flag to the right of his desk. The importance of his childhood days showed on his face as the memory of such times came to life.

#

He folds his right hand over a left fist and shoves them both up under his chin. Then he begins recalling the past. "Being poor was not so terrible. I wouldn't say that I've ever been in a position where I was not able to eat. It so happened that my father was a farmer in the Depression. We were poor, like all people were poor in the South in the twenties and thirties as a result of the aftermath of the War Between the States. You know, our region came back on its own. We had occupation and no Lend Lease and no Marshall Aid, and we had vengeance and reconstruction. Many generations suffered because of this."

His bottom lip pushes upward and the cleft in his chin becomes more pronounced. "We had a lack of industry, the discriminatory freight rates (the South had higher freight rates supposedly because they had less freight to offer) and matters that we could not overcome at the time but did eventually overcome. Our people were proud people like all Southerners, but they were poor." He sticks his chin upward and runs a hand through his hair. "Having farmed, we were always able to raise something to eat. Our society was not as urban as it is now in that more people lived rural. While there was a great lack of money in the Depression, we were always able to eat. I think that was true of most rural people during those years. We didn't feel sorry for ourselves and blame our plight on anybody and want to destroy anything. We just all prayed for a better day and worked harder. And the truly great epoch in American history is the comeback of the people of our region to the position we now occupy. I'm talking about economically and industrially."

Removing his glasses, he wipes them with a clean, white-cotton handkerchief. Then he continues. "My family were good people and wanted us to go to school and learn how to make a living and not be dependent. My father felt that way although he died at an early age. My mother went to work when he died in 1937 and had worked for thirty years when she retired. I was the oldest—eighteen. I would attribute our drive and push to the fact that my family wanted us to accomplish something and pointed out the necessity of doing something and not remaining status quo."

After his father's untimely death at age forty, George began to worry about his own health. Sometimes a case of sniffles would cause him to moan, "I think I'm getting pneumonia." And, although rain never bothered him before, he started wearing a raincoat in bad weather.

Even though he was away at college when George, Sr., died, George often wrote Mozelle suggesting ways to settle Jack and Gerald's squabbles. During the summer break, he sat under the big oak in the front yard with his brothers telling them, "You got to get a college education if you want to amount to anything nowadays, y'hear?" His younger sister, Marianne, would sidle up and lean on his shoulder and he would pull her down into his lap and smooth back her silky blonde hair. The Wallace siblings were close.

His mother and father always saw to it that other youngsters felt welcome in their home. They encouraged neighborhood children to play in their yard and they asked them about their schoolwork as they fed them cookies and Kool-Aid. They kept a close watch on them, too. One day when George was ten his mother heard loud screaming outside. Dropping the dishtowel she'd been using, she threw back the screened front door, dashed across the wooden porch, and leapt down the three porch steps. Nothing bad was wrong, though. Her relief turned into dismay, however, when she discovered that George, Sr., had built George a boxing ring in the only available space—right in the middle of her flower bed. About fifteen neighborhood children were stomping on her zinnias. George and a friend had charged them a penny admission to watch the boxing match they were having.

After putting the fifteen cents he collected into a Mason jar, George straddled a kitchen chair and watched silently while Mozelle set the kitchen table with mismatched plates, odd knives and forks, and clear glass bowls gotten as Crystal Oats premiums. "Mother," he said, running his left thumb over a chip on the rim of the solid white dinner plate in front of him, "tomorrow, I'm gonna take that fifteen cents and buy you some dishes all alike."

George also recalled humid August evenings when his parents sat on the front steps watching him and his brothers kicking a football around. And he remembered his sister Marianne, thirteen years his junior, tugging at his sleeve and begging him to play hide-and-seek. Sometimes he granted her wish; other times, he'd sit down by his father and talk about politics instead. Now he feels that those chats helped direct him and that his father's involvement in politics led him into a political career. "I think I was interested in government from the time I was interested in anything," he said. "My father was chairman of our local county commission when he died—he was forty. Even in junior high school, I thought about running for the legislature of the state when I finished college." George seemed to want to take up where his father left off.

In Barbour County High School, George was very popular. He constantly had a group of his peers hanging around him. He was always the leader and always talking. Physically, he might have been looked down on since many boys his age were much taller than he was, but neither that nor a lack of monetary advantages deflated his ego. Both apparently added to his momentum. He strutted around the schoolyard as if he were six-feet tall, cock-of-the-walk. Besides, as captain of the football team and president of the twenty-three- member senior class of 1937, he was the Big Man on Campus.

Whatever he started, he finished. Mildred Laird, an old friend from Clio, said George was compulsive. "He wouldn't leave things undone. He felt obligated to finish a task once started," she said. She recalled George sitting around the wood stove at Rosa Rush's Market arguing with men twice his age about the merits of the university system and never being intimidated by them. At ten p.m., when Rosa closed the store, George would plead, "Just give us five minutes longer," waving his spread-open hand in her direction." Mildred smiled.

"He hated to leave before he won over his audience."

Though segregation was in vogue, particularly in the South, Clio had its own form of integration. The small town didn't have much in the form of entertainment. Other than participating in sports, teenagers had to make their own ways of having fun. When they tired of playing on the baseball diamond behind the Wallace homestead, they'd go to the Quarters and play ball with the blacks for a change of pace. George and his brothers would be right in there with the group. Nobody gave that phase of integration a second thought.

George became interested in boxing and worked at it. He practiced sparring, jabbing and footwork, planning someday to enter the Golden Gloves competition. His friend, W.S. Strickland, worked as a telephone operator in the Telephone Exchange on the second floor across the street from the Wallace home. From his window he could see the Wallace yard and past the big oak tree to the front porch. After six p.m., the phones seldom rang. Since Strickland's job was a little boring, he was pleased when young George called him late evenings asking him to time boxing matches. He had plenty of time to officiate at the fights. They got together and figured a way to work it out. W. S. would ring the Wallace's telephone bell to start and end rounds. W. S. did try to keep it safe, though. He made them promise if the fighting became too rough, they would heed the bell. Evening after evening this went on. As George's skill developed, he took on bigger and better opponents. Two years later, as a hundred-and-eighteen-pound student at the University of Alabama, he won the 1936-37 Golden Gloves Bantamweight Championship.

Nevertheless, his main interest was in politics. His grandfather had served as Probate Judge of Barbour County one term in 1928, and then he returned to being a country doctor. So, George's roots in politics went back two generations.

In 1932, as a spirited thirteen-year-old, George first became involved in a political campaign. He enjoyed going door-to-door soliciting votes for Fred Gibson who was running for Alabama's Secretary of State. Gibson got a majority in Clio, but he lost statewide. Yet, before the race was over, George had a taste of politics, and he liked it.

In 1935, he sought work as a Senate Page. Thirty-five senators had to elect the pages and, from the forty boys applying, only six or seven would be chosen. George's father brought him to Montgomery, introduced him to a couple of senators, and left him on his own to court their votes.

George dug right in. He scurried around the long corridors of the capitol hoping to catch senators as they left their offices. "I'm George C. Wallace from Clio," he'd announce, popping right into their path. "I'd like you to vote for me for Senate Page."

In his first direct contact with politicians, one of the senators young George impressed was Jim Simpson. He became one of George's main supporters and constituents. Taking over as George's promoter, Simpson persuaded other senators to vote for the boy from Clio.

Politics appealed to George even more now. After a week's campaigning, he was successful in obtaining the appointment as a page. When he returned to Clio, nobody there was surprised he'd been selected. They expected it. It only served to intensify their belief he was, "Somebody who wanted to be more than a small-town boy." Right then, he announced that he might run for the legislature someday. Being a page whetted his appetite for a career he already knew he wanted.

George lived in Clio eighteen years. When he left, he told his high school buddies, "When you see my name on the ballot, I want y'all to vote for me, y'hear?"

Time proved they heard.

Old Clio

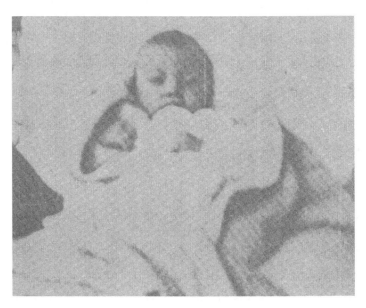

Wallace as a baby

Wallace at about 3 years old

Wallace with his Dad

Wallace in the first grade

Boxing at 15

Wallace in High School

Wallace as Alabama
Senate Page

CHAPTER TWO

ONE OF THEM

In September, 1937, with four twenty-dollar bills in his pocket, George Wallace climbed the steps to the red-brick Administration Building at the University of Alabama. He was wearing the only suit and the one pair of shoes he owned. His cardboard suitcase held three changes of underwear, four pairs of socks, and half-a-dozen white-cotton handkerchiefs. It was light enough to carry in one hand.

The summer had been busy. As a brand-new high school graduate, George sold magazines in North and South Carolina. He and Ralph Adams, a Birmingham Southern student, alternated weeks in making the most sales. George became the youngest crew chief in the bunch. Sometimes they took chickens and vegetables for payment, but it helped feed them, which was as good as cash. Once, when they were hungry, Ralph said, "I got an idea, I'll pawn my razor." With the quarter he got for the straight razor, he bought a meal—roast beef, potatoes and fresh snap beans. He split it with George.

Nights, George picked up extra money boxing. He went to the "smokers," and if the trainer asked, "How old are you, son?" he would stiffen, jut out his chin and answer in the deepest voice he could muster, "I'm twenty-one." Often, he stepped into the ring with men ten years his senior, including some pros. George would dance around with his head cocked to the right and dare his opponent to smash him one. If his arrogance scared them off, fine. If it did not, he was willing to take a few punches to add to his textbook fund. Most of them hurt his ego more than his jaw anyway. It did not pay much, but it helped.

By the middle of September, George went back to Clio. He fanned out a little over a hundred dollars and told Mozelle and his father, "I did it. Look, I've got enough to pay the registration and tuition." George, Sr., slapped him on the back. Mozelle wondered how her son was going to eat and where he was going to live, but she did not ask.

George struck it lucky in the fall. When he told his friend, Ralph Adams, that one way or another he was going to college in September, Ralph came up with an idea that would enable George to live rent-free. "Why don't you go to the University and live in my rooming house?" asked Adams, telling George of the house he had bought with loans from relatives. It was the beginning of a relationship which would span many decades and prove helpful to them both.

Soon George became a partner in helping Adams rent rooms and serve meals. During the bleak days of the Depression, many boarding houses in Tuscaloosa were empty. But George worked hard at keeping every room occupied. He bummed a ride sixty miles to Birmingham, caught students at the railroad station before they boarded trains or buses, and handed them a card with the boardinghouse address. Then he would follow along saying, "We got nice, big rooms and good meals." He would catch up with them again in Tuscaloosa and take them to see the house. Standing back in a bedroom corner, he would spread out his hands. "Look here," he would say. "Look at the size of this room." Something was always cooking. So George was safe in sniffing and asking, "Don't that make ya' hungry? Only eight dollars a month." Not many got away. For every roomer George got, one dollar was taken off his bill. He always managed to live rent-free.

George also had a National Youth Administration job lined up. It paid fifteen dollars a month for fifty hours' work. Working three jobs was not the easiest way to get through college, but when he graduated, he would not owe anybody anything. Although neighbors claim that the Wallace family could have paid for George's education, he refused their help. After he earned his degree, George did not want anybody to feel that they had the right to tell him what to do. He planned to be the one who gave orders.

It did not take George long to meet other students. "In fact," Adams recalls, "a few days after George arrived as a freshman before school started, we got the people in our house to get behind him and he got elected president of the freshman Arts and Sciences Class, the largest class at the University." Adams punctuated his words by tapping his desk with the point of a lead pencil. "It was a tremendous accomplishment since, at that time, George was not affiliated with any organization or fraternity. As a matter of fact, he was elected as an independent over and above the sorority and fraternity candidates who had a 'machine'."

George was a threat. The power structures on campus were in a dither. They did not know what to make of George or how to deal with him. They could not take him into their flock; National Youth Administration rules prohibited his joining a fraternity, and they knew that he was not about to give up that job. They just had to tolerate him. But it irked them. When George walked by with a cigar popped in his mouth, strutting like a miniature tycoon, fraternity brothers, all dressed in three-piece suits, would cluster in a circle. "Look at that," one would say, pointing at George and the dozen colleagues half-a-head taller than he trailing behind. "All country boys like him." But, whether they liked it or not, before long George Wallace had his own clique of fiercely loyal supporters.

When the fraternity members snubbed him, George acted like he did not care. Twenty-five years later, though, when Delta Chi president Dr. Claude Layfield "discovered" records which showed George had pledged Delta Chi at the University of Alabama, George accepted the unanimous invitation of the national board to be initiated into their fraternity.

In college, George stayed busy. During the day, he attended classes, studied, worked at the boarding house, conducted meetings, and planned activities as class president. At night, he would "work out," boxing in the University gym.

One person who went to see him fight was Glen Curlee. He had heard about "a little fellow around who is a terrific boxer" and he wanted to know if it was true. It took only a few minutes for Curlee to see "this guy was tough." He wanted to meet George so he hung around until the practice session ended. Curlee told Wallace that he liked his boxing style and would be back again. George squared his shoulders and said, "Thanks."

Having an audience gave George someone to show-off for. He started going to the gym five minutes earlier and staying until the janitor turned out the lights. Week after week, Curlee watched as George got better and better with his punches. During that time, Wallace and Curlee became fast friends.

In November of George's freshman year, his father died from Brill's Fever. At the time, George did not realize that his father, at forty, was very young to die. Nevertheless, his entire first year of college was blighted by the death. It worried him that mortgage holders foreclosed on the Wallace property. All they had left was the house in Clio. But if George ever considered dropping out of college, he did not say so. Instead, he told his friends who asked if he would have to quit, "My daddy wouldn't want me to do that. He always wanted us to accomplish something and not remain status quo."

His mother took a job as a sewing supervisor for young girls. Marianne, whose birthday was in June, was barely four years old. Jack was fourteen and Gerald was still in high school. It was not easy for Mozelle to rear them alone and keep the family intact.

But George wasn't a burden. He paid his own way. In the summers following his freshman and sophomore years, he worked as a "dog man" for the county. Under the compulsory inoculation law, he inoculated dogs against rabies. In high school, he had been the inspector's assistant one year, and since he had experience, he got the appointment from the County Health Officer. For the job, he received two to three hundred dollars per year above expenses.

George worked hard in his pre-law classes, borrowing Glen Curlee's textbooks because he had none of his own. Curlee joked that "George said he had a law book once, but I never saw it." He borrowed a tux from his classmate, Irving Bergbauer, so that he might attend the free sorority and fraternity dances. But that was the extent of George's social life.

He was much more interested in his studies. In the classrooms, the young men sat side-by-side at double desks. Squinting, George would lean over, read ahead, and be prepared to answer questions. During the ten-minute break between classes, he would dash into his pre-law class, slide into the seat beside Curlee and say, "Quick, gimme your book." Curlee said that George would "read the first case and, if he got called on, he would get up and explain it; if he didn't, then he'd read the second case from his seatmate's book while the first case was being explained."

Curlee recalled, too, that George would come over to his place and "read the whole book at a glance." He said, "George

could remember cases and rulings from September until May."
With a little envy, he added, "While I studied and got a 'C,' he
read it once and got an 'A.' He'd be moaning and groaning,
saying, 'Curlee, there's just no way I can pass,' but he'd
always come out on top."

Once, when Curlee checked the posted grades of a law
class, he saw that George got a 'B.' Glen was so sure that
George had been cheated out of an 'A' he asked the professor
to let him see George's paper. After looking at it, Curlee was
sure his suspicions were justified. He told the professor, "I'm
sure there's been a mistake." The teacher shook his head, "I
couldn't give George an 'A'. It wouldn't be fair to those who
study." Chances are that Curlee never told George what
happened. If he had, it is unlikely that George would have
accepted the professor's reasoning without a fight.

George won the Alabama Bantamweight Boxing
Championship in 1936 and 1937. His friends cheered him on.
But in 1939, as a hundred and twenty-seven pounder, he lost to
a boxer named Jim Mobley of Mississippi State College
fighting in a Southeastern Conference Tournament. Curlee
patted him on the back. "Aw, George, don't worry 'bout that,"
he said. "The referee was way off. Anyhow, that fight didn't
amount to anything. Next time, you'll cream 'em." George
climbed back up. In 1940, as a junior, he was captain of the
squad of Alabama Battlers at the University. They finished
third in the conference standings.

In addition to his boxing, George held office as the
president of the Spirit Committee his senior year. They had to
plan football pep rallies and parades. Then he tried twice for
the presidency of the Cotillion Club and lost. He sloughed the
loss off, claiming, "I really have too much to do to take on
another job anyhow."

After graduating in 1941, he chose to further his career and increase his opportunities in politics by entering law school. He soon became a member of the Law School Honor Court.

He completed college and finished law school in May, 1942. His old friends say that he did not get his diploma until much later—when he could raise the money required to receive that piece of paper.

Wallace in College

Boxing at Alabama

CHAPTER THREE

SPINAL MENINGITIS AND ARMY SERVICE

When he received his LL.B. from the University of Alabama Law school in 1942, George Wallace could not afford to set up a law practice. Before he found a job, one of the ways he survived was by selling some of his clothes and a hundred coat hangers from his closet for four dollars and fifty cents.

George took the first job he could get—driving a dump truck for the State of Alabama in Tuscaloosa. It did not matter that he had never driven a truck like that before. George got around that problem. He found the state prison convict in charge. "Hey, boy," George called to him from across the street. The driver turned and looked at the black-haired man headed in his direction. George walked over, leaned against the door on the driver's side of the truck, and asked the young black man inside, "You wanna make a quarter? How 'bout showing me how to double clutch this truck?" The convict nodded and George slipped in beside him. After a couple of times around the block, George took the steering wheel. Ten minutes later, he hopped out. Making a circle with the thumb and index finger of his right hand, he told the driver, "Thanks. See ya' payday." He paid off the debt when he got his first check. George worked an eleven-and-a-half hour day for thirty cents an hour.

He next got a job as a tool checker at the government aircraft school in Tuscaloosa at higher pay—fifty cents an hour.

"I felt real lucky," he said later. "I got a pay increase of twenty cents an hour and worked inside, to boot."

In October, 1942, he met Lurleen Burns who would become his first wife. At sixteen years old, she had graduated from high school and had taken a business course but she was working as a clerk in Woolworth's. George shopped there. As a truck driver, he went where he could get the most for his money.

That fall, George was in and out of the dime store almost daily. Even though state vehicles were not for personal use, the State of Alabama dump truck would be parked out front. George had no other means of transportation. He used the truck to court his sweetheart. Later, it was said the first order he put out after he became governor was that no one could use state vehicles for personal business.

On October 20, 1942, George was sworn in as a private in the Army Air Corps Reserve.

While he waited to be called up, he continued to live in Adams' boarding house. Adams was off in the service and had turned everything over to him. George managed to keep the rooming house full, but he failed to collect the rent. Then men left for the service, and the few remaining stragglers living there refused to pay. So, George had the utilities cut off. He said later, "I was not going to let Adams' property be lived in by people who would not pay the rent when they were able to."

Closing the house meant that he did not have a place to live. Glen Curlee invited him over to spend the night, offering to let George sleep in his bed. "No, no," George insisted. "Just throw a blanket on the floor for me." The overnight stay turned into a six-month visit. Glen said that before long "George got so spoiled he complained of the accommodations and we had to get a bed instead of his pallet on the floor."

26

In 1943, George was called into the Army Air Corps for Cadet training. He took basic training in Miami Beach. In order to get the pilots needed at the height of the war, the U.S. Army Air Corps lowered their standards. Requirements were not as stiff as they had been. They took in cadets and trained them rigorously, beginning at Miami Beach where all the hotels were taken over by the military.

To regiment the men and prepare them for active duty, the carpets were cut out and the elevators were shut off. George Wallace had to climb stairs and get down on his hands and knees and scrub floors.

The academic work was tough, too. One of the men, Albert Johnston, said, "We crammed four years of college into five months, going from simple arithmetic to spherical trig. And they were bringing pilots into the Air Corps at a rate of ten thousand at a time, and whether you had, or didn't have, a college education, you went through this course. They called it 'raising your I.Q.' It was something to do with those of us who had college," said Johnston.

The Southerners in the group had to tolerate one other thing. Northerners insulted them by implying if they had not gone to Yale or Harvard, they "had not been to college." Wallace shrugged his shoulders or responded with a snort to such remarks. Sometimes he let them enjoy their superior attitude by acting the part of an uneducated redneck.

Johnston remembered one incident particularly about Wallace. "In the barracks, there'd be five-hundred men trying to shave and we had somewhere in the neighborhood of seventy-five lavatories," he said. "Of course, we had to line up and wait our turn. George had come down and was in the midst of shaving when I came in. He hollered at me and said, 'Al, I just found out why the whole world's afraid of Switzerland.'

"I figured it was some kind of joke and I took the bait and

said, 'Yeah, George, why in the world are they?' He told me his uncle wrote him a letter and he had just received it and it told him why people were all afraid of Switzerland and he said, 'Oh, yeah! Russia's afraid; Germany's afraid; China's afraid; England's afraid; even the United States is afraid of Switzerland. Nobody ever jumped on Switzerland. They never did get in the war.'

"By that time I was ready for him to get to the point and I said, 'George, my God! Why is everybody afraid of Switzerland?' And everybody's ears were plucked up. They could hear us talking across the rows of men. Then George turned around, looking like a country bumpkin, and said his uncle wrote and told him Switzerland had 'the largest underground Navy in the world.' Oh, you could hear the razors falling into the lavatories and all that. By that time, George was through and he just eased out.

"Of course, I was still there. They believed Southerners were rather stupid and I almost got into a fight. They crowded around, trying to convince me there wasn't any such thing as an underground Navy and I was telling them, 'Hell, I don't think so either,' all the time knowing they didn't quite believe I knew better. Out of the corner of my eye, I could see George walking out, laughing." George had pulled two jokes—one on the men, the other on his friend left looking like a fool.

George was shipped to Ouachita College in Arkadelphia, Arkansas. The 67th Cadet Training Group, of which George was a member, was the first group to be stationed there. There were two-hundred and fifty men from each area, almost too perfect a balance to be mere coincidence. It appeared to the men that the Air Force was integrating the North with the South. But even if integration was the purpose, the men from the same areas segregated themselves. Those from Mississippi, Louisiana and Alabama clung together. And in that relatively small group Albert Johnston from Carthage, Mississippi, and George Wallace from Clio, Alabama, became close friends.

Members of their Cadet group rented a house and established a club called the 67 Club. They put in a juke box and the men and their wives spent weekends decorating it. Mr. and Mrs. Clark Sanders who lived nearby brought sandwiches to the gatherings. She would help scrub floors while her husband painted the walls and fixed leaky faucets. For many of the young couples, it was their first time away from home, and they missed their families tremendously. The young cadets welcomed the attention of Wynnie Dea Sanders and her husband. And they enjoyed the dances and barbecues at the club. Mrs. Sanders became known to the 67 Club as "Mom" and she called them all her "boys." The off-campus club became a home away from home where the homesick were comforted and those with domestic troubles could be counseled.

George Wallace and Mom Sanders met March 1, 1943. He must have impressed her because she wrote of him twenty-four years later, "Among the cadets was a skinny little fellow, chewing a pencil-size cheroot cigar, with the brownest eyes in the world."

George was lonely, and when he would come into the clubhouse and tell her, "I had another argument with my history professor today about government—that man just can't understand states' rights," Mom had no way of knowing where it would all lead.

One day, quite suddenly, right in the middle of the training period, George had a much more serious need for the aid of Mom Sanders. After he had flown a Cub ten hours, he "fell out on campus." No one knew what was wrong. Mom Sanders took him to the Base Hospital where a young captain, fresh out of medical school, checked his temperature. It shot up to a hundred and six.

Medical facilities at the base were limited. They were equipped to care for broken arms or colds, but this problem was beyond them. They packed George in ice, but before they determined exactly what the illness was, he grew worse. Getting him to the Army-Navy Hospital at Hot Springs fifty miles away was imperative. It turned out to be spinal meningitis. The immediate fear was of brain damage.

It was difficult to get George accepted as a patient in the hospital at Hot Springs. Although this was an isolated case of meningitis at Ouachita, nationwide, Army bases had many such cases and the hospitals were crowded. But Mom would not be put off. She got on the phone and insisted, "This boy needs help. You can't just let him die. You've got to take him." The Army doctor kept telling them they had no room. Finally, at her insistence, they agreed to admit George, and he was transferred to Hot Springs where he received proper treatment. He had to stay in the hospital several weeks, however. Following this, he had a recuperative furlough and was able to go home to Tuscaloosa on thirty days' leave.

But when George got there, he just could not be still. The first Glen Curlee knew of George's return was when he and a friend were leaving a building in downtown Tuscaloosa. All of a sudden, his friend grabbed his elbow and pointed to the corner. "Look! There's George C.," he said. "He's supposed to be in bed."

Curlee darted down the steps and caught up with George, offering, "Ill fix up your old bed."

George declined. "No, I'm fixin' to get married," he said. "That's the best way to stay home—get married." He had returned to Tuscaloosa with a purpose in mind.

George and Lurleen were married in May of 1943 in a simple ceremony. It was the middle of World War II. An Air

Corps private drawing about twenty-five dollars a month marrying a dime store clerk was lucky to have any money. Wallace said later, "We picked our old friend, Adolph Foster, a justice of the peace, to perform the ceremony 'cause we wanted him to have the dollar we could pay."

George and Lurleen went back to Arkadelphia and spent their honeymoon in the home of Mr. and Mrs. Sanders. The newlyweds had a small apartment and Mom took Lurleen under her wing. Later, she explained her concern for the teenaged bride: "Imagine your own sixteen-year-old daughter, or granddaughter, in a like circumstance, and you will know how my heart and love went out to her. She didn't miss many days being in our home, and she helped me can fruit and vegetables, wash dishes, cook, sweep, mop and do just about everything there was to do in a home. When I protested, she got around me with this: 'I've got to live in a small town all my life, and I need to know how to do all these things.'" Mom Sanders was a good teacher, and Lurleen learned her lessons well. She also had to learn how to economize.

On a serviceman's pay they had to skimp to get by, and Lurleen did not have many clothes. Robert Rapier used to joke about it later, telling Paul Tardy, "I don't remember George, but I remember that cute little green dress he carried around with him that had Lurleen in it."

Since he was married, George did not try to get back into cadet training. He was transferred to San Antonio, then to Amarillo to Aircraft Mechanics School. Mom knew that George and Lurleen were leaving and she rented their apartment. Then Lurleen could not go with George because his check had not arrived. She moved in with Mrs. Sanders' foster daughter, June Lee, until his check caught up and she could follow her husband. Soon, Lurleen joined George in Amarillo and got a job as a clerk in a clothing store.

Nothing was fancy. Lurleen lived downtown. George was in school during the day, and worked at the Army Ordnance Plant stacking TNT on his day off and at night. Lurleen did not get much of his attention. Most of her days and nights were spent cleaning the apartment, fixing meals and reading—alone.

When he graduated, George was sent to Denver to attend Flight Engineers School, and Lurleen, who was pregnant, went back to her parents' home. At the time, Henry and Estelle Burns were living in Mobile, Alabama, where Mr. Burns was working as a crane operator in a shipyard. In October, 1944, Lurleen Wallace gave birth to their first child, Bobbi Jo, at Brookley Air Force Base hospital.

George was still in Denver. Over a year had passed since he had been critically ill. One day, he and Al Johnston bumped into each other at Lowery Field. Al said, "Gosh, George, it's good to see you, I didn't know what happened to you." Al thought that George looked all right. "At that point," he said, "I became convinced George was going to make it. I could see that he was snapping out of it and working like hell to do it. He was working to get his personality back. He was not the same jovial kid I knew back at C.T.D. His mind was good but he wasn't as friendly, not as outgoing and a little more subdued. Before, he was full of mischief." Johnston said that he got that impression because he could not get a response when he began rehashing George's joke about Switzerland's "underground Navy."

It disturbed him when George solemnly nodded and said, "Yeah." But, even if George seemed to lack some of his keen sense of humor, Al was glad to know that the brain damage they feared had not occurred.

From Denver, George was sent to Alamogordo, New Mexico. Lurleen rejoined him with their new baby. It was only for a short time, but they wanted to be together for the few days before he went overseas.

There was a problem. Housing was at a premium. Everything available was rented, even trailers, tents, or anything people could possibly live in. The three Wallaces spent one forty-degree night sleeping on a front porch with the baby nestled between them. They finally ended up in a converted chicken house with concrete floors. It had been cleaned up and fumigated, but it was a one-room affair with no bath. They had to use the bathroom inside the main house. The only cooking equipment was a hot plate. But they considered the chicken house a luxurious accommodation compared to what many had at the time.

As primitive as their living conditions were, this time may have been the happiest of Lurleen and George Wallace's entire married life. They were together, and George's ambitions had been put on "hold." He cooed at the baby and the three of them ate meals together as a family. George sat beside Lurleen and held her hand while she told him about Bobbi Jo's birth. With only minor outside influences to concern him, for once, George gave Lurleen and the baby his attention.

After he finished his training, George was made sergeant as a B29 flight engineer, operating engine control and the other electrical functions of the aircraft. In Topeka, his crew collected their airplane, *The Sentimental Journey*, then went to Sacramento to receive their overseas assignment. They went to the Aleutian Islands, landed in Hawaii, were stationed in Saipan, then Tinian with the 20th Air Force, 58th Wing 468 Bomb Group, 795th Squadron.

His crew flew ten missions over Japan, coming back with spent anti-aircraft flak marks on their plane. After flying a mission on Air Force Day (August 5), they found that they had been chosen to train for the merit position of lead crew. The selection was made on the basis of record and percentage of strikes on the primary target and other factors. *The Sentimental Journey* did not lose one of their eleven-member crew.

On August 6, 1945, Hiroshima was bombed. Three days later, Nagasaki. The crew was sent back to the U.S. They landed in California on August 13, 1945. The next day the war was over. George Wallace went to Mobile to see his family. But the night the end of the war was celebrated, he stayed home. He said, "I was real lucky to get back from the war safely. I didn't want to go downtown in the middle of that celebrating crowd and get hit on the head with a brick." Recalling his father's untimely death, George did what he could to avoid the same fate.

George Wallace had a scar from his hitch in the Army. Working near engine test blocks caused him to become hard of hearing. Instead of letting this interfere with his plans, he later made it work for his own benefit. During campaigns, when he wanted extra time to consider newsmen's questions, he used the defense as a ploy. Cutting his eyes sideways, he would cup his hand behind his right ear and ask, "What's that? I didn't quite hear you."

His discharge would not be processed until December. He went to Muroc Lake, California, and was hospitalized for combat fatigue. After spending several weeks there, he was discharged December 8, 1945, with a ten-percent disability for what he termed "residuals of spinal meningitis." Once again he returned to Mobile. Then George hitchhiked alone to Montgomery to see Governor Chauncey Sparks about a job. They needed an assistant in the Attorney General's office, a position for which George was qualified. He had no trouble getting the position. At last, he had a chance to use the law degree for which he had worked so hard. At a salary of a hundred and seventy-five dollars a month, he moved to Montgomery. Lurleen went to work at J.C. Penney.

But living accommodations were still scarce. To solve the problem, George went to see Mrs. Metcalfe. "Remember me?" he asked when she opened the door.

"Well, I declare," she said. "George Wallace."

George threw his arms around her. He had not seen her since he boarded there when he and her son were both senate pages. But that did not matter. "I got me a wife and baby and a job in the Attorney General's office," he bragged. Squinting, he took both her hands, "I know you rent mostly to railroad men, but could you put me and Lurleen up—just for a while 'til we get settled?" She opened her mouth, but George rattled on. "Lurleen'll keep the baby quiet."

Mrs. Metcalfe's shoulders relaxed and she laughed, "Oh, George. You always had a way with me. All right."

Mrs. Metcalfe soon grew fond of Lurleen and the baby, but she seldom saw George. He spent most of his days and nights at the office. As Assistant Attorney General, George wrote briefs on criminal appeals and informal opinions on questions propounded by officials in the state. George worked hard and learned from every case. He served in that capacity from January to the middle of March, then took leave to run for the legislature from Barbour County, hoping to go on to bigger and better things.

That was when two-hundred Christmas cards George sent began to pay off.

Wallace's Plane

Wallace with Crew and Plane

Wallace in Uniform

Wallace with
Lurleen and
baby
1940s

First Apartment

CHAPTER FOUR

A HANDSHAKE AND A SMILE

The Christmas when George was in the Pacific fighting the war, he sent Christmas cards to everybody he knew in Barbour County. Some read the greetings and were surprised to see his sprawling signature. They were pleased and flattered that George remembered them. When he came back and put his name in the pot as a legislator from Barbour County, he hoped the name "Wallace" would be familiar. George was determined to win.

In March of 1946, on a three-month leave of absence from the Assistant Attorney General's position, he started campaigning for the Democratic primary.

George had developed an ability to remember names and faces and he knew many of the twenty-eight thousand, eight-hundred and ninety-two Barbour County citizens. People felt important when he asked personal questions like, "Did Uncle Bob get over his bout with the flu?" and "Whatever happened to cousin Maybelle who sold her beauty shop and moved down to Magnolia Springs?"

George had the full support of Governor Sparks. He was grateful to have the governor as his advisor and confidant. From the beginning of the race, George was extremely optimistic. He had no doubt that he would beat his two opponents, Ernest Norton and Colvin Caudell. Nevertheless, he kept on tromping down the dirt farm roads of Louisville,

Bakerhill, Brundidge, and Clio, pumping the hands of everyone he could get to come to the door or catch out in the field plowing.

Leaning over a barbed-wire fence, George would yell out to a farmer, "Hi, I'm George Wallace, live right over in Clio. Got a minute?" By then, the man would be curious enough to head in his direction. "I'm running for the legislature," George would begin, "and I'm gonna get your children some trade schools to go to. Say," he would interrupt himself, "Aren't you Winn Martin's cousin?" By the time they shook hands, George Wallace had another avid supporter. By May, he had finally reached eighty percent of the voters in Barbour County. And he told them all what he planned to do as a legislator.

During the trying college years, George became convinced that not everybody should go to college. He saw a way to improve conditions for middle and lower class citizens by establishing trade schools. Back in the late thirties and early forties, he and Glen Curlee had many discussions about the need for trade and technical schools. "We would see so many individuals in colleges taking courses that just weren't their cup of tea," recalls Curlee. "We saw the futility of this especially in the case of one young man. That guy, who was extremely talented in taking a radio apart and putting it back together again, was in college, following in his father's footsteps, trying to be a lawyer." George had worked hard at using his own abilities to achieve goals. He hated to see waste, especially in the form of unused talent.

George and Glen felt then that people were usually better off pursuing their own interests. They began to make plans to provide the education necessary to enable young men and women to enter technical fields. "We realized the time was coming when there would be a need for skilled people working with their hands," Curlee said. He recalls that even then

George was thinking about how to carry out those plans. That year, 1946, was the right time for this type of platform. The people responded with support for Wallace.

On May 10, 1946, *The Clayton Record* gave the following results for Legislative Place Number Two:

Colvin E. Claudell	134
E.W. Norton	833
George C. Wallace	1,585

Being the last name on the ticket had not hurt George one bit. In the run-off, George beat Norton and prepared to take his place in the Legislature of the State of Alabama.

George did not get his wife's vote. Although she was married and had a baby, Lurleen Burns Wallace was only nineteen years old. But she had done her part. Lurleen had taken care of the baby, put out the garbage and paid the bills all those months while her husband was running around the state. But nobody clapped for Lurleen when the election results came in.

George had not won by chance. It had taken a lot of hard work and well-laid plans. During the campaign, he had let it be known that he had sold subscriptions to *The Clayton Record* back in college. "I didn't do it for the money," he said. "I did it because it's my favorite paper." Most Barbour Countians agreed with George's view. He got the support of the periodical and its editor, William Lee Gammell.

Another factor played a part, too. As a candidate, Wallace's appeal to Barbour County inhabitants lay in the fact that he had held up to them the hope of a better life. And the lifestyle he proposed suited their unsophisticated ideas. He talked of trade schools and two-year colleges. In a populist farm community, residents could more readily see the need for technical schools and junior colleges than for expensive expansions of state facilities which did not touch their lives.

When George stood on the courthouse steps and told a gathering, "The people working with their hands create the wealth. The people who drive the nails, the plumbers and electricians who build the buildings enable industry to come to Alabama, or any other state," and of schools that would be closer to home and not as expensive as universities, they felt that he understood. Maybe George really would do something for them.

After winning the primary in May, George had no Republican opposition in the general election. He returned to his job in the Attorney General's office for the rest of the year. George began his term as a legislator in January, 1947.

At that time, the salary for a legislator was eighteen dollars a day, including expense money, when the legislature was in session. They met every two years for about five months, plus one or two special sessions that lasted a couple of months. The total pay for a two-year term amounted to approximately three-thousand dollars. It was not enough to live on, so George and Lurleen rented an upstairs apartment in Clayton, and he opened a law office. During legislative sessions, they took a room across the street from the Jefferson Davis Hotel.

Eddie Anderson, a black porter who had worked at the hotel since 1930, recalled that "George ate at the boarding house, too, but he got his mail here so people wouldn't know where he was living. George would always holler at me. I consider him a personal friend." Then, scratching his gray hair, he added, "There's more good about him than bad."

In Clayton, the Wallace's lived a quiet, small-town life. Lurleen took part in church plays, and George taught Sunday School at the Clayton Methodist Church. Jere Beasley (later Lieutenant Governor of Alabama) was one of his students. "We'd get unruly at times," Beasley said. "Then George would point to me and say, 'Let me tell you about the time my plane,

The Sentimental Journey, almost went down. Those Japs were coming at us...' and on he'd go with his World War II story. Those wide-eyed fifth and sixth graders would slide over to the edge of their seats," Beasley recalled. "I guess he picked on me because he knew me best. My mother ran a grocery store five houses down the street from the Wallace's. And I used to tote groceries to their house every other day."

Charlie Weston, who had been a member of the House of Representatives from 1939 to 1943 under Governor Frank Dixon's administration, knew that Lurleen did without to help George reach his goals. "When Lurleen went to town to shop," he said, "she'd be wearing a cotton dress so thin you could almost see through it. They were dirt poor."

Five-foot-two Lurleen, who weighed less than a hundred and fifteen pounds, did not count on clothes to make her glamorous or enhance her appearance. She was neat, but not beautiful. She wore her brown, shoulder-length hair brushed back in a page-boy fashion. And Lurleen preferred simple, straight-line dresses in blue, green or beige cotton over flowery, silk designer patterns with gathered skirts. Flashiness did not suit her taste or style.

Other things, however, concerned Lurleen more than clothes, especially her children's future. She wanted the best for them. But could George provide it? Lurleen, serious and sensible, knew that no matter what, her husband was going to pursue his political goals. It would be up to her to ensure stability in the family.

Weston urged Lurleen to "...make George take out an insurance policy to pay for the children's education because he'll never have any money." His assessment of the situation was likely to be true. George was already putting everything he could into a fund for his next venture into politics.

In 1948, George met Billy Watson, who was to have a

tremendous impact on his political future. Watson was about twenty years older than George—old enough to project a father image. He could provide the counsel and approval lacking in George's life since his father's death. He did not always sympathize with George, nor did he give in to him. He was gruff talking and seldom complimentary, quite unlike George's contemporaries Glen Curlee and Ralph Adams. George kept himself psyched up, but he still looked for a pat on the back from his friends, particularly after a successful speech.

Watson could not be counted on to give praise. It took more than talk to impress this hardened old warhorse. Billy had been in the political arena almost twenty years, and had seen the workings of many a campaign, including one of Governor Sparks'. Although he had never held public office, he had taken an active part in several campaigns and had been interested in politics all of his adult life. He took a special liking to the young lawyer from Clayton and followed his early political career closely. He saw that George followed up his speeches with actions. With a father-like pride, he watched while George pursued his goals.

Watson saw that George's eagerness and enthusiasm were contagious. During legislative sessions, George ran back and forth from the house to the senate, cornering fellow legislators and senators. He would tell them, "I want you to support me on this, y'hear?" First, he would go to lawmakers he knew, but the older, more influential politicians did not frighten him with their seniority. Sooner or later, he got to all of them. In the house chambers, he would get on the floor and push. "We need more payrolls in Alabama," he would shout, pulling the mike down to his level. "Folks here want a way to make a decent living. This Industrial Act is needed." He would slam his fist on the podium and speed up his speech so other legislators could not interrupt. With such action he was often successful in wearing down objections to the bills he proposed.

George was a workaholic who seldom relaxed. But in the evenings, he would sometimes go to the Elite (pronounced E-light) Restaurant at 129 Montgomery Street, within a mile of the Capitol. The Elite had been there since 1911. It had the usual hanging baskets of fern scattered around the dining room. Triple A rated, it offered some gourmet dishes like Shrimp St. Jacques and Crabmeat au Gratin, but its only real distinction was that all the politicians gathered there.

George would bounce in, glance around to find the table where his friends were sitting, and drag up a chair. "Gimme a hamburger, hon," he would tell the waitress, "Lotsa ketchup." But when it arrived, George would be so engrossed in the discussion of "the Anti-Lottery Bill," or his pet project, "the Wallace Industrial Act" that he hardly knew what he ate.

Most of his political cronies drank highballs. But George always had a plain Coke. Then he was so busy making points about his Industrial Act that the Coke got watery. When he absent-mindedly took a sip, he would push out both lips, shove the glass to his right, and grip the shoulder of the man next to him. Sometimes it was Governor Folsom. Turning and looking straight into Folsom's eyes, he would say to the governor, "Jim, I sure hope you can help me get this through the legislature."

With the support of Governor Jim Folsom, the Wallace Industrial Act passed and it brought new industry to Alabama, resulting in millions of dollars in payrolls for the state. The standard of living immediately rose in Alabama, and along with it, the prestige of George C. Wallace. Senior representatives and legislators began to take a closer look at the young legislator with the dark hair and deep-set eyes. His height and slight build were deceiving. They found out in a hurry that he was not afraid to stand up to them.

The Wallace Industrial Act helped label George a progressive. The bill was innovative in that it allowed the floating of municipal bonds to build industrial plants and equip them for the purpose of getting new industry and business to the community. This was quite an unusual thing, and a far-reaching measure. Since its adoption, hundreds of new companies located in Alabama, including the Armour Plant, the International Paper Company and ninety-eight other industries.

Different bills sponsored by Wallace—the Anti-Lottery Bill, the Highway Responsibility Law, the Natural Gas District Act, the Alabama G.I. and Dependents Scholarship Act, and an act bringing Social Security protection to city and county employees—also helped provide better living conditions for Alabamians. At the same time, Wallace led innumerable fights for vocational rehabilitation, mental hospitals, old age pensions, tuberculosis control, and education.

During Governor Jim Folsom's administration, new people began to come into Wallace's life. One of those was Albert Patterson of Phenix City. He was a member of the state senate, an experienced politician. He recognized the potential of George Wallace when they first met. Even though George looked young, he was soon considered one of the floor leaders of the administration and, as such, persuaded Patterson to co-sponsor a Trade School Bill he had authored. The dreams that George Wallace and Glen Curlee had talked about over late-night cups of coffee at the University of Alabama were about to come true.

In 1948, George Wallace became known as a southern spokesman. It happened during the National Convention in Philadelphia where the Democratic Party split over the issue of civil rights. Eleven Alabama delegates walked out and formed the States' Rights Party.

Jimmy Faulkner, a state senator from Bay Minette, Alabama, and George Wallace were two of the thirteen Democratic delegates who stayed and fought on the Convention floor trying to nominate a candidate more acceptable to the South. It did not work.

In spite of strong opposition from many groups of his party, Truman was re-nominated and later re-elected.

Integrationists abhorred the position of Wallace. George took a different stand. He was proud of his achievements in government and of his attempts to preserve what he called, "the way of life of the South." If this meant segregation forever, it was all right with him. Even then, he continuously maintained that he was misunderstood. Wallace insisted he was not against citizens because of their color. Big government interference was what he claimed he objected to.

Meanwhile, Lurleen sat home. She had heard legislators' wives whispering about George's escapades with other women. And she knew that he had the nickname "Peter." She did not like it at all. Lurleen was extremely jealous. But she had little chance to do anything about it. Even when George was in Clayton, he did not stay home. When they were together, Lurleen tried to tell George, "I'm so tired of being alone."

"Well, you're not really alone," he would reply. "You have the children and your mother's around a lot to help."

Her brown eyes would begin flashing and she would snap at him, "Look, you're not fooling me. While I'm raising the children by myself, you're up there in Montgomery running around."

He would lash back, "Well, maybe if you'd come up there more..." Then he would soften. Holding out his arms, he would say, "Oh, I didn't mean that. C'mon over here, sugar." For a while things would be all right.

Lurleen tried hard to please George. In 1949, while she

was pregnant with her second child, she went to Montgomery to attend social functions. But things did not change much. When they went to a party, as soon as they got in the door, George would wander off with Jimmy Faulkner or Albert Patterson. Standing in the corner with a half-empty punch cup in her hand, Lurleen could hear George say, "Yeah, Jimmy, we got that G.I. Bill through, didn't we?" Then he would slap Faulkner on the back and move over to the opposite side of the room without even glancing in his wife's direction.

In January of 1950, Peggy Sue Wallace was born at Salter's Hospital in Eufaula, Alabama. George and former Governor Chaucey Sparks hopped into a car and rushed there as soon as they got the news that Lurleen was in labor, but they did not arrive in time for the birth. George checked on his wife, shook hands with the doctor and the nurses, and took a look at the baby. Then he got right back to politics. Lurleen consoled herself with the fact that George's work was important to many people. What he did was far-reaching and affected more than just the four members of the Wallace family.

The same year, he won re-election in the primary. After winning the general election, he returned to Montgomery to his seat in the legislature.

Their only son, George, Jr., was born in October, 1951. This time George beat the race with the stork. But he did not spend much time with his family. The father of three had to get on with the business of politicking. After six years of ramming through every bill possible, he felt that he had done about as much as he could in the legislature. Besides, he had another excuse for wanting to progress. His growing family needed food, clothing and shelter and Wallace said, "I need a higher-paying job to support them." Foremost in his mind, though, was the desire to move ahead politically. Lurleen and the children could manage without him. After all, they always had.

In 1952, he ran for judge of the Third Judicial Circuit comprising three counties—Barbour, Bullock and Dale. If he was elected to the judgeship, he would receive an annual salary of eight thousand five-hundred dollars. That would help. George justified indulging his ambitions by telling himself the increased income benefited his family. But the main consideration was that he would have a position of greater control in the State of Alabama.

People back in Montgomery were taking a hard look at the young politician who stood up to members of the National Party. Later, after George was elected Governor, the 1963 Inaugural Book explained what their reactions were: "The fomenters of integration and excessive federal power first felt the punches of the Barbour County fighter...though he was regarded by national boss politicians in the throne room as a country boy come to town...they became increasingly wary of the little delegate as he refused to stay off his feet and characteristically challenged every proposal and bulldogged every asterisk of the infamous Civil Rights plank.

"Refusing to be pushed out of his delegate seat and out of the Convention, Wallace forced recognition of the nomination of Senator Richard Russell, a loyal Southerner, for president. After prolonged speechmaking, marshaling of forces, and pure political battling, the powers wrangled the nomination down, only to look up and find the same Wallace, on his feet again, nominating Senator Richard Russell for vice president."

There was no doubt about it: George Wallace was becoming known.

MARY S. PALMER

CHAPTER FIVE

THE FIGHTING LITTLE JUDGE

As the incumbent, Preston Clayton had the edge in the 1952 race for judge of the Third Judicial Circuit. The town was named for the Clayton family. Preston's father had been President of the University of Alabama, and later a Congressman. Clayton traditionally supported members of its founding families to keep the power within their own ranks. Winn Martin, President of Clayton Banking Company, as did many of the old, established citizens, wanted Clayton to stay in office and planned to back him.

This was the second time Martin was unable to support George. In the 1946 legislative race, Martin had told George Wallace he would have to support his opponent, Ernest Norton, an attorney for Clayton Banking Company.He remembers, "That didn't bother George. He'd still come and tell me things, or ask for advice. There was no resentment, or if there was, he didn't show it."

And now, six years later, he again had to tell George that he could not vote for him, but would be obligated to vote for Preston. "George didn't get mad, really," Martin said with a shrug. "He was a good sport. I admired that, even if I couldn't support him."

Martin's response certainly came as no surprise. But George was shrewd enough to wait until he got in the back room to spout out, "Old fool. Clayton'll never change long as he's around." He knew how politics worked in a small town. He kept trying, nevertheless, to win over the old-timers, confidently telling his supporters, "Don't worry, now, ya' hear? I've beaten die-hard politicians before."

Claytonites watched the progress of George Wallace with interest. Charlie Weston noticed early in the campaign that at local activities, "People gathered around George, not Clayton." He recalls, too, that while Preston was receiving few contributions, "They were coming in daily for George in amounts of one to twenty dollars." Weston felt that people were beginning to see Wallace as a winner, and they wanted to get on the bandwagon.

George thrived on publicity and personal approval. Often, after a speech, he would turn to Weston and ask, "How did I sound? Did it go all right? Did they like me?" The more applause, the better he liked it.

George won the position of the Third Judicial Circuit Judgeship. In 1953, he vacated his seat in the legislature to take his place on the bench. His district included Barbour, Bullock and Dale Counties. Being a judge was just another stepping stone. He used the position cautiously and kept local customs, oftentimes outspokenly defending them. Claytonites were proud of their choice when George said, "I don't feel right sitting in judgment without a prayer first."

They nodded and solemnly bragged, "I voted for that man."

His rulings were traditional, and he was known as a judge who did not lean toward favored cliques. He admitted that he drank socially up until this time. But, in order to fit the image of a judge, he stopped drinking altogether. George was planning for the future. The Wallaces bought a house in Clayton on Eufaula Street and the family became part of the community life.

Since Bobbi Jo's sixth birthday was not until October, she missed being admitted to public school. So Lurleen sent her to a private kindergarten run by Mrs. Ruth McDonald in her home. With only six students, Mrs. McDonald was able to teach the youngsters enough to allow them to enter public school the next year at second grade level. Peggy Sue, who was born in 1949, and George, Jr., often invited other preschoolers to their home. Sometimes the Wallace yard was full of children playing football. George was often out there huddling with the boys. On Sunday, the family attended church together. But George was gone much of the time, and Lurleen had most of the responsibility of rearing the family. Her support came from her mother. Mrs. Burns visited and helped with the grandchildren. Yet family decisions lay mostly on Lurleen's shoulders. She had to stretch the grocery budget, buy shoes for the children, and help with their homework.

George had to travel to the other counties in his care, but even in Clayton, he spent much of his time away from home. The three Wallace children were small and noisy, and George felt that he had to have a quiet place to work. After dinner, he would gather up a stack of papers and peck his wife on the cheek. "I'm going over to Billy Watson's, hon. Be home about ten," he would tell her. Alone again, Lurleen had to put the children to bed. Then she sewed dresses for the two girls until George got home or she became too sleepy to wait up any longer.

Many nights George sat on an oak, straight-backed chair in the back room of the Watson's red-brick home on Louisville Street. As he pecked away at the manual typewriter, preparing speeches to give to clubs and civic groups, the rickety metal typing table rocked back and forth. George ignored it. Billy often left George in the den and went to bed before ten p.m. His wife, Frances, stayed up until she finished her mending.

Even when she nodded off, and then got up and left the room, George hardly noticed. He kept X-ing out some words and adding others until he was satisfied. Then he folded up his papers, stuffed them into the pocket of his sports shirt, and slipped out the back door. Still, most of the time, even after all the preparation, he went to speaking engagements with only a few key phrases jotted down on a slip of loose-leaf paper.

Once, Billy found a wadded-up note that George had dropped by the wicker wastepaper basket. He un-crumpled it, looked at it in dismay, then handed it to his wife. "Look how he makes his speeches!" he said. The scrap of paper contained only key words, no sentences.

Lurleen often went along with George to speaking engagements. It was one of the few outings in which she indulged. Even so, she went more to please George than for her own enjoyment. Her being there looked good. It gave George the image of a "real family man."

Lurleen sat beside him, smiling as he spoke, but she seldom said a word. Some people did not see her presence as an advantage. A *Montgomery Advertiser* reporter once told Charlie Weston, "Lurleen will never be an asset to George." George and Billy Watson thought differently and they were right. Lurleen became governor in 1967 after George was ineligible to serve a third term. It was the only way George could hang onto control in Alabama. Without his wife to take over, George would have been sunk.

When George stopped by Billy Watson's on the way to speaking engagements and pleaded, "Come go with me, Billy," Billy, one of the few persons not awed by George, often growled back at him, "I don't want to go with you to speak!" But most of the time he ended up tagging along anyway.

During the day, in the courtroom, George was trying cases which ran the gamut from criminal to civil. As an inexperienced judge, he did not know all of the law. So he spent hours studying briefs filed by lawyers in the circuit, poring over them at night before making a judgment. By skipping dinner at home and eating a hamburger while he worked, George learned much about the law that he had not been taught in college. George always said, "The next best thing to knowing something is knowing how to find out."

In 1953, George faced a new problem. Liberal groups took strong steps to implement integration. Wallace did not like it at all. He proved how much he objected by being the first judge in the South to issue an injunction against the removal of segregation signs in railroad terminals.

Black citizens who had waited one hundred years for their freedom to be a reality were outraged. They would not be pushed aside again. All over the United States, they joined forces in an effort to force integration. They wanted to be treated as first-class citizens.

In December, 1955, a black woman got on a city bus in Montgomery, Alabama, and was immediately ordered to move to the rear. It was one year after the "Black Monday" edict was issued by the Supreme Court. Rosa Parks wanted to test that law. When she refused to budge, she was arrested. The uproar that followed brought a boycott of the bus lines which lasted a year. Out of the shadows and into the limelight came the pastor of the Dexter Avenue Baptist Church.

Twenty-five-year-old Martin Luther King, Jr., organized and led the boycott. His church was only a short distance away from the Capitol, and the controversy began to focus on him.

George Wallace followed all this at the same time he was campaign manager for Jim Folsom. Big Jim Folsom had just completed the first year of his second term as governor. After Folsom's re-election, no one in Alabama admitted having voted for him the second time around. But somehow he had won. George Wallace had been his South Alabama campaign manager. Wallace's position caused an estrangement with Jimmy Faulkner, who had also been in the race. Faulkner believed that if Wallace had not supported Folsom, he would have won the election. Still, all three expressed the same feelings about the integration issue now facing the state. None of them liked it. They had hopes of reversing some of the decisions.

In December, 1956, the Supreme Court intervened in the bus boycott matter, issuing an order to desegregate all Montgomery buses. It said, "The court found Montgomery's 'Jim Crow' law, requiring Negroes to occupy the back of the bus, violated the 'equal protection of the law' clause of the Fourteenth Amendment and hence was unconstitutional." Race was obviously going to be a large issue.

By then, Folsom's term was nearly complete, and time was drawing near for those planning to enter the 1958 governor's race. George had decided to run. He had a difficult opponent and he knew it would not be easy. John Malcolm Patterson had been elected Attorney General following the murder of his father in 1954. (Albert Patterson was Attorney General until he was killed in an alley adjoining his office). Now John Patterson hoped to become governor so he could "clean up the state."

Back in Clayton, Billy Watson encouraged George Wallace to run. He egged George on, but George did not need much prodding. He knew the race would be a hot one. Issues were plentiful—state government spending, integration, cleaning up vice and corruption, and the war against the loan sharks—among others. The winner would have his hands full for four years if he followed through on campaign promises.

The big issue was segregation and Patterson had a continuing advantage. The battle over segregation of the races in public facilities was being vigorously fought in Virginia, and

Patterson had been assisting the Attorney General of Virginia in every way possible. Action was also beginning in Alabama. Patterson was defending segregation in several federal suits attempting to integrate public facilities. His activities were getting publicity and keeping his name right in the middle where the public could not miss it.

Then a suit was brought to enjoin the activities of an organization formed in 1909—the National Association for the Advancement of Colored People. It was operating in Alabama as a foreign corporation without having complied with Alabama corporation laws. The state won; the N.A.A.C.P. was ousted and that put a damper on their activities for several years. The ruling made a hit with Alabama citizens who favored segregation. They felt that Patterson had the best record and was the strongest candidate on the integration issue.

Wallace conducted a mud-slinging campaign from the start. While Patterson was busy being dignified, Wallace kept running around the state, name-calling. Wallace used vicious publicity that *The Montgomery Advertiser* printed. He would hold up the newspaper clipping and say, "You folks ought to know that Patterson's got Robert Sheldon, the Grand Dragon of the Ku Klux Klan, behind him."

Toward the end of the race, Patterson gained confidence. It was the working class, whose support Wallace had strongly counted on, that turned to Patterson as their hero. As Attorney General, he had vowed to put loan sharks out of business. And he was successful after getting a Small Loan Law passed. This netted him additional votes. Patterson was elated. He recalls, "Everything seemed to jell. It was obvious out there running for governor. You could feel it and sense it. Young people and old people would come up to me and express an interest in my campaign. Sometimes they'd slip twenty-dollar bills into my hands with no strings attached, often leaving without even telling me their name. When this happens, you know you've got it."

The primary was held September 2. Faulkner, with the most money and the largest organization behind him, came in third. Patterson and Wallace were in the run-off. There was still hope for George. But whether it was a get-even measure or not, Faulkner announced he would throw his support to John Patterson. But Wallace still counted on votes from another quarter. By appointment of Governor Folsom, he was serving on the Board of Trustees at Tuskegee College, a well-known black school. He expected this to net him the support of registered blacks.

Wallace lost. It was the first race he had lost since his senior year at college when he tried unsuccessfully for president of the Cotillion Club.

George brushed off the dirt of the campaign and gave his attention to hearing cases as a judge. One of his first major decisions involved integration. The last month of that year, members of the Civil Rights Commission came to Alabama. They were concerned that blacks had been kept from voting by a poll tax and a literacy test.

The Civil Rights Commission asked that voting records be brought before them at a meeting in Montgomery. Judge George Wallace objected. "This was contrary to state law, which says the records cannot be carried out of the county. Moreover, we had them impounded in two counties for other purposes; we told the Civil Rights Commission they could have the records when we got through with them, that they were impounded for the grand jury. With that, the federal judge [Judge Johnson—who was a former friend of George Wallace's] issued an order for me to appear before the Civil Rights Commission which, in my judgment, was illegal."

George felt if Judge Johnson thought the records were

improperly impounded, he should have filed a proper motion in court. So Wallace said, "No." Then an order was issued to force him to bring the records and George said, "No!" a little louder. He gave the records to the grand jury and they, in turn, allowed the commission to see them but only in the county where they were. At this point, Judge Frank Johnson cited Judge Wallace for contempt and set trial for January, 1959. When the trial came up, Wallace pleaded "Not Guilty" of contempt but "Guilty of violating the court orders."

"I told them 'Yes, I'm guilty.' I didn't obey the order," he said later. "Johnson had no right to issue such an order."

George had hoped for a conviction and a chance to get to the Supreme Court to test whether or not a federal judge can take over the functions of a state judge. In the end, George was found "Not Guilty" on both counts. Wallace felt Johnson backed off because he feared repercussions if federal judges started trying to jail state judges.

There was some name-calling on both sides—in Johnson's written decision and by Wallace in speeches and on television. Wallace admitted it. "I called Johnson some strong names, including 'liar,' on television and in two-hundred speeches, for I resented this man, a federal judge, involving himself in politics." From Johnson's point of view, it did not ever seem to be his intent to actually put Wallace in jail. The whole incident commanded statewide and national attention and resulted in being a publicity bonus for Wallace.

He would need it for the 1962 governor's race.

CHAPTER SIX

"PARK YOUR CAR IN THE BACK, GEORGE"

George remained in Clayton and worked as a judge another year, but the mud-slinging campaign of 1958 had taught him a lesson. Even though people listened with relish to his angry remarks about opponents, they had not voted for him. Between the 1958 and 1962 races, George planned a different kind of campaign. Bob Ingram, editor of the *Alabama News Magazine*, was not surprised. "George always flowed with the tide," he said. "Wallace has never been reluctant to change his thinking when the public demanded it."

But George worked through words and not through appearance. He took a shower every morning, kept his shirt tail tucked in, and re-combed his hair whenever the wind blew, but he did not consider fancy clothes or a Cadillac necessary. As long as his shoes were polished and his Sears Roebuck suit was pressed, appearance did not bother him. He wore clothes until they literally fell apart. In the 1958 campaign, Emma Teal, the sheriff's wife, worked for Clayton Dry Cleaners. She remembered George bringing his navy blue pants to her for repair. "He would bring in his britches with so many holes in them they looked like a pin cushion. He'd ask me to see if I could 'patch them one more time.'" She chuckled. "It became such a joke around town for a judge to wear patched pants that one day a photographer from *The Clayton Record* came in and asked me to hold up the pants I was fixing for George. He took a photograph, but I don't know whether it ever got published."

During that 1958 campaign, he drove an old Chevrolet that did not run too well. When he went to Mobile, he would park it a block from the Cawthon Hotel, where his campaign headquarters was located, just in case he had problems getting the car started. His workers thought that he should keep it completely out of sight. They cautioned him, "Park your car in the back, George," because they were afraid the shoddy old car would make him look unsuccessful.

After the voting records incident in 1959, George resigned as Circuit Judge and his brother, Jack Wallace, stepped into the position. George opened a law office in Montgomery in partnership with his other brother, Gerald, and then he began to travel the state and sell himself.

By 1962, George had built up his law practice and had a better income. The fourth and last of the Wallace children, Janie Lee, had been born in 1961. Family expenses were higher, but the Wallaces were managing very well. Things were looking up. All over the state, George had a better image. And there was an extremely strong supportive attitude in Clayton. "Everybody went overboard for him," said Mrs. Teal. One of their own as a contender raised interest in the 1962 governor's race to a record high.

George had made a name for himself by publicly taking stands and by spending time between campaigns increasing his contacts. People no longer asked, "George who?"

Though he was getting all the material and moral help he needed from his friends and supporters, George was doing his part, too. With Seymore Trammell masterminding the campaign, George steadily stumped the state and never let a day pass without exerting every effort to shake one more hand, gaze into one more face and commit it to memory, hopefully picking up additional votes and new campaign workers. After a while, more and more people recognized him and stopped to listen to his booming voice.

Since George was better off financially, he dressed nattier and he drove a better automobile. He would jauntily spring out of the car, rake a comb through his hair and hop up on a platform or a flat-bed truck to give his speech. "It's great to be here in Grove Hill," (or wherever it might be) he would begin. "The town I came from—Clio, in Barbour County is—(either bigger or smaller)" and he would rave on, working up the interest of the people until the right moment came to switch to the political theme. By "feeling" the audience, he could gauge what to say and what not to say. If they clapped, he was like a talking doll wound up. If they yawned and shifted from one foot to another, he would change the pitch of his voice, and try again.

For bankers or Rotary Club members, words like "sovereignty" and "integrity" came smoothly rolling out of Wallace's mouth. But when his audience was a group of shipyard workers in Mobile or farmers in Baldwin County, the Southern drawl became more pronounced and the "y'all" and "folks" followed the grits and gravy speech. He preached "returning the country to the principles upon which it was founded" and he repeatedly called for "state sovereignty." Many Alabamians believed in that. In their sparsely inhabited state, they thought they could overcome the evils of big city ways if they could maintain segregation and class distinction.

Prior to World War II, there had been little change in the black-white situation since the Civil War. Negroes were free, but from that point on, not much progress had been made. Whether it was because of lack of educational opportunities or failure to take advantage of opportunities, the black people still had not gotten into the mainstream of life. A few had risen to the top of their professions in the seventeen years since the second world war. Some had become teachers and doctors or lawyers. But even those individuals remained within their own special circles in the black community. If a black man was a high school principal, he was a principal of a black high school and a member of a black teachers' association.

The same practice applied in all fields. Churches were nominally integrated, but in the overwhelming majority of cases, they were not. So when Wallace banged his fist on a podium and said, "I believe in States' Rights," blacks saw a threat to the limited recent progress they had made. They were against him.

Lack of black support did not even slow George down. He went on and on, repeatedly defending himself against charges of racism: "I do not dislike any of the handiwork of God," he insisted. He stressed that he wanted "equal but separate rights." Blacks could not accept this. Even if they liked other parts of his platform, they saw him as a completely unacceptable candidate.

Many white Alabamians felt differently. Segregation was on the top of their list of crucial issues, followed closely by the need for law and order. Wallace hit a nerve when he said that "changing labor union seniority lists, open housing, and some of these other things they're shovin' down our throats are wrong and unfair." These were issues Southerners felt posed threats to their existence. Their way of life, full of social and class distinctions, was going down the drain and taking with it many of the customs Southerners had worked so hard to preserve. It was all being done not by choice of the majority of Alabamians, but by federal judges.

They did not like it. Many citizens looked to the country boy from Clio to be their rescuer. He could call their names and remember where he had last seen them. "Oh, yeah," he would say, "I saw you in March at that rally in Greenville."

Whether the person was a mayor or a carpenter made no difference to George. He committed their faces to memory.

John Pemberton, Alabama Clerk of the House, remembers how much being known made one young lady feel important: "Once at a barbeque during a statewide rally in Montgomery in 1962, Wallace went through the line. A seventeen-year-old serving girl in a white uniform was quite surprised when Wallace stopped and said, 'Hi, Sue'." She told Pemberton that Wallace had seen her but once before, dressed in ordinary street clothes, in Bay Minette. She could not believe he remembered her."

In '58 and again in '62 a tall, successful-looking red-haired man traveled everywhere with George Wallace. Oscar Harper was a country boy, too, from Geneva County. He had no interest in a cabinet position since his firm, National Services, Inc., in Montgomery, operated in twenty-eight states and kept him occupied full time. But he liked the association with George and the excitement of the campaign. He stood by, listening to crowd reactions during as many as ten speeches daily. In his successful advertising career, the lanky six-footer had learned to "read" people, too. He was an asset to George.

Harper and Wallace thought alike. Politically, they both felt that the South could handle its own problems. But Harper did not give his opinions by making speeches; he just stayed in the background and found out what the audience was thinking. He felt that after people heard Wallace speak, "the crowd thought more of him." It impressed Harper that George was able to stay calm, even in tense situations when the audience became antagonistic. George took it coolly, and Harper felt that proved he was a stable individual.

But George could be inconsiderate and impulsive. He often created a problem for his campaign workers. They would try to keep up with him, but he would go way down into the crowd to shake a farmer's hand or to sign an autograph for a ten-year-old boy. Then he would disappear. The workers would skirt around frantically trying to locate him. By that time, he might be half a block away, heading for the car. They would have to run to catch up with him. George was in excellent physical condition and he often left some members of the group panting behind. It became such a problem that new workers were told, "Now watch the car or George. That's how you'll know when to leave."

The 1962 race had its share of contenders. Among these was a hard-drinking, colorful character named "Shorty" Price. "Shorty" was a perennial runner. The bleary-eyed man from Louisville just could not seem to make a lasting impression. He ran for governor four or five times and tried countless other offices. He never even placed. But occasionally he could draw a crowd.

One day Wallace was in Brundidge, Alabama, with a street full of interested citizens listening to his speech. Suddenly, Oscar Harper pointed to a group migrating towards the barber shop located at the back of the audience and asked, "Where the hell are they going?" Harper and a couple of campaign workers walked around to see what the attraction was. Sure enough, there was "Shorty" standing in the barber shop doorway, talking up his platform to the back of Wallace's crowd.

In those days, George was not always able to draw large numbers of people. Sometimes, he would look up to see only ten or fifteen pairs of eyes looking back at him. Some of these stared vacantly, and it appeared that they were there because it was all they had to do. But whether the crowd was large or small, the speech went on. George gave them every phase of his platform just as if a thousand persons were present.

On cold and rainy days, Wallace plodded along. He worried about his health a good deal, but he kept up his pace.

He had passed the age at which his father died, and he was living with an extraordinary amount of tension. When Lurleen saw how tired he looked as he shaved at five a.m., she would plead with him, "George, can't you just stay home one day?"

His answer was always the same, "I gotta keep going." His image in the mirror told him that he needed rest, too. But George Wallace would not slow down. He knew that the winner of this race was obviously going to be the candidate who reached the most people.

This time, since a governor was only allowed to serve one term, Patterson could not seek re-election. Speculation by the political experts was that if Folsom entered the race he would be the winner. He seemed to be a shoo-in for governor. Everyone pooh-poohed the chances for Wallace, or anyone else, to be elected.

Then Ryan deGraffenreid moved over from the House to the Senate and began to emerge as a leader. He was attractive and expressed himself well. He was also dedicated to progressive issues such as education and economic development. Beginning late but with much to offer, he prepared to enter the 1962 race.

Albert Brewer, a legislator from Decatur, supported Wallace, but was not confident that he was backing a winner. Recalling his concern, Brewer said, "DeGraffenreid caught on in North Alabama. He was young, made a very good appearance, a good presentation. A lot of things played in the race. It was difficult for Wallace to get off the ground. His workers didn't feel good about it at all."

Brewer need not have been concerned. George was about to find a need and fill it. People in Alabama were extremely concerned about segregation, and they were waiting for a candidate to speak out on the issue. Up until this time segregation had been somewhat soft-peddled. Then about five weeks before the election, George attacked Judge Frank Johnson on the contempt issue of 1959. This caught on, and he coined the slogan: "Stand Up for Alabama." Wallace, playing to the white majority, used segregation to stir up the crowd.

In the meantime, some of the underground forces who work in campaigns painted deGraffenreid as a liberal. On top of that, Folsom gave away the election on pre-election night when he appeared on television seemingly under the influence of something. His slurred speech and uncoordinated motions shocked Alabamians. The next day the word was out. Those who had not seen the program heard about the unbelievable indiscretion of the former governor. That was it for Folsom. Wallace and deGraffenreid came out in first and second place. Folsom, the sure winner, had lost.

In the run-off, Wallace came out on top. His administration as the Governor of the State of Alabama would begin January 14, 1963, with the formal Inauguration Ceremony.

CHAPTER SEVEN

"SEGREGATION NOW, SEGREGATION TOMORROW AND SEGREGATION FOREVER"

The Wallace family had come from a converted chicken coop to the governor's mansion. Club memberships and fancy food had never interested George and Lurleen. George preferred sports and hamburgers with ketchup. Lurleen was happily occupied with taking care of her children. As Alabama's first family, they chose to live simply in the fifty-six-year-old colonial structure. Governor Wallace was more concerned with affairs of state than with impressing people by his social status.

He looked upon the money which came with the job as just a nice lagniappe. His opponent Ben Stokes said, "George never did care anything about money. To him, it's just something you need to run a political campaign." His friends thought George might splurge some of the $25,000 a year salary by moving up from King Edward to English Corona cigars.

January 14, 1963, was Inaugural Day. The twenty-eight-degree temperature had a chill factor of zero. Members of the new first family tried to keep warm with electric blankets covering their laps while they watched a five-hour parade pass in review. There were one hundred and seventy-four bands and ninety-three floats. No Negro bands were invited to join the march. Two former governors, Frank Dixon and James

Folsom, were on the reviewing stand and remained seated during the ceremony, but the new governor chose to stand most of the time. Ten-year-old George, Jr., who had made campaign speeches for his dad, now shared the glory. He wore a top-hat, frock-tail coat, striped trousers, wing collar and ascot tie, exactly like his father.

Former governor, Chaucey Sparks, who helped Wallace get a start in politics, was suffering with the flu and was unable to appear in person. Nevertheless, he introduced Wallace on this Inaugural Day by long-distance telephone hook-up from Eufaula.

At one twelve p.m., George Wallace took the oath of office. It was administered by his brother, Circuit Judge Jack Wallace. He stood on the precise spot where Jefferson Davis had taken the oath as President of the Confederacy one hundred and two years before. Wallace placed his hand on the Bible Davis had used and pledged faithfully "to perform the duties of his office, and to defend the state and the federal constitution."

The Governor's Inaugural Address thrilled Alabamians and has been much quoted through the years.

First, Wallace acknowledged the home folks who gave him his start: "I want to thank those home folks of my county who first gave an anxious country boy his opportunity to serve in state politics." He mentioned specific areas such as "Suttons, Haigler's Mill...Beat 6 and Beat 14...And Clio, my birthplace." He made a special reference to "Blue Springs, where the vote was three hundred and four for Wallace and one for the opposition...and the dear little lady who I heard had made that one vote against me because she couldn't see too well...and she had pulled the wrong lever. Bless her heart."

Next, he thanked his family, his supporters and even his opponents: "And I wish I could shake hands and thank all of you in this state who voted for me...and those of you who did not...for I know you voted your honest convictions...and now, we must stand together and move the great State of Alabama forward."

Then he got down to his campaign promises. Dramatically spelling out his intentions, he said, "I shall do my duty to you, God helping...to every man, to every woman yes, and to every child in this state. I shall fulfill my duty toward honesty and economy in our state government so that no man shall have a part of his livelihood cheated and no child shall have a bit of his future stolen away.

"I have said to you that I would eliminate the liquor agents in this state and that the money saved would be returned to our citizens...I am happy to report to you that I am now filling orders for several hundred liquor agents and stamped on them are these words...'for liquor agents...destination...out of Alabama.' I am happy to report to you that the big-wheeling cocktail party boys have gotten the word that their free whiskey and boat rides are over...that the farmer in the field, the worker in the factory, the businessman in his office, the housewife in her home, have decided that the money can be better spent to help our children's education and our older citizens...and they have put a man in office to see that it is done. It shall be done. Let me say one more time...no more liquor drinking in your governor's mansion." That was a promise George Wallace never broke.

He said he would seek new industry, dignity and enrichment for senior citizens, better markets for farmers and help for struggling laborers. He also promised to raise educational standards.

Hitting hard at federal interference in state affairs, he took a strike at President John Kennedy who had recently signed an executive order against racially segregated housing and who put troops in Mississippi. "The federal troops in Mississippi could better be used guarding the safety of the citizens of Washington, D.C., where it is even unsafe to walk or go to a ball game...and that is the nation's capital."

Wallace blasted big government by saying: "We find we have replaced faith with fear...and though we may give lip service to the Almighty...in reality, government has become our God." He compared the Constitution to the Ten Commandments by saying, "But the strong, simple faith and sane reasoning of our founding fathers has long since been forgotten as the so-called 'progressives' tell us that our Constitution was written for 'horse and buggy' days...so were the Ten Commandments."

Referring to what he termed a "might makes right" philosophy, he charged that men were attempting to "play God." The South would not stand for it, he said. "Let us send this message back to Washington by our representatives who are with us today...that from this day we are standing up, and the heel of tyranny does not fit the neck of an upright man ...that we intend to take the offensive and carry our fight for freedom across this nation, wielding the balance of power we know we possess in the Southland...that we, not the insipid bloc voters of some sections...will determine in the next election who shall sit in the White House of these United States...that from this day...from this hour...from this minute...we give the word of a race of honor that we will tolerate their boot in our face no longer...and let those certain judges put that in their opium pipes of power and smoke it for what it is worth."

Wallace had faith that others would join the fight. He saw the issue as national. He said: "And you native sons and daughters of old New England's rock-ribbed patriotism ...and you sturdy natives of the great Mid-West. ..and you descendants of the far West flaming spirit of pioneer freedom...we invite you to come and be with us...for you are of the Southern mind...and the Southern spirit...and the Southern philosophy...you are Southerners too and brothers with us in our fight."

Switching to the threat of Communism, the new governor rejected the view that poverty, discrimination and lack of opportunity cause people to turn to Communism. He denied that it was a problem in the South. "There aren't enough Communists in the South to fill a phone booth," he said.

The best-remembered and most-often quoted part of his speech dealt with segregation. Governor Wallace said: "Today I have stood, where once Jefferson Davis stood, and took an oath to my people. It is very appropriate then that from this Cradle of the Confederacy, this very Heart of the Great Anglo-Saxon Southland, that today we sound the drum for freedom as have our generations of forebears before us done, time and again down through history."

His voice got louder and with his right fist pounding the air two feet above his head, Wallace challenged: "Let us rise to the call of freedom-loving blood that is in us and send our answer to the tyranny that clanks its chains upon the South. In the name of the greatest people that have ever trod this earth, I draw the line in the dust and toss the gauntlet before the feet of tyranny...and I say segregation now, segregation tomorrow and segregation forever."

The crowd yelled, whistled, and applauded. George had to pause until they calmed down.

A Birmingham attorney said that twenty years later George admitted it would have been better had he said, "States Rights today...tomorrow...forever," but he got excited and said "segregation" in all three places.

At the end of the speech, however, Wallace directed his

remarks to blacks. He offered an invitation to the "Negro citizen of Alabama to work with us from his separate racial station as we will work with him to develop, to grow in individual freedom and enrichment."

He ended with a prayer "that the Father who reigns above us will bless all the people of this great sovereign state and nation, both white and black." He used this kind of line to end many of his speeches.

The headlines spread the news. *The Mobile Press* and *The Mobile Press Register* headlines read: "Big Government Blasted by Wallace," and "Incoming Governor Hits Desegregation." Some reports picked up Dothan attorney Richmond Flower's statements in support of integration, "Flowers Flays Wallace Plan." The papers attempted to give a clue as to what the administration would do during the next four years. They could make educated guesses based on campaign promises, but what would actually happen nobody knew.

Immediately after assuming the governorship, Wallace defied the federal court integration orders. He ignored Alabama Attorney General Richmond Flowers who had warned that such actions would "bring nothing but disgrace to our state, military law upon our people, and political demagoguery to the leaders responsible."

Sometimes, George took time out to do ordinary things. Shortly after he was inaugurated, he took his sleek, black Lincoln limousine and drove to Billy Watson's house. Billy had put him down many times when they traveled together on the campaign trail. Once, when they were at a gospel singing, George leaned forward to hear the words of his favorite song *How Great Thou Art*. Billy knew that George had a hearing problem and had to strain to hear the music. But he ignored that and blurted out in a loud stage whisper, "Sit back, George.

They're not talking about you!"

Remembering the days when they told him to "park around back," George pulled up right in the driveway and called Billy out to see his fancy car. Strutting around to the driver's side, he opened the door and reached over to flick his cigar ashes in the ashtray. "When the cigarette lighter goes bad," he told Billy as he exhaled a puff of smoke, "I'll just get me another car." It was one of the few times George seemed to enjoy any luxury.

The Wallace's moved into the mansion and began living a different life. The antebellum home with its thirty by sixteen-foot rooms and beautiful winding staircase was a far cry from the one-story house in Clayton. The dark mahogany wood of the ornate bedroom furniture was quite a contrast to the straight lines of the mismatched twin bed, walnut headboard and dresser set Lurleen and George had when they first married.

One policy of the governor's mansion was to have servants who were convicted murderers, because experience had proven they were the best risks. Social statisticians say that someone who kills in a moment of passion makes a much better employee than one who steals, forges or robs. The murderers were considered to be more trustworthy than thieves. So the system was to use inmates from Alabama prisons as maids and cooks in the mansion. Now they had two brand-new bosses.

George's sister, Marianne, knew Lurleen had dual obligations. She still had children to rear and she had to be First Lady. George was gone much of the time. Marianne defended George's absence: "You can't make a speech long-distance. He had to be gone."

With reservations, Lurleen accepted her role as Alabama's First Lady. She knew that she would have to move about in society. A longtime friend, serious-minded Mary Jo Ventress, recalls Lurleen's awe of people more educated than she. "She always felt a little withdrawn, kind of cowed by other people who professed educational degrees—uncomfortable with them," she said. "She didn't want to make any mistakes that would embarrass George. All of her little life her main concern was to work for his welfare and his good, really." Even if Lurleen felt insecure at times, now, as the governor's wife, she would be thrown with some of the greatest "brains" in the state time and again. Later, as governor, she would be responsible for accepting or vetoing their recommendations.

People responded to Lurleen's humbleness. In 1966, a Gallup Poll named Alabama's lady governor sixth in the top ten most admired women in the world. Her showing may have been partially a spin-off from George's immense popularity, but her charm and personality and the courageous spirit she showed in the face of personal illness impressed many people.

If Lurleen had problems living a life of luxury, George had them, too. With his background, he had always considered himself a champion of the poor. He did not want to splurge with their money now. The bill he sponsored as a legislator, the Wallace Industrial Act, helped improve the standard of living for the lower class. The new industries it brought to Alabama prevented many previously unemployed farmers from having to leave the state. As a gubernatorial candidate, George had stumped the state, promising to use the Act to bring more payrolls to Alabama. As a legislator, he had made good on that promise. He could do more now from the governor's chair.

Though Wallace was helping the lower and middle classes and receiving praise from them for his efforts, others were very vocal about being anti-Wallace. Some said they "hated his guts." He had brought it on himself. In the 1958 campaign, when Patterson waved the bloody shirt of segregation and won, George Wallace saw that he had been "out-segged." He vowed then that it would never happen to him again. Because of that, he had not had the support of blacks. He had also turned many white integrationists against him. One was State Representative Ben Stokes of Mobile who charged that "a public figure who preys upon the worst instincts of man is not a good public figure or a good leader." He agreed that Wallace had kept his promise in the 1962 race—to pursue segregation relentlessly, but he didn't approve.

During the 1950s, President Eisenhower showed little concern with matters related to segregation. According to Stokes, "that just paved the way for guys like George Wallace to walk on the scene and arouse the passions of people."

Legal-minded Stokes saw George's actions as indefensible. "George knows the importance of upholding the law," he said. "He's even been a judge." Charging the governor with being responsible for others breaking the law, he added, "I think the actions of Wallace during those years helped set the pattern of disobedience to law and disrespect for the law."

In 1962, George was not about to change his pattern. He had set his course and had no intention of swerving, much less turning around.

Things changed when John Kennedy became president. The first Catholic Chief Executive was a man with new and different ideas. If integration was to be fully implemented, it would be during his term. From his position as holder of the highest office in the land, President Kennedy had made much progress in the area of desegregation before Wallace took office as governor. During the Oxford riots, Kennedy sent troops to the University of Mississippi to integrate it. Wallace did not become involved directly. He did, however, side with Governor Ross Barnett in speeches. He also studied the incident to plan strategy if he got tangled up in a like situation. Before long, Attorney General Robert Kennedy, brother of the president, was sent to Alabama as a mediator.

He came to seek Wallace's cooperation in implementing

integration at the University of Alabama in a calm and peaceful manner. Nationwide newspapers publicized George's defense of Barnett and the Attorney General's upcoming visit. Kennedy was the first such visitor, but through the years, other dignitaries would follow him. Alabama was on the map and recognized because of her governor's outspokenness.

Attorney General Robert Kennedy arrived on April 26, 1963, and a meeting was set up with Governor Wallace. Wallace was concerned. He feared being misquoted by Kennedy, and he also wanted to ensure the safety of the Attorney General while he was a visitor to the state. Public Safety Director Al Lingo was ordered to have full security forces around the Capitol. Upon his arrival, Kennedy was escorted with state troopers flanking all sides. Wallace's executive press secretary, Bill Jones, officially greeted Kennedy and escorted him to the office of the executive secretary, Earl Morgan. Then Morgan took Kennedy to the governor's office.

After welcoming amenities, Wallace asked Ed Reid, director of Alabama League of Municipalities, and Alabama Finance Director Seymore Trammell to stay. Kennedy had Circuit Judge Thurgood Marshall at his side. Then Wallace told Kennedy, "Just to be sure there's no misunderstanding about what's said here, this conversation is going to be taped. We'll give you a copy." Wallace knew that leaks of alleged conversations between Kennedy and Governor Ross Barnett of Mississippi made it appear that Barnett was merely pretending to fight integration; later, he would step aside. Nobody believed Barnett's denials. Wallace did not want that to happen to him. Kennedy opened his mouth to protest, Wallace raised his hand and said, "The press won't get it unless you agree."

It was not long before Kennedy brought up integration. He asked Wallace, "Will you give me your word that you will not block the plan to enroll Negro students in the University of Alabama?"

The governor replied, "I can't do that."

Kennedy tried again. He leaned across the mahogany table and glared straight at George Wallace. "Governor Wallace, you realize that it is going to be done, I'm sure." Kennedy emphasized each word.

George shook his head. "Not if I can help it." He rose from his chair. Kennedy remained seated and George sat back down. After an hour and a half, the meeting was a stalemate. Kennedy left that afternoon, dissatisfied with his failure.

On Saturday, May 18, President John F. Kennedy came to Alabama for the Thirtieth Anniversary of the Tennessee Valley Authority. Wallace was uneasy about Kennedy's attendance, but he had to attend even though he did not want to.

Wallace greeted Kennedy with a wave of his hand as the helicopter whirled to the ground behind the TVA building at Muscle Shoals. When it landed, the two men shook hands and walked a hundred yards to the outdoor platform where a crowd of fifteen thousand awaited Kennedy's speech in the blazing summer sun.

The president got a howl of approval when he waved to the audience. George Wallace was not about to be upstaged. He raised both hands above his head in greeting and the crowd shrieked with delight. Then he had to step back and let Kennedy have the podium. While Wallace grimly listened, the president said: "The people of this area know that the federal government is not a stranger and not an enemy." Wallace clenched his fist. He did not agree, but he could not say a word.

Afterward, Wallace and Kennedy rode to Huntsville together in the presidential jet-powered helicopter. It was awkward for the two men. Both seemed uncomfortable. Wallace kept adjusting his tie and Kennedy repeatedly straightened his shirt collar. The president was pushing for the employment of blacks in Birmingham businesses. But Wallace turned toward him, looked him straight in the eye and told him: "Look, this has already been done."

Kennedy's Bostonian accent became very pronounced when he replied, "The fact is that in Alabama, blacks generally hold menial jobs."

Wallace cocked his head and retorted, "Now that's up to the employers and, in my opinion, it's not a matter to be decided by governmental rulings." Once again, a confrontation ended without anything being resolved.

Regardless of Wallace's feelings, Judge H. H. Grooms ruled, in Birmingham on May 21, that Vivian Malone and James Hood, both Negroes, must be admitted to the all-white University of Alabama.

There was loud applause from the black community. White Alabamians became indignant. They huffed and puffed at the intrusion by the federal government, and their governor screamed "interference." It did no good. It was clear that integration was not going to be confined to Alabama. Before long, all the schools of the South would be involved.

Integrationists insisted that it was about time Alabama and the South caught up with the rest of the nation. Segregationists complained that this would only be the beginning of federal intervention, that soon every phase of people's lives would be subject to the whims of Washington.

Throughout the controversy, Wallace protested vigorously, but got nowhere. He knew full well what he would have to do to keep his promise to "Stand Up for Alabama." He would have to give his message all over the country.

Nationwide fame for Wallace began when Lawrence Spivak invited Alabama's governor to appear on NBC's Meet the Press June 2, 1963. Bobby Kennedy had come to Alabama without a fear of appearing publicly. Yet New York might be dangerous for Alabama's governor. For safety's sake, Wallace went to New York City under an assumed name. The nation waited for NBC to produce the "mob leader" from Alabama.

Wallace was ready for them. The pugilist had his "dukes up" and was prepared to meet the formidable interviewers. The discussion centered around what was later to become known as "The stand in the schoolhouse door."

On the panel were Anthony Lewis, from *The New York Times*; Frank McGee, an NBC news reporter, Vermont Royster of *The Wall Street Journal* and Spivak. They tried to catch Wallace off guard on constitutional law, but he came back at them with cases and rulings on "separate but equal facilities." Wallace repeatedly rejected the notion that he advocated violence. "To avoid confrontation," he said, "I've been urging Alabamians to stay away from the campus on registration day." George added, "By standing there, I'll represent the people of the state."

Six days before registration, Federal Judge Seybourn Lynne in Birmingham ordered Governor Wallace not to physically prevent the Negroes' admission to the University. This did not keep him from attempting to stop them from enrolling. Still, it was clear if he did not allow them to pass by him and enter the college, he would be subject to arrest and federal imprisonment.

The events of registration day were dramatic. Federal men were clearly in control on June 11, 1963. They worked to avert a riot, perhaps a bloody confrontation. Wallace alerted law enforcement officers and ordered five-hundred guardsmen to Tuscaloosa. If there was anything the two sides had in common, it was a desire to keep the peace. Notices had been sent to newspapers requesting that people stay at home. The Governor wanted to stand alone.

The national press and the Wallace staff had never met before. Reporters wrote later that Wallace cooperated fully with the press. He even arranged a truck to carry TV cameras to the scene at seven a.m. so they could have a clear view of the barring process.

Assistant Attorney General Nicholas Katzenbach held in his hand a proclamation from the president. He began reading but was interrupted by Wallace who squared his shoulders and drew up to his full five-foot-eight inches. "Now you make your statement, because we don't need your speech," he told Katzenbach. When the governor's turn came, Katzenbach nodded, curled the corners of his mouth slightly upward, and stepped aside. He knew all along that he was going to be the winner.

Wallace tilted his chin up as high as it would go and said, "I'm appearing in behalf of the people of Alabama." He called his action "not defiance for defiance's sake but for the purpose of raising basic and fundamental constitutional questions." His appeal called for the stoppage of illegal usurpation of power by the central government and he went on record denouncing it.

All the nation heard. Katzenbach was right, Wallace would not win that day. But he had made his point. His message, one of many, had been sent to Washington.

When the recently federalized Alabama National Guard arrived at the scene, Governor Wallace reminded them, "Except when you're under federal orders, I'm your commander in chief." There was not much more he could say. But he had the last word, and he left with the politician's diplomatic phrase, "I am returning to Montgomery to continue working for constitutional government to benefit all Alabamians—black and white."

Different reporters reported the incident differently. Their viewpoint seemed to depend on what they wanted to believe.

The national press saw the test as a big victory for the cause of integration, and it was obvious that the University of Alabama would be integrated from then on. Integrationists had won round one. The fighter was down for the count, but he and his people did not seem to know it. Those who agreed with Wallace felt he had been successful in drawing attention to the dangerous power of the central government. The Wallace corps bragged that they had proved to U.S. citizens that the federal government had over-stepped its authority and misused its power.

With public opinion hanging in the balance, President Kennedy did not want a head-on clash with Wallace. Wallace could have been hit with contempt proceedings in federal court but this was avoided. Still George was not ready to let the matter end. He had hoped for a subpoena. He wanted an opportunity to make his case public and to bring the question of state sovereignty to a test. But he did not get a chance. Nothing further was done.

Barely six months into his term as governor, Wallace began gearing up for the presidential campaign. After his famous stand at the University of Alabama, many Americans knew him and his concerns. Whether they agreed or not, they were interested in hearing what he had to say. Colleges of many states invited him to speak.

The college students may have merely wanted someone to challenge or laugh at, but George did not care. It gave him a chance to air his views. Once he got on stage, he did whatever it took to begin or finish a speech. Even though he was controversial, he had a big group of people who followed him around and helped him send his message.

One man who helped him was Doug Benton, who weighed in at about three hundred pounds. The usual line was that Benton "carried a lot of weight in Alabama." Benton, a

Barbour County boy who refined his accent with fifteen years in radio and television, was born in Louisville, Alabama. He had known George Wallace all his life. His voice matched his physique; it was deep and booming and carried well. Soon he would put it to good use.

Doug had followed Wallace's career and had gone to work for the campaign during the first governor's race. He was still with the group in 1962. When Wallace took office, Benton was appointed to the State Licensing Board for the Healing Arts. Before long, he became known as "The Voice of George Wallace" because he introduced Wallace at most of the rallies.

After the successful governor's race, all of Wallace's workers expected to get some rest, but the action was just beginning. Because of the influx of offers from well-known universities and colleges, he decided to tour the country. It took him away from Alabama and left the administration of state affairs to his subordinates. Some of his political opponents felt this suited Wallace fine, that the day-to-day routine of running state government did not interest him.

Somber, grey-haired Robert Vance, Alabama National Democratic Party Chairman, believed that. He saw Wallace as "the ultimate candidate for governor" but he said that "presiding over some hassle between two departments of state government, resolving some personnel question, or handling a purchasing matter where he doesn't have any direct interest are just not the sort of things that appeal to him."

Others felt the same way. Ray Jenkins, Managing Editor of *The Alabama Journal* in Montgomery said, "He seems to kind of lose interest in government once he gets there." *The Alabama Journal* had supported Wallace in 1958, but it and *The Montgomery Advertiser* both broke with him over the issue of school desegregation. They worried about his intentions "to take every step conceivable to maintain segregation, even to the point of calling out state troopers after a local school board chose to desegregate its schools."

Jenkins recalls the paper's stand, "The position the papers took was that this stand by Wallace was a violation of everything Wallace stood for concerning local government. Even when the local government made its decision, Wallace overruled by using state authority." He shook his head: "The analogy was precisely the same analogy he used with the federal government stepping in, forcing unpopular decisions. The papers broke with him then. Relations since that time have been going downhill. The papers have not supported him since then in any of his campaigns, including his presidential campaigns."

Alabama State Representative Ben Stokes remembers Wallace in the same way. "I happen to know that back in 1963 the powers that be in Mobile urged George Wallace not to intervene in our affairs down here," he said. "We were ready to comply with the federal court order to desegregate the schools." Stokes said that the County Board of Education, the City and County Commissions and "a tremendous number of influential people holding office and others tried to get Wallace not to interfere in our problems down here." Nevertheless, Wallace dispatched the National Guard to Mobile to prevent the entry of black school children in white schools. "It was at that point that my antipathy towards Wallace was at its greatest peak," Stokes said later.

Despite criticism of his bold self-righteousness and for his lack of attention to state affairs, George was still set on telling the nation's youth what he had to say. An Alabama governor had never before undertaken such a plan. It was an innovative move. Wallace aides were not sure what would happen, and no one knew how it would turn out. However it worked out, they felt it was sure to put the spotlight on Alabama.

The Civil Rights Act was in the works. Some saw it as an infringement on the personal rights of people, as a way the government could gain control of property rights and seniority lists of labor unions. Others took it to mean that there would be equal rights under the law. Black leaders felt that it would bring about the end of segregation.

About the time Wallace began planning his tours and deciding to enter Kennedy territory for his first speeches, newspapers across the country were giving the other side of the picture. Frank Holeman of *The New York Daily News* wrote, for example, of the twenty million Negroes who "served notice that they were intensely dissatisfied with their lot."

It was Sunday, September 15, 1963. A bomb had killed four black girls as they were putting on choir robes in the cloak room of the Sixteenth Street Baptist Church in Birmingham. Carole Robertson, Cynthia Wesley, Eddie Mae Collins and Denise McNair never knew what happened. But their parents would never forget.

In the violence that followed, two black boys were shot to death by whites. Rev. Martin Luther King, Jr., a leader of the Southern Christian Leadership Council, was with the two hundred and ten thousand Negro and white sympathizers during the March on Washington for Freedom and Jobs.

On August 28, 1963, at the Lincoln Memorial, King spoke out to them: "When the architects of our republic wrote the magnificent words of the Constitution and the Declaration of Independence they were signing a promissory note to which every American was to fall heir. Instead of honoring this sacred obligation, America has given the Negro people a bad check, a check which has come back marked 'insufficient funds.' But we refuse to believe that there are insufficient funds in the great vaults of opportunity of this nation. So we have come to cash this check—a check that will give us upon demand the riches of freedom and the security of justice." King would have much more to say. Meanwhile, Wallace's men set out to make arrangements for his speaking engagements.

Without preplanning and playing it by ear, Bill Jones, his press secretary, flew to Boston in October, 1963, to survey the areas the governor was to cover beginning in early November. By then, Wallace's planned trips had begun to be thought of as pre-campaigning, and trouble began to brew. Civil Rights leaders looked right past the Junior Colleges and Trade Schools being built during the '62-'66 administration which would benefit minorities, and saw a picture which scared them to death. George Wallace looked like a serious candidate for the office of the President of the United States.

Wallace blocking the schoolhouse door

Wallace Speaking to Veterans

Wallace Addressing joint session of legislature

Inauguration with Lurleen and 3 children

CHAPTER EIGHT

A KING, NOT A KINGMAKER

George's brother Gerald was one of his political liabilities. But despite Gerald's shady dealings, George adamantly defended him.

Bob Ingram, a political columnist for *The Montgomery Advertiser*, saw what happened any time attacks were made on Gerald. "If you start picking on Gerald, you've got to fight George, too," Ingram proclaimed.

Yet everyone saw that Gerald and George were not alike. Ray Jenkins, an avid opponent of the governor, did not hesitate to spell out the differences: "The secret of it is purely and simply that the two men have different aspirations, aims, and ambitions in life," he said, adding, "Gerald is an alcoholic; he tells it himself. He's also had three divorces—things like that. But blood is thicker than water, and George is very protective towards Gerald."

Gerald was unconcerned about living up to his brother's standards. He used his position as an attorney and the governor's brother to make an enormous amount of money. *The Alabama Journal* Editor, Ray Jenkins, offered proof of Gerald's unethical actions. In the mid-sixties, *The Alabama Journal* and *The Montgomery Advertiser* found that Gerald had an interest in a plant selling asphalt to the state at higher prices than the competitive bids. "We also know his income in one year in particular reached $135,000, although he had no visible law practice and no visible income. He has, from all indications, become a fairly wealthy man without any visible means of support."

Bob Ingram pointed out another incident. He said that "Gerald was paid enormous fees for getting some bond issues from another lawyer, but even there he's never been indicted or tried in any light. So for the record, he's never done anything." And, there has never been a case. Somehow it has been side-stepped. Even when the contracts in question were voided by court action, Gerald Wallace remained scot-free.

"There's a double standard in Alabama politics," Ingram added. "George Wallace can do things and things can happen in his administration which would destroy any other public official. Gerald and all the things he's been involved in apparently have not hurt his brother. The record shows, and I've heard other politicians say, 'How is it that these things go on?' For some reason the people just say, 'Well, George didn't know anything about it'." He concluded, "It's wrong," shaking his head in utter disbelief. Evidently, many Alabamians believed George Wallace could do no wrong.

Ray Jenkins put the blame on George's loose governing policies. "That's how such political scandals crop up," he explained. "When you don't have a firm control on it [state government], they [wrongdoings] happen. Underlings begin to get greedy." He implied that if the governor had been doing his job right, things like that would never have slipped by unnoticed.

Although others were using the power of their position to amass a fortune, it was clear that Wallace did not. By satisfying his burning ambition to be governor, he had what he wanted. He ignored criticism because he knew that, no matter what accidents or scandals occurred in state government, he had loyal supporters who would still defend him by shrugging it off and saying, "You can't blame George for that. He just makes poor choices in the people he surrounds himself with sometimes." It never occurred to them to expect George to exert better judgment. Not only did these people absolve George of all guilt, they also kept urging him to make country-wide speeches and "at least consider" running for the presidency. By chance more than design, the speechmaking became a sounding board to see whether he would have a chance if he should choose to become a candidate.

The timing was perfect for George to present his ideas. In 1963, the country was just beginning to feel the impact of the Kennedy administration. The war in Southeast Asia was being escalated. Voters felt that Kennedy had been in office long enough for his plans and programs to take form. He was accused of not being sufficiently committed. But the truth was that he had problems getting his programs through Congress. The narrow margin by which he had taken office gave him no mandate that Congress felt bound to respect. Nevertheless, U.S. citizens wanted action and improvement, not excuses. They were disillusioned and dissatisfied. Governor Wallace could take these facts to the people to prove his points.

He did. In 1963, what became cross-country tours began in the East. Wallace talked and talked. In early November, Wallace took his fight for States' Rights out of the South into Boston for a speech at Harvard, Kennedy's alma mater. Although it was reported that Governor Endicott Peabody gave Governor Wallace a cool reception, Peabody assigned an aide to Wallace and put his limousine at Wallace's disposal during the course of his stay in Boston. George Wallace pulled no punches, he made no apologies for Southerners. He told the intellectuals at Harvard the same thing he told the crowd everywhere: "We got people in Alabama as intelligent and refined and cultured as you are, and don't you ever forget it."

Bill Jones arranged every appearance he could for the governor. Wallace welcomed the opportunity to take his cause into Indiana, Maryland, Ohio, North Carolina and Wisconsin. He fielded all the questions of newsmen and batted them back as quickly as they came. He talked about big government and the bureaucrats taking over the lives of citizens. He constantly denied being a racist and repeatedly warned that "central control is leading to a police state in the Americas." He remained committed to segregation for Alabama, always adding, "The rest of the states ought to decide for themselves what is best for them."

What had begun as an "Ivy League Tour" (so named by the press) had spread into other states and captured the attention of the national press.

The questions flowed freely, and day by day, Wallace's answers became more polished and detailed. The challenge seemed to stimulate him.

The South was stirred politically, watching one of their own men go crisscrossing over the country. It pleased them to pick up their newspapers in the morning and read that the governor had unhesitatingly told a Boston Rotary Club group: "I'm proud of the South and I'm proud to be a Southerner." George was just the man who could do it. Known to be a real Civil War buff, he would go into a discourse on history, referring to the position the South was in following the wrath of the Civil War. Then he would point to the "great comeback of the South in spite of the strenuous efforts required to bring about a change during the reconstruction period." He would deliberately note that "all this was done without the benefit of Marshall Plans or federal aid of any kind." After ten such speeches daily, he left the last one, exhausted.

Those traveling with him would be tired out, too, and often weak with hunger. But they could never be sure that they would end the day by getting a good meal. For Wallace, eating was just a necessary evil, and he did not care too much what he had, as long as there was plenty of ketchup to put on it. On one occasion, after a grueling day driving from Maryland to North Carolina for ten different appearances, the group left the last engagement and went to a nearby restaurant. The speeches had gone well, and George, standing beside his chair, congratulated campaign workers as they passed. "Fine job," he would say, steadily pumping their hand up and down. By the time half the corps went by, the men were famished. They wished that he would stop talking and sit down to order so they could, too. One of the aides whispered to the photographer, "Now you just watch. Here we are starving and Wallace will order a hamburger." He was right, and as protocol would have it, they all felt they could order no more. That night most of them went back to the hotel still fairly hungry.

Some audiences were hostile. The Wallace group sometimes had tomatoes and eggs thrown at them. They would go outside to leave and find the air let out of their tires. These and similar actions were taken, according to Wallace observers, by "hippie types" who saw Wallace as a dumb Southerner without enough sense to stay away from places where he was not wanted. Many Alabamians were dissatisfied, too. While Wallace was out of the state chasing after the presidency, Alabama was being ruled with substitute leadership. They felt that the governor was neglecting the job that he had been elected to do. George responded to their complaints with the excuse, "I'm doing it for you."

George Wallace was accused of many things but never of being a snob. Whoever walked into his office got a warm greeting, even political opponents or senate pages. George wanted to be liked by everybody. It disturbed him to think someone disliked him. He spent extra time just trying to convert them. And he always felt that he could.

Self-confidence was a characteristic George had in full-measure. Even when eggs and rocks were thrown at him during campaigns, he thought if the antagonists would just let him finish his speech, he could win them over. If not, he ignored their jeers. He had good reason to believe that he was liked and respected. A 1967 Gallup Poll asked 1,526 adults the question, "What man that you have heard or read about, living today, in any part of the world, do you admire the most?" Mr. Wallace tied with Richard Nixon for seventh place.

During Wallace's first presidential campaign, a tragic event took place. On Elm Street in Dallas, Texas, November 22, 1963, the President of the United States was assassinated. It shook the world, shocked the country, and gave the U.S. a new and different leadership. Americans stood aside helpless and sad while the funeral procession carrying the casket of their slain president passed by on the television screen. Those who might have wished to see John F. Kennedy out of office did not want it to happen that way.

Lyndon Baines Johnson entered the White House to complete the remainder of Kennedy's term. He jumped right in on the integration question, and five days after the death of Kennedy, President Johnson declared to a joint session of Congress that there had been "enough talk about civil rights" and that it was "time now to write the next chapter, and to write it in the books of law." As the first Southerner in the White House since immediately after the Civil War, he committed himself completely to follow through on Kennedy's program.

Integration was enforced in the North as well as the South. There was an unexpected spin-off effect. Interestingly, when open-housing regulations applied in the North, George Wallace found himself with new allies.

There were four major civil rights organizations: The National Association for the Advancement of Colored People, with Roy Wilkins as executive; the Congress of Racial Equality, whose director was James Farmer; the Southern Christian Leadership Conference, with King as its head; and the Student Non-violent Coordinating Committee, with James Forman as executive secretary. The latter had branched off from King's group and was the most militant of the four.

From these organizations flowed the inspiration for Negroes to fight for their rights. These groups claimed to be non-violent. Yet there was always a chance that wherever they went, they would leave in their wake a rash of destruction. It often happened. This had occurred in Alabama, Tennessee, Illinois and Washington, D.C. Emotions were stirred, and both sides often lost control. Wallace's campaign for the presidency continued. Jimmy Faulkner and George Wallace had patched up their differences, and Faulkner was placed in charge of three states, California, Washington and Oregon. As an influential newspaper publisher, he was a great asset to Wallace. He and his campaigners worked hard and kept long hours. Wallace carried his cause to the West and Northwest. Sympathizers of the Negro Revolution cringed when Wallace referred to blacks as "unambitious Africans" who had to be educated by the white man of the South. They screamed "racist" and tried to break up the meetings. But the Wallace group was not easily dismayed. However, when the crowd became uncontrollably antagonistic, the Wallace people would get upset. George kept his composure. He could usually calm them down. "Now, let's all be in a good humor," he would say. "Don't get in an uproar." And tempers would cool off.

Doug Benton, another state official traveling with Wallace, helped keep the peace in a special way. The team had run into the problem of which dignitary in each town would introduce the governor. Always, more than one person wanted to do the honors. So, to solve the problem, the Wallace group imported Benton.

Then, when the question, "who'll do the introduction?" came up, the press secretary would say, "Look, we've brought our own M.C." And that settled the matter. Benton's job was to go out and do the money pitch and warm up the audience. Next, the governor would come on stage. Early in the game Benton discovered that one thing he always needed to know was where they were. When he introduced the governor as "America's greatest living statesman" and turned to meet him halfway on stage, Wallace would often ask, "Where are we?" and Benton had to have the name of the city ready. It was not easy because they were making ten or twelve stops a day.

Before Wallace got to center stage, he wanted to be sure about things. He would say, "It's good to be here in Belle (or wherever they were) tonight," and the speech would begin.

Doug had another job, too. After introducing the governor, he would exit via the stage door. The "crazies" who threatened to blow up the building or kill Wallace usually hung out there. Benton went to check on them. "Somebody was always going to get him, and they wanted to talk about it," Benton said. And they would talk to him, because he was a member of the governor's party. All they wanted was a chance to brag. Sometimes the group of antagonists would get angry, and a little fracas would start. If the chatter developed into a potentially explosive situation, Doug would motion to Skeets McDonald (an entertainer, now deceased) to come over and help him out. Benton was big at three hundred pounds, but he could not take on a dozen men. So, instead of fighting, McDonald would appear at his side, and together they would go into a standard act.

Benton laughed when he told about it. "It was a real loony

routine, and it always scared off the kooks," he said. "Skeets would start talking about something completely unrelated to the threats of the crowd and we'd go into the nervous bit." By then a whole flock of hippies had gathered, enough to warrant Benton and McDonald's putting on a good show. Doug would put his coat on backwards, and Skeets would point his finger at him, jump up and down, and say, "Up, Shelia." Then Benton (the right size for it) would rise up like an elephant. "It scared the mob," he said. "But sometimes they just laughed."

Benton recalls several occasions when the people who were warning they were going to do something to Wallace would go get the security men and point out McDonald and him, saying, "Listen, you'd better watch those guys. They're a couple of kooks!"

One way or another the act always worked. Once, it led a man who had threatened to blow up the entire building to become so frightened he jumped a six-foot fence. Then he brought a security man back with him and peeped around the comer of the building searching for "the dangerous people." Suddenly, he had become concerned with his own safety and turned to law enforcement officials for protection.

Other places, too, were hazardous for the conservative group from Alabama. According to John Pemberton, Clerk of the House, who traveled with the group, it was risky to "say you even lived in Alabama." So wherever they went, aides elbowed their way through the crowds first, clearing a path for Wallace and hoping that the friendly people in the audience outnumbered the hostile ones.

Lurleen went along for the first time on a trip to South Bend, Indiana. The militants were there, too. They brought their signs and were ready to have their say when the governor spoke at Notre Dame University. John Pemberton, a big, lumbering country boy who would make two of Wallace, looked at the mob coming over to the car. He did not mind admitting that he was afraid. "They beat on the car and almost turned it over," he said. "Everyone was frightened—except George Wallace. He didn't care."

Pemberton did not speculate on whether it was a true lack of fear or just an arrogant show. All he said was, "It was amazing to see how that group drew strength from George's attitude. Why, in no time at all, they completely calmed down."

Many people were involved in this campaign. One was soft-spoken Emmett Eaton, Executive Director of the Commission on Aging, who had first worked in Labor Relations with Governor Wallace in 1958. In 1962, Eaton had become very active politically, and by 1964, he was excited about Wallace's prospects and was ready to go all over the country campaigning. He was one of the first to go to Wisconsin and he divided his time between that state, Indiana, and Maryland. Eaton was convinced that Wallace was the best man for the job and explained his reasons for working in the campaign. "I believed in his theory and in his stand," he said. "So, I wanted to do everything I could to help."

When they did well in the presidential primaries, Emmett was proud. "I knew we were successful in 1964 when we got one quarter of a million votes and they were predicting we would get ten thousand. We didn't have any money and we didn't have any resources," he said, illustrating how they had to "just tough it out."

While they were glorying in their successes, other camps were seething at having a third-party movement gain so much recognition. President Lyndon Johnson did not want to be bothered with the little group of zealots. Also, Martin Luther King had to be contended with. He had won the Nobel Peace Prize, and was very active and respected. All over the United States, people who had not taken a position on civil rights before read and heard so much about it they were forced to take a personal stand. Members of the clergy had more and more to say about the issue, and most of them praised King. Pope Paul granted the black minister an audience when King was in Europe accepting the Nobel Prize. King was also a guest speaker at St. Paul's Cathedral in London.

Wallace had faced strong opposition just as determined as he was. But he had been duly warned. At the time of the famous stand in the schoolhouse door, Reverend William Griggs, an open-minded Clayton minister, ran into George at Huntingdon College. George was on his way to the University of Alabama. They stopped and talked briefly about the situation at the University.

Almost with regret, Griggs recalls their conversation, "I talked with him and I told him he was doing more to integrate Alabama than anybody else in Alabama. And he asked, 'William, why is that?' I said, 'Well, you're saying things and doing things that's going to bring all the pressures of the civil rights groups on you and on the state. Of course, personalities like you give them a way to be able to dramatize it, you see, because with moderate or liberal governors you don't see this happening. You're going to the University of Alabama, a public institution, to prevent a citizen of Alabama from attending. You know that's not right.'"

The Methodist minister had known George since 1952. Griggs considered it his duty to admonish him. They had a great deal of close contact when George was a judge and Griggs was pastor of Clayton United Methodist Church. He had been with George on speaking engagements at Masonic ceremonies, and their paths had crossed frequently. Even though they were good friends, George did not listen. Griggs had hoped to stir George's conscience. He was disappointed because he felt George was compromising his principles. "He knew what he was doing," Griggs said. "But he was a politician; he knew how to get elected in Alabama."

Ideologically, Griggs and Wallace differed, but their friendship continued. George selected his course of action and stood by it. But Griggs felt safe in the knowledge that not everybody in Alabama followed the governor. Some of the boys George taught in Sunday School had a different philosophy. They marched in civil rights demonstrations and worked for the cause. A couple of them were put in jail at Kilby prison after an uprising in 1964, and a black attorney, Fred Gray, had to bail them out. Among them was a minister's son.

If George knew about that or other incidents, it did not stop him. No matter what happened or how many insults or questions were flung at him, nothing seemed to discourage him or slow him down. Newsmen asked him about financing, and he very frankly told them, "Yes, Alabama taxpayers are paying for this campaign trip." Senator Wayne Morse (D-Oregon) cornered him on the ten percent disability check he received from the U.S. government. He implied that George was not mentally fit. The governor fired back, "I'm ninety percent all right; the senator might not be as well off." And when Wallace was pushed to the wall with questions concerning racial equality, he would twist things around and cloud the issue by comparing civil rights with the formation of central government and unbridled federal executive power. He warned repeatedly: "We are headed for a dictatorship and it's not going to be far off."

Then, in the spring of 1964, he asked students at Whitewater State College [Wisconsin] if they were aware of the "Communist Party's approval and support of the Civil Rights Bill." He said, "I'm telling you now, this is going to be the means by which private property can be transferred to public domain." Wallace called it a vehicle which would be used "to permit a few men to form a national police force."

If all this was not frightening enough, Wallace brought up various ways that a citizen could be investigated, arrested, charged and tried without benefit of a jury and how American citizens were threatened by a tyrannical form of government. Listeners may not have agreed with him or liked what they heard, but the words commanded their attention.

By the first of June, Wallace was still in the presidential race, but he seemed to be waiting for something to happen. He stated he hoped to make both parties more conservative, but there was no evidence this goal was occurring. Then at the Republican National Convention held in July, 1964, Senator Barry Goldwater was named the Republican presidential candidate. He was known as a conservative who spoke his mind. His nomination seemed to satisfy Wallace and many Southerners who feared that Nelson Rockefeller would be the nominee.

This turn of events made an appreciable difference. All the Wallace efforts had been made with the thought that the balance of power lay in the vote of the South—that the Democrats could not win without its support. The Democratic Convention was only a month away. A decision had to be made fast. On July 19, Wallace picked up a short statement written on Washington Hotel stationery, checked it over, and okayed it for release to the press. It said he had decided to withdraw.

In withdrawing, Wallace alluded to the impact his campaign had on the Democratic and Republican parties. He gave the people hope for a new and different future in the brief statement: "That this message will be heeded is evident." At the same time, he promised Goldwater nothing and skillfully evaded the question put to him by Ben Franklin, a *New York*

Times reporter, "Will you actively campaign for Senator Goldwater?" Wallace mumbled something the reporter did not catch. But he really gave no definite answer.

Those results did not satisfy Alabama's National Democratic Party Chairman Robert Vance. He was unhappy. Because of a credentials dispute at the Democratic National Convention in August, the state-enacted law barring the National Democratic ticket from being on the ballot under a party label kept Johnson electors from appearing. So Vance felt that "In 1964, the people of Alabama were not even able to vote for President of the United States. The so-called Dixiecrats working for Governor Wallace kept Johnson electors off the ballot."

Regardless of his resentment, there was very little he or any other Alabamian could do about it. The damage was done and it was irreversible. When Johnson was re-elected anyway, it made no difference—except to the Alabama voters who felt thwarted.

Presidential campaign Photos

CHAPTER NINE

FIFTY LONG MILES

Selma, the seat of Dallas County, had long been queen of Alabama's grain and livestock empire. Just forty-two miles east of Montgomery, it moved at a slower pace than the capitol city. Serene and sleepy on the exterior, the town retained the tradition of Southern gentility closely protected by a small group of elite families who boasted that their ancestors had lived there since the Revolutionary War.

In 1964, Selma's population of twenty-eight thousand, three hundred and eighty-five was one-half black and one-half white. A majority of wage-earners were agricultural laborers who barely supported themselves and their families. Many blacks had never voted. Literacy tests and a poll tax kept most Negroes in the Deep South away from the ballot box. Now, much to the chagrin of the ruling class, a Voting Rights Act was in the works.

Selma foundries and factories made half the cannons and two-thirds of the fixed ammunition used by the Confederates in the last two years of the Civil War. In 1865, it was captured and burned by U.S. troops. Now it was in for a new and different kind of fight between the races.

In December, 1964, Governor George Wallace was forced to grant the Dallas County Board of Registrars ten additional days for voter registration.

Under pressure from the federally-sponsored social

revolution, some Negroes registered. Up until that time, Selma was unknown to most Americans. Then cars, trucks and hordes of protesters flooded the streets. They came from the south, north, east and west of Alabama—Mobile, Prichard, Huntsville and Sunflower. Martin Luther King, Jr.'s demonstrators began arriving in January, 1965, to plan a massive nearly fifty-mile-long march from Selma to Montgomery. In eight weeks' time, Selma's population was upped more than two thousand. Most of the newcomers were black.

Joe Smitherman, Selma's new mayor, had a good working relationship with the governor's office. Nevertheless, he told Wallace's people to butt out. He said the town's authorities could handle the situation. George Wallace could not do that. He was watching every move that King's group made. By the end of the first week in January, the attention of the nation's media turned to Alabama. NBC, CBS and ABC carried it on the six p.m. news, day after day. Selma became almost a household word.

Public opinion was intense on both sides. The national press generally took the side of the underdog—the Negro. They ignored the fact that many blacks became registered voters in Alabama. They headlined that few Negroes were registered in a dozen of Alabama's sixty-seven counties. They quoted President Lyndon B. Johnson who said, "The real hero of this struggle is the American Negro. His actions...have awakened the conscience of this nation." But *The Alabama Journal* editor, Ray Jenkins, tried to remain unbiased. He commented that "Poor blacks and poor whites are in the same boat." Jenkins saw those two groups as equals, both needing help. But he thought that the governor felt differently. "Poor whites come first with Wallace," he said.

From January until the end of March, King's demonstrators could be seen wandering around downtown

Selma. These integration supporters had a hippie-like appearance and wore the raggedy-edged jeans and flip-flop sandals which were a sign of the times. But when the cameras picked them up on television, some who were sympathetic to their cause were not favorably impressed. Their boots and beards, tight-fitting dresses and stringy hair tended to mark them as members of a radical group. Some saw people that they recognized. Waiters, telephone linemen, teachers and Baptist ministers with ragged beards and unwashed clothes did not look like people who represented moral authority. This turned some people against them. Their demand for a change in Alabamians' way of life appeared to many citizens to be a change for the worse, not better.

Conservative citizens began to scream "Communist" every chance they got. The movement, nevertheless, received support from the clergy. Many priests, ministers and nuns were genuinely concerned about obvious inequities. They backed up their words with actions, marching alongside their black brothers. But Wallace workers insisted some of them were fakes. Doug Benton, a member of George Wallace's cabinet, said many of the clerics who participated in demonstrations were impersonators. Also, not all bona fide clerics who demonstrated had the sanction of their superiors.

The Most Reverend Thomas J. Toolen, Bishop of the Mobile-Birmingham diocese, objected openly to nuns and priests roaming the streets of his diocese. Certain parish priests also deplored the idea of a brother priest behaving like a radical.

The Reverend Hinton Lipscomb, a Mobile-born and bred Catholic priest—who knew the pain of being different since he lost both legs to a disease—expressed his opinion vocally and in a letter to a Bishop of Houston. "In a march marked with incidents of fornication, law-breaking and the like," he wrote,

"I see no reason for Catholic priests and nuns to take up such a cause and flaunt themselves for all the American public to see." He spotted his correspondence with a few "damns" and "hells" for emphasis.

Underneath the turmoil, a search for truth and justice was being conducted. The truth of what took place was being recorded as it happened. History would have the notes of the press and the tape recordings of national television commentators to refresh memories.

For two months, King's demonstrators blocked Selma streets. They wandered in and out of stores, handling merchandise and saying, "We're just looking." During lunch hour, local citizens had problems getting served at Kentucky Fried Chicken or McDonald's. The serving windows were full. Black visitors crowded out the regulars. Often, demonstrators would take boxes of chicken or hamburgers and sit on the carpet-like grass of Sturdivant Hall at 713 Mabry Street. Selma citizens disliked their museum's lawn being used as a public picnic area. It damaged the grass and discouraged paying customers. But there was little they could do about it.

The prime concern of the demonstrators was getting nationwide attention for the voting bill. And they made a lot of noise about it. They chanted their cause all over town: "We want to vote, we want to vote." Selma residents closed their windows and stopped up their ears. But the media paid attention. For weeks on end, hardly a day passed without a mention of Selma, Alabama.

Throughout the period, George Wallace appeared to keep his hands off the situation. As governor, he had an excuse to interfere. It was his responsibility to maintain law and order on the one hand, but he also had to allow local authorities to take care of their own business in their own way. After all, he was the one who said levels of authority should be respected.

So he sat back, tapped his feet, and bided his time. Selma swarmed with strangers who came and went as they pleased. Their numbers increased daily from six hundred, to seven hundred, to a thousand. Martin Luther King, Jr.'s group moved forward with steady progress.

King announced that he would march to Montgomery.

The prospect of one thousand people led by King from Selma to Montgomery had Wallace clenching his fists. Busy Highway 80, down which they would travel, would become a bottleneck. In addition to the normal flow of traffic, curiosity seekers were bound to turn out in huge numbers. Wallace consulted with many of his advisors and asked their opinion about trying to stop the march. He got "yesses" and "nos." The buck had to stop somewhere, and Wallace knew all along that the decision was really in his lap.

The governor said "No." He avoided the true issue and warned that Alabama highways must not be blocked. State Troopers would be there to stop the march. The marchers vowed to march anyway. The ultimatum neither stopped nor discouraged them.

On Sunday, March 7, 1965, King was not there to lead his troops into battle. Hosea Williams of Atlanta, and John R. Lewis of Selma led the march. James G. Clark, the sheriff of Dallas County, had the villain's role when police power confronted Civil Rights forces.

When the marchers came face-to-face with the Alabama State Troopers east of the Edmund Pettus Bridge across the Alabama River in downtown Selma, they were told, "Turn back." Ignoring the command, they surged forward as a group. Billy clubs, wielded by angry lawmen, came into contact with heads. Whips struck backs, arms and legs. Blood began to flow. Two hundred state troopers and sheriff's deputies "employed whips, night sticks, cattle prods and tear gas."

People screamed, cowed or tried to run. But unarmed and defenseless, many had to take the blows. Seventeen were hospitalized and sixty-seven others received emergency first aid.

The world watched on television. Many viewers were horrified. Not Governor George Wallace. He praised police efforts and claimed that their action saved many Negro lives.

Despite a federal court order, on March 9, King led fifteen hundred blacks and whites on a token one-mile march. Again, Alabama State Troopers stopped the group. King turned back, but his effort was effective. Right away, thousands of sympathetic integrationists conducted similar marches in New York, Los Angeles, Detroit, Chicago and Boston.

Two days after the confrontations, a tragedy occurred. The Reverend James J. Reeb, a Unitarian minister from Boston, was attacked by three white youths on a Selma street. Within two days he died from his wounds in a Birmingham hospital. Immediately, twenty-five thousand Civil Rights demonstrators conducted a sympathy march in Boston. President Johnson thought that was enough. On March 15, he told a joint session of Congress that "Every American citizen must have a right to vote." Hoping to put an end to the violence, he stepped in, ordered the Alabama National Guard federalized, and directed them to protect the marchers on March 21 when they tried again to go from Selma to Montgomery.

Johnson sent a thousand Army military policemen, plus dozens of FBI agents and U.S. Marshals, to Alabama. Soldiers guarded every crossroad on U.S. Highway 80. But they were not needed. This time, there was no violence. As it turned out, a heavy rain caused more problems for the marchers than anything else.

Despite that, this time it worked. King, who lead this march, proclaimed victory. When he arrived, he was elated to find a crowd of thirty thousand flag-wavers gathered on the steps of the capitol in Montgomery. However, the exuberance was short lived. Spirits were dampened that night. Thirty-nine-year-old Viola Liuzzo, a white woman from Detroit, was shot and killed while driving two Negroes from Selma back to Montgomery. She left five children motherless. Johnson's intervention had not prevented another fatality.

Shortly afterward, President Johnson appeared on TV and announced the arrest of four Ku Klux Klansmen charged in connection with Liuzzo's murder. The accused, LeRoy Wilkins, Jr., William Orville Eaton, Eugene Thomas and Gary Thomas Rowe, Jr. were all from Alabama. Johnson called the Klan a "hooded society of bigots" and said it should be investigated. King clapped, and Klan Imperial Wizard, Robert M. Sheldon, called the president a "damn liar."

Rowe was revealed as an FBI informer. Wilkins, Eaton, and Thomas were convicted on an accusation of conspiring to deprive Mrs. Liuzzo of her civil rights. Federal Judge Frank M. Johnson, Jr., sentenced each man to ten years in prison, the maximum sentence for the offense.

By the end of March, the demonstrators finally left. Wallace and his political contemporaries heaved a sigh of relief. So did the citizens of Selma. But they regretted that the town's dignity and refinement had been destroyed.

Selma's aristocracy was shaken. How could they ever bring back the poise and gentility they once claimed so proudly? Now "Selma" would be synonymous with words like "bigotry" and "violence."

Even people who had not been involved in the action felt its upsetting impact. For over two months, Selma had been in a state of turmoil. Knowing it was almost too much to expect, now citizens hoped that their town would return to normal.

CHAPTER TEN

A WONDERFUL WOMAN

Instead of being dismayed and disillusioned by the turmoil of the Selma-to-Montgomery march, George Wallace was invigorated.

At that time, an Alabama governor could not succeed himself. Wallace immediately got busy implementing a way to keep the governorship four more years.

Late in September, 1965, with the heat of Selma barely cooled, a bill was introduced in the legislature of the State of Alabama proposing that "the people of Alabama be allowed to vote on whether they want a governor to succeed himself in office." The ears of the nation perked up.

Liberals became alarmed. They thought they were almost rid of George C. Wallace. All indications were that if he ran, he would be governor again. From that position, he could continue his argument in favor of states' rights.

After the bill passed the Alabama House of Representatives and received support in the senate, a small group of senators filibustered and blocked the measure. On October 22, 1965, the senate adjourned, refusing to allow Alabamians to vote on the succession bill amendment. George lost.

What was left to do? It was inconceivable that George would give up what he had worked all his life to attain. He found an alternative, a way to keep the power—through

Lurleen. So Lurleen, unassuming and ill, was groomed to become the first woman Governor of Alabama. George had to keep control of the State of Alabama and that was the only way he could do it.

The question was—did she want to run? Was she willing to make the sacrifices and fulfill the obligations of the office, in addition to her job as a mother? Lurleen, a once child-bride of George Wallace, had ridden with him to the top. As a strong-willed person, he had always been the dominant figure in the family. She knew this would persist, and that she would be governor in name only. Consciously or unconsciously, nearly all her life she had bowed to his will. Only in the rearing of the children had she taken complete responsibility. Perhaps that gave her some degree of self-confidence.

The issue was complicated by the fact that Lurleen had cancer. She had gotten the first diagnosis of a malignancy in 1961 when Lee, her last child, was born. Those close to the family knew it then. They wondered if she was physically able to be governor of a state. Did she want to be Governor of Alabama, or did she run just because George said so? Probably no one will ever know. It is possible that Lurleen herself, whatever she might have said, did not really know.

But she did enter the race, and many thought it was willingly. Catherine Steineker, Lurleen's secretary, said her personal entry into the political world seemed like a joke to Lurleen at first. She didn't take it seriously.

Catherine felt differently. She knew George Wallace. He was determined to keep the power any way he could. She also knew Lurleen. They'd been friends before she became Lurleen's secretary in 1964. Their first work together began on Thanksgiving night during the middle of George's first term as governor. The telephone rang, and when Catherine answered it was Lurleen Wallace. Lurleen told Catherine that they were running behind with mailing out Christmas cards and other things and asked her to come help until Christmas. They were having parties at the mansion, and Lurleen's secretary, Sibyl Simon, needed some assistance. Catherine said she would be glad to help. Then Mrs. Simon had problems at home and decided to leave her job. Right after Christmas, they were writing "thank you" notes when Lurleen asked Catherine if she would like to be her secretary permanently. Catherine told her, "I don't take dictation."

Lurleen replied, "I don't give it."

So Catherine agreed to take the job but laid the ground rules. "I'll tell you one thing," she said to Lurleen, "when the time comes that I can't look you in the face and tell you to 'Go to hell,' then I'm leaving. That's going to be the last day I work for you. I don't know anything about this and you don't know very much more and we'll learn together." That was the way they went into what Catherine called "this thing." Then Catherine added that "It was just one of the most delightful relationships you could ever have with anybody in this world. She was a joy to be around. She really was.'"

Catherine was there when talk of Lurleen's running began to become serious. It was not a joke long. First George and some of his political cronies began to throw out feelers through the newspapers to see what the public reaction would be.

Then, just before the deadline for qualifying, George had second thoughts. On George Washington's birthday he came home for lunch. He never did that unless it was a holiday and the Capitol cafeteria was closed. Usually, he used that time to be with employees and talk with them. He found that the grass-roots level chatter was often informative. But since George was dining at home that day, Lurleen invited Catherine and her husband, Al, to come join them. Mr. Steineker also worked for the state as Chief Examiner of Public Accounts. Lurleen knew that George enjoyed his company. As always, the talk would be politics.

Sure enough, when George came in, he had a specific subject on his mind. He made an announcement: "Well, sugar, I've decided we are not going to run. There is an awful lot of legislation to be passed, and I just don't think I can go through with it again. I'm tired. I'm worn out. We'll go back to Clayton and I'll run for judge again and I'll practice a little law and you can go back to fishing."

Lurleen perked up. She had made a decision on her own. She looked down the table at him and said, "I'll tell you right now, I'm gonna run. And if you want to sit up in that Capitol and not help me campaign, that's just fine with me. I'm gonna run for governor."

She'd had a taste of power and liked it. "George was floored," Catherine recalled. "Until that point he had not realized Lurleen was that much in favor of running. I think he felt he had sort of pushed her into this thing."

They questioned Lurleen about her health. Catherine and George asked her if she felt up to it. She was still recovering from a hysterectomy, and Catherine was concerned, especially since a malignancy had been found. She spoke directly, trying to talk Lurleen out of it, "Listen, Lurleen," she said, "you don't feel like running. This will be a hard campaign. You can't just sit here in Montgomery and win it."

But Lurleen was convinced that the cancer was gone. She told Catherine, "I feel great. My doctors told me they have gotten it."

Catherine said she believed this, too. Doctors had tested and tested and had done everything and assured her the cancer was under control. They could find no sign of it, nothing.

"They were good doctors, not some jacklegs. They knew what they were doing," said Catherine, who added that she later wondered if it was, in fact, two separate cancers, two entirely different malignancies.

Lurleen's mind was made up. Catherine knew Lurleen well enough not to argue with her.

She knew politics, too. It was in her blood. In 1935, when Clarence Norton, Catherine's father, ran for tax assessor, George's father managed his winning campaign. And in George's first legislative race, Uncle Ernest Norton upset the family by opposing him. So Catherine could understand Lurleen's attraction to politics.

Still, Catherine felt that George was really ready to quit. She recalls, "Really and truly I think at that point—now I don't know whether later on this would have been true—but at that point George C. was perfectly willing to give it up. 'Let's go home,' he said. 'I have had it.'

"If Lurleen had said, 'All right, that's what we'll do,' that would have been the end of it." But if this was true, it certainly would have been out of character for the former fighter. To believe that George Wallace would have been satisfied to move out of the capitol and return to country life just did not make sense.

Others felt differently. They thought that George made the decision for Lurleen. Reverend William Griggs was one who said he "doubts that Lurleen wanted to be governor but Barbour County men are persistent." He said he knew Lurleen as "conventional, traditional but not aggressive." To him, she didn't seem to be the type to be that kind of leader.

Regardless of what anybody thought, the governor's wife prepared to run. And the effort seemed against her own nature. Mary Jo Ventress, a longtime friend, said Lurleen always let everyone else do things. Now she had to be at the center herself. "Basically, Lurleen was always interested in the other person's welfare," she said. "She never did try to push herself.

She wasn't a pushy type, and she preferred to stand back and let others take the limelight."

Mary Jo spoke of how Lurleen had a lot of innate ability but always was a little shy. "Lurleen was constantly on guard so that she'd make the right impression. She realized that whatever she did reflected on George. So she tried very hard to present a perfect image," Mary Jo said.

#

While George was on his way up, things were hard in Clayton. Money was scarce and Lurleen learned to "make do" with what they had. On those few occasions when Lurleen had the opportunity to buy something new, it was an important event. Mary Jo recalled one such time when "Lurleen's excitement over a new dining room suite prompted her to call George at the office the minute it was delivered. She just could not wait until he got home to tell him," she said. "It didn't take much to make Lurleen happy."

Later, as a judge, George splurged and gave Lurleen mink kolinskys for her birthday. Mary Jo laughed, remembering the reaction of Lurleen's friends. "With a little envy, the other ladies in her circle just thought that would be the finest thing— to have a little mink collar scarf. Lurleen did, too. She was so proud of them she kept them in the box all the time so they would be safe. Her friends joked and laughed that she would never get to wear them. They thought she would wear the box." But through years of struggle, Lurleen had grown to be very protective of the valuable things she acquired because luxuries, for her, had come few and far between.

This simple background led her from the streets of Clayton, as a young mother in bobby sox—the "just a housewife" type—to the role of First Lady of the state and on to become a candidate for the governorship. Lurleen of Alabama would soon be known across the nation.

She began to campaign without much change in her appearance or her personality. Somehow she found the self-confidence necessary to a politician, and a strength she did not know she possessed. She kept her simple attitude and Alabamians liked it. Still, George really carried the brunt of his wife's campaign. He made most of the speeches, and whatever Lurleen added was usually received as secondary. But she did have to make a good impression, or people would not have accepted her, no matter whose wife she was.

During the campaign, Lurleen had substantial opposition. Her opponents for the Democratic nomination included Ryan deGraffenreid, Attorney General Richmond Flowers, former Congressman Carl Elliott, State Senator Bob Gilchrist, former Governor John Patterson, and businessman Charles Woods. Then deGraffenreid was killed in a plane crash in February, 1966, while engaged in a pre-campaign organization effort. This left one fewer candidate vying for the governor's chair. The other five campaigned actively but there was no need to worry. Lurleen captured fifty-four percent of the vote and won the primary without a run-off. This sick woman had entered a field against nine male opponents and had beaten them all, calling herself "an instrument whereby you, the people of Alabama, have an opportunity to express yourselves..." Alabamians expressed themselves very clearly. Her closest opponent, Richmond Flowers, received 172,385 votes. Lurleen received 480,841.

Newsmen came from all over the United States to cover the event that put the first woman ever in the Alabama governor's chair. Headlines proclaimed the victory. *The Chicago Tribune*: "Mrs. Wallace Big Winner." *The Kansas City Times*: "Mrs. Wallace by Landslide." The Wallaces had successfully stumped the state. They were a team now. She was Governor of Alabama, and George would run the state.

If Lurleen's being governor did anything for her marriage to George, it had to be that it gave her an opportunity to understand what a politician's life was really like. Lurleen and George had the problems most couples do. Catherine Steineker referred to one of the reasons for disagreement between them. "Lurleen couldn't understand why it [politicking] took so much time," she said. "This was the thing she and George had not seen eye to eye on for years." When she hit the campaign trail, however, Lurleen realized how many hands had to be shaken, how many people had to be smiled at and greeted warmly, and how many hours it all took.

Being governor, however, did not change her values. It made her more cautious in the things she said and did, but she was no politician. Catherine said, "She just loved people. She was warm, she was just so warm. The only thing Lurleen regretted about being in politics was that it did take her away from her family so much."

Lurleen had always liked casual clothes and simple styles. She never spent much money trying to be fashionable. This was reflected in the way she dressed for the inauguration. Her friend, Mary Jo Ventress, made the pillbox hat she wore on Inauguration Day, January 16, 1967. And that day is vivid in Mary Jo's memory.

Mary Jo remembers Lurleen's promise to Alabama citizens. "The most memorable moment I have of Lurleen is that I can just see her as she took the Oath of Office," she said. "Tears well in my eyes and my throat gets lumps in it because she was sincere in what she said that day when she promised Alabamians, 'With God's help, I'll make you a good governor.' She meant that thing. It wasn't lip service to her. It was sincere dedication. She would have done anything in her power had she been given the opportunity. I do think she would have made a profound impact on the people of Alabama. I can still see her in a little black suit with her head held high, tears in her eyes, with the firm conviction that this was something she fully intended to do. It was a real desire for her to do what she thought would be necessary to make a good governor."

Years later, after Lurleen succumbed to cancer, Mary Jo had not forgotten her friend. She recalls, too, that Lurleen had her make the gown for the Inaugural Ball. The portrait taken of her in that gown was Alabamians' favorite of Lurleen Burns Wallace.

There were many dignitaries present at Lurleen's inauguration, but none more important to George and Lurleen than one guest they invited personally. "Mom" Sanders from Arkadelphia, Arkansas, had been a surrogate mother to George and Lurleen when he was stationed in Arkansas in World War II. She had kept in touch with George through the years and attended his inauguration in 1963. She often wrote him to say she had seen him on TV and she would express agreement with his position.

In her letters, sometimes Mom would mother him a bit. George appreciated her interest and understanding. Once, when she defended his position against that of *The Arkansas Gazette*, he wrote back:

> "Regarding the Arkansas Gazette editorial - this is typical of them. However, I have found that, insofar as this position of the press is concerned, they can 'fool some of the people some of the time but not all of the people all of the time.' I do not feel that too many people are being fooled now by *The Arkansas Gazette*. However, it does not even concern me—my hide is getting pretty tough."

Each time George received a letter from Mom, he answered. Probably the one she treasured most was written May 9, 1966. It was very sentimental, reminiscent of the days he spent at Ouachita and with high praise for his adopted mother:

Dear Mom,

I would like to take this opportunity to express to you my sincere gratitude and appreciation for the many kindnesses that you have shown to me throughout the years. I will always remember the fine days I spent in Arkadelphia and the help you gave Lurleen and me.

You are the most unforgettable person that I have met during my entire Army-Air Force career. I remember how homesick and blue I was there in Arkadelphia, and you not only helped me over this but also looked after Lurleen when she came there as a young bride.

Much has happened since those days in Arkansas at Ouachita College, and 1 am grateful for the fact that you have made it possible for me to stay in touch with many of the fine young men I met there by sending me their addresses and informing me of their whereabouts.

Again let me thank you for helping a homesick youngster and his bride many years ago in Arkadelphia. We will always have a warm place in our hearts for you.

With best wishes to you and all your family, I am,
Sincerely yours,
George C. Wallace, Governor

George did not forget the lady who had befriended him.

When the inaugural invitations were mailed, Mom Sanders was among the first to receive one. And when she arrived in Montgomery, the red carpet was out. The day before the inauguration, her assigned escort took her to the Wallace home on Farrar Street. Lurleen's parents, Mr. and Mrs. Harold Burns, were living there and taking care of the house until George and Lurleen could move into it. On the walls, Mom could see mementos of the life of her protegé and she found it all "incredible."

Many years had passed but memories remained, and as Mom Sanders witnessed the swearing-in ceremony on that January day in twenty-eight-degree temperature, the shivers that went up her spine were as much a result of pride as they were of the freezing cold.

So Lurleen took office with the confidence of her friends, at least. They knew she had the benefit of George's past experience and felt that would help tremendously.

In many ways, George and Lurleen were alike. Money, and the things it would buy, did not interest them. As a woman, Lurleen probably realized more than George that she had to have clothes appropriate to the occasion, but she kept her taste for casual wear during her term as governor. For special occasions, when she did need to be smartly dressed, she chose dresses from Miller's, a fashionable shop in Montgomery. "Then," her secretary recalled, "she would pay as much as was necessary, but it nearly killed her to have to do it." During the time she was First Lady, however, Lurleen still shopped at Sears.

When she took over as governor, the duties of George Wallace were reduced only slightly. Lurleen took care of vice-presidential-type chores. She attended groundbreaking ceremonies, ribbon cuttings and personal appearances when it was important that the governor be present, but George continued to do most of the administrative work. People around the state began to call them "the Governors Wallace."

While Lurleen kept up a good front, by the end of March she looked tired out. Even a healthy Lurleen was not accustomed to being a head of state. She was a homebody type. Her friends in Clayton remembered her as "brown as a berry hanging out clothes...she loved to get to the clothes line even when she had a dryer." They couldn't picture her as the Governor of Alabama. A Lurleen turning away from her family to preside over affairs of state was an improbable reality.

But Lurleen did do her share. As governor, she did much to further favorite causes. The children's mental institution at Partlow in Tuscaloosa received her full attention. Her compassion for the patients brought her to tears and moved her to see that many improvements were made in the children's behalf. She resolved that if there was any way to improve the conditions, she would do it. She initiated one of the finest mental health programs in the nation.

All during the first six months of Lurleen's term, she was losing weight and becoming increasingly ill. The cancer had come back. On the sandy shores of the Gulf of Mexico one warm June day, she told her friend, Catherine, that she would not be around another year.

While Lurleen was committed to her job, she realized that she needed some time to rest and she had no qualms about taking an afternoon off. She loved hunting and fishing, and Capitol employees were not surprised to see her "sneaking out the back door" around one p.m. But George stayed available, and visitors at the Capitol were just as satisfied to shake his hand as they would have been to shake the hand of the current governor.

George had a reason for holding on to the governorship. He was keeping his name in front of the public lest they forget him before the 1968 presidential race came up. Right now, he was just biding time.

George was not just sitting back looking at the school buildings, junior colleges and trade schools he had helped build. His concerns were much bigger. He maintained that the race problem would be solved only by education. More schools had been built. Hopefully, all who desired to learn could now obtain an education of their choice. Though many of the minority groups remained dissatisfied, most citizens felt Alabama's educational system had been greatly improved during the Wallace administration.

With this to his credit in Alabama and the nationwide recognition of having once run for the presidency, speculation began about whether the former governor would try again. George had dropped out of the 1964 presidential race, but he had long since learned to cope with disappointment. His life had never been without peaks and valleys, and even the distressing news of Lurleen's cancer did not impede his political career. He seemed to be able to separate his private life, with its personal worries, from his political life and its demands upon his time and energy. It was almost as though he lived in two distinct worlds.

For Lurleen, the reality of cancer neutralized the joy of the high honor of being governor. She was sick and she was scared. When she felt very ill, she was helped by her minister. The Reverend John Vickers came to offer consolation and hopefully to strengthen her faith and give her courage. It looked hopeless but the doctors kept trying. In another effort to arrest the malignancy, Lurleen went to Houston to the University of Texas M.D. Anderson Hospital and Tumor Institute. George, their oldest daughter Bobbi (now Mrs. James Parsons) and Mary Jo Ventress went along. Despite efforts to prevent her having to face people at the airport, a crowd still showed up to see Governor Lurleen. With forced determination, she shook their hands, then said a private goodbye to her children.

Medical bills mounted. Friends of the Wallaces maintained that "there was never a lot of money...George had good insurance but the premiums took a big bite of his income." That probably saved him from bankruptcy. A small fortune was spent on Lurleen's medical care, but it was all useless. Even though she would live long enough to be a part of the 1968 presidential campaign, nothing could be done to save her.

The people closest to her realized that the end was drawing near and they were sad. Lurleen's associates and those who had come to know her through television, radio and the newspapers held her in high regard. News reports of her weakening condition caused Alabamians to fear that Lurleen would not serve out her term. Some people did not like her being the shadow of George Wallace when she was governor, but many judged Lurleen on her own merits. Alabamians still echo the opinion of Derryl Gordon, Wallace's Executive Secretary, given shortly after Lurleen's death. He said, "Now that was a wonderful woman."

Lurleen's Inauguration

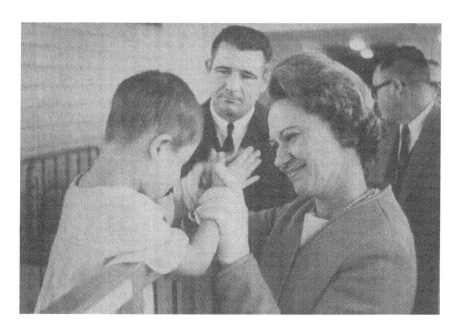

Visiting Bryce speaking with a child

Official Portrait of Lurleen

CHAPTER ELEVEN

THE DOLLAR BILL CAMPAIGN

The 1968 campaign was George Wallace's most successful try for the presidency.

Early in the game, a trial run was planned to get Wallace on the ballot in California. This was hard to do. Registering Californians had to fill out incredibly complex forms. They had to be explicit about their street address, a lot number, names of cross streets, and provide other information which most people would not have at their fingertips. If one thing was wrong with the application, the applicant was refused. Also, when a person registered as a member of the American Independent Party, he relinquished his right to vote in the primary. Some people got the impression that they would not be able to vote in the general election either.

At the first hint that Wallace would try to get the American Independent Party on the California ballot, newspaper columnists ridiculed his effort. Wallace had no money and neither did his party. The Wallace camp claimed that Rockefeller and several others had spent millions of dollars attempting to get on the California ballot and had failed. How could this Alabama ex-governor expect to succeed where dynamic business tycoons could not? Rumors were flying and people were laughing. Newspapers scoffed as they printed the small numbers pre-registering—so far. That was the beginning. There was much more to come.

While the mechanism for the California try was being set into motion and the campaign crew prepared to go into high gear, Lurleen was getting sicker day by day. For her, Christmas had begun in July. "She was worse than Lee about Christmas," her secretary, Catherine, said. "In the middle of the summer we would decide on some small gifts—which couldn't cost much because they had to come out of Lurleen's household money— but these were selected to be distributed to all the children in orphanages in the state." It was a custom Lurleen had begun as First Lady and wanted to continue as governor.

On long September nights, Governor Lurleen would go out to the guest house alone and sit at the table set up especially for the purpose of gift wrapping. Bogged down in ribbons and Santa Claus red and green Christmas wrap, she lovingly took the little gift (Lifesavers, perhaps) and carefully packed each one, night after night, until the two thousand were done. The next day she would brag to Catherine, "I wrapped a whole case last night."

Beginning right after Thanksgiving, Lurleen and her secretary personally delivered as many packages as they could to orphanages. When time ran out for her, Lurleen sent the rest by her personal representative.

Another project of Lurleen's was to have the retarded children of McInnis School in Montgomery come to the mansion for a Christmas party. The Christmas tree was always up and beautifully decorated. On Lurleen's last Christmas she chose a flocked tree that reached to the mansion ceiling. It was totally done with pink decorations. Catherine recalled how it looked. "For some years Lurleen had been collecting little hand-made jeweled balls—the ones made with Styrofoam then done with velvet ribbons, pearls and different colored stones," she said. "She used those and nothing but pink balls, pink bows and pink birds. It was lovely." And the pleasure in the eyes of the little children admiring it was Lurleen's pleasure, too. But their plight disturbed Lurleen and her secretary remembered how, "after the party, Lurleen went back and sat in the den and sobbed like her heart would break."

The memory of it all was vivid in Catherine's mind: "The children always brought a gift which Lurleen put with all the beautiful things people had sent and all the things the florist made—they would bring a Christmas tree with little ornaments on it. That was in a place of honor up in the front of the house with all the gorgeous stuff. Boxwood and fresh holly were all around and right in the middle of it would be whatever those children brought from the retarded home. It was there. Children were just her greatest joy."

But the pleasure of gift giving was not all Lurleen had to think about. There was medicine to take and trips to Houston for chemotherapy. There was also her children's future...and George's presidential campaign.

As governor, it was important that Lurleen be a part of that campaign. When George decided to tour California in November, she agreed to go along. She packed the clothes that now hung loosely on her frail body and vowed to conceal her suffering behind a smile.

As Governor of Alabama, the first in Alabama and only the third woman governor in the nation's history, Lurleen lent support to the campaign in California. Support was what they needed most. The Wallace troops had to persuade over 66,000 people to go to city hall and fill out a complicated form to be able to vote for the American Independent Party (A.I.P.).

One of the men who traveled with the Wallace group in 1968 was Roy Dobbs, Accounts Manager for Southern Bell Telephone Company. He was in the position of being right in the middle of the campaign. He always had to arrive early and set up the telephones. From the inside he could see what it took to achieve their goal in California. "It took a lot of people working," he said. "We needed them to pass out leaflets and answer phones." At the grass-roots level he saw they would need cold, hard cash. But that could and would come in one dollar at a time. It was to be a "Dollar bill campaign." The money was funneled from Montgomery into a general campaign fund. Finance Director Seymore Trammell and Cecil Jackson were trying to hold everything together and it was a tremendous undertaking. Looking back, Dobbs recalls just how big it was: "When you're trying to do a program of that magnitude and depending on finances from people sending in dollars, it's pretty tough. You don't know the outcome or what the candidate's going to do." The uncertainty of success added anxiety to an already difficult task.

George just kept plodding along, refusing to believe he could not make the California ballot. The more the news reported his task as impossible, the more determined he became. The Wallace group set up headquarters all over the state, saturating the Los Angeles area particularly. But the movement was not just other people doing all the work. The governor made up to twelve appearances daily. Co-workers remembered that even under so much strain, George remained congenial. His efforts were rewarded; the personal meeting with "the man" made the difference. By the deadline for citizens to register as members of the American Independent Party in California, George Wallace was indeed on the ballot, and TV and newspaper reporters had to change their tune. Self-assured as he might have seemed over the victory in California, *The Advertiser Journal* (Montgomery, Alabama) reported December 24, 1967, that Wallace revealed plans to go to Ohio next but that he appeared less than confident. He said, "You've got to have close to half a million signatures there. I'm going to try to get on the ballot, but it's very difficult to get signatures."

Nevertheless, the third party became a genuine force. Reporters all over the nation had to acknowledge that the Alabama governor had done what he had set out to do, at least in California.

After her return from California in November, Lurleen and her secretary, Catherine, made another trip. It was to be her last, other than going to the hospital in Houston. Lurleen, Reverend John Vickers and Catherine went to Selma to the Methodist Children's Home to deliver presents to the children. They had been together so much, Catherine could look at Lurleen and know how bad she was feeling. That day she knew Lurleen was obviously suffering.

Recalling how much effort the trip must have required, Catherine said, "By the time we got to Selma, she was in so much pain she couldn't hide it too well. But she walked all over the grounds at that children's home and went in every one of those cottages to see their Christmas decorations and to have pictures made with all the children." Like George, Lurleen would not give up.

On the day before Christmas Eve, the Wallace corps arrived back in Montgomery following their California campaign. Elated that the signature gathering was a success with over the 66,059 voters necessary to get his American Independent Party listed, George smilingly greeted Lurleen when she met him at the airport. She was a little peaked, but she did not look like a dying woman. George's good news and her attention to others, particularly children, had revitalized her.

Lurleen's love for Christmas did not rub off on George. His campaign continued right until the day itself. Even then, much of the activity surrounding a political candidate did not change.

For one thing, George still had to have protection. A

would-be assassin would hardly be concerned with Christmas. On Christmas, the four security men decided between themselves who would work. Since Wallace was at the mansion, Dave Harwood had guard duty there on Christmas day.

Inside the house that morning, the governor's children were eager to open their presents. Six-year-old Lee was out of bed by six-thirty, shaking her father until he agreed to get up, too. They went downstairs. Forcing herself, Lurleen exclaimed with surprise and pleasure as she opened her gifts. Pulling out a robe and a white blouse, she said, "Thank you" to George and hugged her children one by one.

When things calmed down, just before their noon dinner, Wallace wandered outside. He was surprised to find Dave sitting in the guard house by the front gate. Without hesitation, he said, "Dave, it's Christmas day. You go home. I'll call you if I need you." His consideration amazed the state trooper. Dave wondered how "a governor and a presidential candidate even had time to remember it was Christmas."

The dollars were coming in. They came from members of AFL and CIO unions wanting to protect their seniority; from Mississippi, Ohio and California parents concerned about school situations, especially integration; from Alabamians and Virginians who wanted to preserve the Southern way of life; from police officers, anti-Communists, and any and all who saw value in the stand of the fiery, determined Alabama governor. While both the Democratic and Republican parties were receiving money in large amounts, the determined Alabamian was getting his one bite at a time. His party was satisfied. As long as the money flow remained steady and the workers stayed dedicated, the American Independent Party felt that they could pull it off and win the election against all odds.

The next move was to go from California into other states.

Traveling fast from one place to another created a problem. George had always been afraid to fly. He worried about bad weather every time they went up. The A.I.P. had old airplanes, which made George even more wary. When he got worried, he would abruptly change travel plans.

One afternoon when Roy Dobbs was flying with them, they zoomed over Nevada. Dobbs recalls that the weather "wasn't that bad." It was clear enough for them to look down and see Vegas. One minute Dobbs was pointing out the Boulder Dam; the next minute he saw they had turned back: there was the dam again. The governor had not liked the way the clouds looked, so he insisted on landing.

The non-scheduled stop put them in a bind. Las Vegas was not prepared for them. "It wasn't real easy to get accommodations for that many people. In fact, it was quite difficult," Dobbs said. "And that night after everybody went out to eat, they came back to the headquarters and found that someone had ordered two hundred orders of Kentucky Fried chicken." Most of it went to waste. Others, too, testify to Wallace's fear of flying. Bill Sellers, a Mobile Press Register political reporter, called it "a mortal fear." He described Wallace as a "white-knuckle flyer who won't drink, but he'll get on the plane with a big cigar and sit there and hold on." One incident in Seller's memory was the time they flew out of Seattle in a Lockheed Lone Star headed for Canada in January, 1964. "We decided to stop over in Bremerton, Washington, to see the U.S.S. Alabama," he said. "Arrangements had already been made to get the ship down to Mobile as a tourist attraction, and we thought it would be good for the governor to go aboard it out there and have pictures made to help promote the fund-raising campaign in Alabama. We took off from Seattle and flew over to Bremerton just a little hop away. It so happened it was rainy and foggy, typical of the winter days in

Washington state. We got down in the pea-soup fog and couldn't see the runway. Everybody was straining and straining, and all of a sudden we passed right over a hangar, missing it about thirty feet. Then Wallace yelled up front to the pilot, 'Jimmy, to hell with that battleship. Let's get that plane back up there where it belongs.'" They skipped seeing the battleship and went into Canada where they found shirtsleeve weather. And the calmed-down governor spoke in Victoria that afternoon.

But George's reluctance to fly did not keep him on the ground. In January, 1968, the Wallace group was off again. They were moving as fast as possible from Montgomery to Dallas and from Massachusetts to California. George embarked on a stump tour that took him over most of the country. His campaign speech remained the same, and many of his crew had it memorized. If he had anything different to add, he would glance down at the rumpled up pieces of paper with his notes on them to be sure he did not forget what it was.

One time, he almost fooled his troops. In Iowa, George's advisors convinced him that it would be a good idea to prepare a printed speech to pass out at the rally. Since Des Moines was in a farming district, they suggested gearing it to the interest of the farmers who were sure to be there. George never used printed copy, so it took much persuasion before he finally gave in. But he did.

When Bill Jones, the Press Secretary, came out that afternoon with a stack of papers in his hand and said, "Here's a copy of the speech for tonight," workers were really taken aback. Many had been with George a long time, and they had never seen a printed text before. Roy Dobbs was shocked. He said, "Man, I've got to have one of those myself. I want to look at what he's gonna say." He got the copy and read parts of it aloud to the group. It concerned all the farming issues and, although it was well-prepared, it did not sound like George Wallace at all.

That night, every member of the Wallace group waited eagerly to hear him begin. This was going to be something new. When Wallace came up, the crowd was applauding and everything was going according to plan. Except when George got to the mike, there was one little flaw: he was empty-handed. Since his talks did not always have logical transitions, it did not matter anyway. He said, "I especially thank people here in Des Moines, Iowa, for coming out tonight and I'm proud of that eighty-six-and-a-half percent vote I got in Selma—my wife got in Selma—and we're proud to have the vote of all the people of Alabama. We want the vote of all the people in this country whether they be black or white, and we're proud to be here in this fine city."

Then he continued to talk about "the recapitulation" that occurred when he was running in Maryland in 1964. "I was doing real fine until the fine Mayor of Baltimore came on the air and said, 'You know Governor Wallace was leading until we had a recapitulation of the votes and after our thorough recapitulation of the votes we find that the governor is now trailing.' So, now friends, if anybody ever tells you they gonna recapitulate on you, you'd better watch out. They gonna do somethin' to you!"

Dobbs and other old-time campaigners looked at each other. They recognized the exact words of the same seven-and-a-half minute speech they had heard a thousand times before.

The incident said a lot about George Wallace. It is characteristic of a man whose ideas never change. He liked "the same old speech." He expected it to get him on the ballot of fifty states, an achievement requiring a mass following of determined voters.

The people came and came. In a little town in

Massachusetts where the people had never seen a political figure as unsophisticated as George Wallace, they were astounded when the Wallace group pulled up in a pickup truck with a trailer behind it and a hillbilly band bringing up the rear. An old man standing on the street corner questioned them, asking, "What's going on?" He could not believe their answer that Governor Wallace would soon climb up on the flat-bed truck and make a speech. The custom in Massachusetts was to rent a hall and have everyone sit down for the political rally. The bystander thought that they were crazy. He immediately told them so. "Humph!" he said. "You won't have fifteen people here." He leaned back against a post and waited to see his prediction come true. Much to his surprise, by the time the band played three tunes and the governor arrived, four city blocks full of people were waiting to hear the rest of the program. The old man just shook his head and walked away in disbelief.

Wallace, like Huey Long, had the ability to stir peoples' emotions, to make them feel. With his confident attitude and magnetic personality, he brought out their strongest instincts of love or hate. By a cock of the head, he roused people to action, even to violence against George Wallace. Crowds became so aroused at times that some wanted to throw bricks while others were moved to a standing ovation by his eloquence. He had audience impact. His typical seven-and-a-half minute speech with all its sameness somehow held listeners captive, possibly because of his strong delivery. Wherever and whenever the governor spoke, all of his energy was directed at that one speech being convincing enough to capture votes.

Back in Montgomery after a tour, George handled his duties as governor and also as a presidential candidate. He kept in touch by phone calls. He would dial number after number. First, he would telephone a leading citizen of a big city like

Cleveland and ask how things were going. Then he would call a clergyman in Massachusetts, asking the same question. Sometimes politics was not even mentioned. But the person receiving the call realized that politics was implicit in every word George Wallace spoke. Each call had a personal touch. They all began with, "This is George Wallace." Whether it was local or long distance, George always dialed his own numbers. He was too impatient to bother with a go-between.

One day his secretary, Sara Crumpton, overheard George reaching a party. By the way he talked, she realized that he had the wrong number. Instead of saying so and hanging up, he identified himself as George Wallace. She could tell by his response that the person on the other end probably said, "Sure you are" but George would not hang up until he "finally convinced the person he called Lana that he was the Alabama governor. The chat was bound to make a few points. George knew that it would also make good conversation over a cup of coffee or a game of bridge. Having his name circulating never hurt a politician."

The Wallace name was slung around. Members of the press gnawed away, repeating that George Wallace was a racist and a bigot, while he proclaimed only to "want this country returned to the principles upon which it was founded." That statement did not satisfy reporters at all.

On the road, George stayed so preoccupied with thoughts of politics that he had no time to think about incidentals. He often overlooked having toilet articles until midnight when he wanted to brush his teeth or shampoo his hair. Then he suddenly realized there was something he would need the next morning. One thing he invariably ran out of was Vitalis. George knew that John Pemberton used the same kind of hair oil. So, since the stores were closed, he would send E.C. Dothard over to John's room to "borrow" his bottle of Vitalis.

This happened almost nightly. Pemberton got so used to hearing Dothard say, "Governor Wallace wants to know if you have any hair oil?" when they were traveling that he quit buying the barber-size bottle and used only the small size because the bottle never came back. Pemberton found it very amusing that "George thought nothing about it." George had more important things on his mind.

If little things like hair oil did not enter Wallace's thoughts, it was not because he was tired and wanted to rest after an exhausting day, for he did not. Many times he would call a campaign aide, rouse him from sleep and say, "Hey, Tommy. Let's go downstairs." At ten p.m., they would stroll through the hotel lobby. Wallace would stop every four steps, walk up to a stranger and say, "I'm George Wallace from Alabama," with emphasis on the "Wallace" and "Alabama." As long as anyone else was there, Wallace would hang around. Sometimes he did not go to bed until four a.m. It was another way for him to meet people other candidates missed. If George Wallace was around, anybody could get to shake his hand.

One such incident happened one night in Boston. It was raining hard the evening Governor Wallace was scheduled to speak. South Central Bell representative Roy Dobbs had finished checking his phones and was standing in the lobby of a Holiday Inn with his Wallace Campaign identification button on his lapel. While he waited for the action to begin, a tall, slender fellow came in out of the rain and walked up to Dobbs.

"Excuse me," the man said. "Aren't you with the Wallace party?"

Dobbs replied, "Yes, I am."

Then the man introduced himself as Bill Heller, an umpire with the American Baseball League. He asked how the campaign was going and what their next stop was after Boston. In the course of the conversation he said, "You know, I would really love to meet the governor."

Larry Knapp, another one of the umpires of the All-Star game, came over and chimed in, "Yeah, man. I'd sure like to see the governor, too." Just then, Public Relations man Bill Jones walked by; Dobbs grabbed him by the arm. "How about you taking these people up and getting them through security?" he asked. Jones answered Dobbs, "You can take them on up. You can get in as easily as I can."

Dobbs agreed. He was security cleared. They got through the maze of Secret Service people and finally inside to the governor, who was leaning back in a lounge chair smoking a six-inch cigar while he talked with his press secretary about football.

Dobbs introduced the two American League umpires to Wallace. The governor gave them a hearty handshake. They discussed a recent call when Heller said Johnny Bench was out and Bench insisted that he was safe. Wallace laughed. "Yeah, I know who won," he said. The officials autographed baseballs for the governor's children.

Then Heller remembered a friend who wanted a Wallace autograph. He told George, "You know, Governor, I have a friend in Florida, a councilman, and I'd sure like to get you to autograph a baseball for him. However," he chuckled. "I don't have any balls left. The only one I have is autographed to this fellow [the councilman] from Mickey Mantle."

Suddenly the solution to the problem hit him. He said, "Aw, the hell with it. How 'bout you just autographing it on the other side?"

Amused, the governor signed it, saying, "That ought to be something." Heller ended up with signatures of both Mickey Mantle and George Wallace on one baseball.

No matter how late they stayed up the night before or how many guests were entertained afterwards, the eleven-hour day did not stop. The troops had to keep up the pace, too. When people would say, "I don't see how the governor can stand the push," they would often get the answer, "Heck, you ought to be with some of us. We have to get up before he does and go to bed after. We whip into a town at ten or eleven at night when everything's closed. They'll have something for him to eat in his room and we've got to go out and fend for ourselves."

Then, if the respondent was Dobbs, he would add, smiling, "Really there's not that much to getting up and giving the same speech over and over. I can give it for him if he falters a little bit."

But a slender, bespectacled Alabama Highway Patrolman remembered more to be done than merely giving a speech ten times a day. Dave Harwood remembered a very serious Wallace who was all business and had to be up at eight a.m. and ready to go every day during the travels of the 1968 campaign. He recalled, too, how George observed the regulations he set for his workers. Despite some objections, a cardinal rule was "No alcohol." They had to survive the ten-hour days on their own. Often the ten hours would stretch into twelve or more. When the security men thought the day was done at five p.m., Wallace would come out of the mansion and kill their hopes of going home.

Instead, they might hop a plane to Birmingham. When they returned to Montgomery late that night, if George thought of something he had not done at the Capitol, they would go back there. It was work, work, work.

In addition to the long hours, the security men did not have an easygoing kind of relationship with the man they guarded. They were not advisors. They took a "speak when spoken to" attitude and never engaged the governor in conversation. Their job was doubly tough because they constantly had to be in the governor's way. But he never became annoyed with them.

Harwood was astounded at the patience Wallace displayed. "Imagine all those hours with faces in your face, feet making every step you make—getting in your way. They're bound to. But that man never said a harsh word. He never told us how to do our job or what to do. I guess he thought we'd run our job and do the best we could."

It was often worse than just having people underfoot. Once, in a tight situation where the crowd was screaming out "Kill Wallace, get that bigot!" only the back door of the governor's car was unblocked. So the four security men got the governor in, scrambled over him one by one, and finally filled up the front and back seats. Although the episode disturbed the troopers who said, "Wallace ought to hate us for the way we shoved him around," it did not ruffle George at all.

What did upset him was the realization that Lurleen had taken his place as head of state. With Wallace, everything equated to politics, and he was very sensitive about anyone else's being in the limelight, especially his wife. The first time it hit him that Lurleen was in charge was immediately after her inauguration. It is customary for the governor to ride in the right rear seat of the car. After the inaugural ceremonies were over, Lurleen arrived and took her rightful place. When George got to the car, he opened the rear door and there she sat smiling up at him. "Go around the other side, George," she calmly told him. When Lurleen later told the story to Albert Brewer, she described the expression on George's face as "priceless."

On other occasions, Lurleen's humor got the best of George. During the time Lady Bird Johnson was carrying on her landscape beautification project in Washington, Lurleen teased George about putting him in charge of state beautification. Those around the Capitol knew it was only a joke, but a Master of Ceremonies at a Legislative Seminar did not. He made a comment that there was "a highway beautification project in Alabama," and added, "We're happy to report that Mr. Wallace will be in charge." Everybody laughed, but George just glared at his empty plate.

Quite suddenly, the whole political atmosphere changed, particularly for Wallace, who was very involved with the race issue. On April 4, 1968, in Memphis, an escaped convict, James Earl Ray, was accused of shooting and killing Dr. Martin Luther King, Jr. It shocked and infuriated the black community. George Wallace deplored the slaying, calling it "a senseless, regrettable and tragic act." He expressed the hope that "whoever is guilty of this act will be speedily apprehended."

There were riots in major cities across the country. King was well respected. He had reached the top of his profession as a crusader who had achieved success and worldwide acclaim. He was in Memphis trying to get garbage collectors an increase in pay. There was no indication that there would be violence. He had been many places before when the situation was much hotter. King had supported the cause of his own ethnic group and for it had died a hero's death. The world would not be likely to forget him.

When James Earl Ray was captured, he confessed and pleaded guilty to the slaying, then recanted his statement. He was convicted and received a ninety-nine-year sentence. That did not ease the pain of Coretta King, his widow, King's children, other members of his family, or followers who depended on him.

Still, in politics, the pause for bereavement is brief. For the presidential candidates, especially George Wallace, the show had to go on. The Democrats and Republicans had strong parties behind them, but Wallace was strictly on his own. George was not looking for party support. What he called "not a dime's worth of difference" between the two parties made their backing lack appeal. He wanted, and received, the support of the average man—the millwright, the policeman, the small businessman, and he claimed,

"They are the mass of people who are going to support a change on the domestic scene in this country."

He still accepted what little assistance he got from politicians. He even bragged about their endorsement. When Lester Maddox of Georgia—who had been elected governor as a Democrat—would not openly endorse Wallace's candidacy, he at least told the Alabama governor, "I commend you for your courage and determination and wish you well." Wallace was happy about that.

In his speeches, George harped on bureaucrats telling people what was best for their children, the antics of pseudo-intellectuals, busing, labor union seniority, high taxes and extravagance in government. But did Wallace expect to win?

Back in Montgomery, Lurleen was losing ground to cancer. Mary Jo Ventress came to the mansion every day. She weighed Lurleen's food and fed it to her.

George was gone. Lieutenant Governor Brewer had taken over many of Lurleen's duties at the Capitol, so Lurleen had some free time. Once in a while, to get her mind off her illness, Lurleen spent the day in the house on Farrar Street they were keeping for their retirement home. By then, she was almost too ill to enjoy being in a home of her own. Nevertheless, it was something to do, something to look forward to, and a link with the past and an uncertain future.

Lurleen had been in and out of the hospitals in Montgomery and Houston but nothing was helping. She had lost over twenty-five pounds. After she came home from St. Margaret's Hospital in Montgomery on April 13, George and the children checked on her day and night. She had days when she could join in the conversation, and days when she could barely whisper up until the last week of her life. Her husband began to lose all hope. He stayed by her side constantly. He was right; this time there would be no remission of her illness. On May 7, 1968 at 12:34 a.m., Lurleen Burns Wallace died.

George and his three younger children moved into the four-bedroom brick house on Farrar Street. Sunday after Sunday, he visited Lurleen's grave in Montgomery's Greenwood Cemetery. He went through the routine of going to his office daily. Many a morning, as he was leaving, he turned back to his security man and said in a half-whisper, "She was here this time last year."

After a thirty-day interval, he once again burrowed into his work. For his own sake, his friends urged him to get involved in politics again. He soon began to get out and see people, hoping to switch his attention from his loss to matters at hand. Some men drown their sorrows in drink; George buried his in a crowd.

Campaign news was taking much of the headline space by now. Robert Kennedy was going strong. But on June 5, 1968, in the Hotel Ambassador in Los Angeles, a Jordanian Arab sneaked into the kitchen and shot Kennedy as he passed through. The candidate did not die on the spot but he died the following day. Sirhan Beshra Sirhan was convicted of the crime, but his death sentence penalty has never been carried out. It was the first Islamic terrorist attack in the U.S.

Wallace stepped up his campaign. He began an eleven-state fund-raising tour. June saw his corps of supporters in Memphis, Atlanta, Charlotte, and in the states of Virginia, South Carolina, Louisiana and Mississippi. Seven thousand and fifty supporters were served twenty-five dollars per plate dinners and a total of 86,300 people attended the rallies. Even if the big politicians were not backing him, he and his colleagues were elated when the Reverend John S. Lanham of

Hays Memorial Methodist Church gave the invocation at a fund-raising dinner in Chattanooga, Tennessee, and told four hundred and fifty persons, "Outside of Christ, the only salvation of the country is the election of George Wallace."

The press remained relentless, and Wallace grew angry when one reporter asked him if he was familiar with U.S. foreign policy. George retorted, "The implication is that us rednecks aren't up on foreign policy, but the folks who are supposed to know it have gotten us into four wars in fifty years. I know as much about foreign policy as anybody in this race." So voters could choose a Republican, a Democrat, or George Wallace.

The public speculated about the alternatives. Failure by any candidate to win a majority of the electoral vote would throw the decision into the House of Representatives, where each state would cast one vote for president. Wallace kept saying this was not his hope. Whenever that question came up, he repeatedly stated he was seeking only the presidency. And he also kept saying he was offering the voters a choice. Some voters were not quite sure just what kind of a choice it was.

At the end of June, the American Independent Party began campaigning in New England. Up there they ran into trouble. Hostile leaflets passed out by an unidentified writer reinforced the theory offered by Ray Jenkins that poor blacks are in the same boat with poor whites but poor whites come first with Wallace. It read:

RACISM IS USED TO DIVIDE BLACK AND WHITE WORKING PEOPLE
   Perhaps the biggest appeal that Wallace makes to white voters is that he is the protector of the white working man against the 'nigger'. This is BUNK. We've all seen that Wallace is no friend of the workingman - whether his

[sic] black or white. Why does Wallace use his racist apeal [sic] to white workers? As William Huie, a native white Alabamian, explains, "He gets the poor white man's vote by yelling nigger, then steals bread from his pockets.

Racism has always been used by bosses and their politicians in the North as well as in the South to keep black and white workers divided to prevent them from uniting to fight for a better living. THE ENEMY OF THE WHITE WORKINGMAN IS NOT THE BLACK MAN. Black people are the most stepped-on group in the U.S. and are leading the fight against slumlords, loan sharks and low paying jobs. What the big business and the government fears is that poor, and working-class whites will stop hating black people and will see that it is to their advantage to support the struggles of black people.

THE ENEMIES OF ALL WORKING PEOPLE ARE WALLACE AND MEN LIKE HIM WHO USE RACISM TO DIVIDE THEM AND PUT THEM DOWN. Let's stop playing into the hands of the bosses and their politicians!

That was not all; it continued:

STAND UP FOR THE AMERICAN PEOPLE - STAND AGAINST WALLACE

Wallace says, "Stand up for America." But his record in Alabama and the slogans he uses clearly make him an enemy of the poor and the workingman. He is not the only politician, however, who wants to keep working people divided and powerless while they pay most of the taxes and do most of the fighting in Vietnam. There are others who accomplish the same thing thru [sic] different means.

In Worcester, where wages are very low and strong unions have been kept out for years, we should not be fooled by Wallace's racist and phony patriotic appeals. Today, we stand up against Georg [sic] and stand up for the American people.

Regardless of such attacks, the American Independent Party movement continued. By the end of July, the Wallace group had moved into Tampa, Florida, and the audience of eight hundred cheered when George charged that "a single federal judge has more power than fifty governors combined." Their shouts of agreement seemed to indicate a surge of concern that the power of federal government was constantly growing and taking away individual rights. George kept telling the people he could do something about it if he were given the chance.

Wallace and his party moved on through Texas to California to attend the state convention. They stopped in Shreveport, Louisiana, and drew an overflow crowd of fifteen thousand at the Coliseum. An overjoyed George Wallace assured supporters that he was gaining the same support throughout the nation and gave them the credit for shaking the major parties. He told his audience: "You folks in Louisiana are certainly shaking the confidence of the Democratic and Republican parties." Men with "Wallace" neckties and women with "Wallace" straw hats led the crowd in applause.

When the Wallace staff and traveling party arrived in California, the oldest daily in the West, *The Sacramento Union*, gave George Wallace good press. The August 3 issue featured a page-one smiling governor standing at the mike. It was a contrast to the many scowling, fist-raised poses which were generally chosen by newspapers around the nation. But even if the city did seem friendly, security measures were abundant at the A.I.P. state convention. A flock of Secret Service men and troopers were right on Wallace's heels every minute. Two major public figures had been assassinated within the past two months, and everything possible was being done to prevent its happening again.

The campaign corps kept going except for a one day break. George Wallace celebrated his birthday on August 25 by enjoying a day of fun at Disneyland with his children, then relaxing at a party that evening in his hotel suite. But bright and early the next morning he was back at the old grind. The August schedule had him crisscrossing the country.

On September 1, National Campaign Director Cecil Jackson announced they would begin the move into an "active campaign." Up until that time, the concentration had been on getting on the ballot. Now, Wallace was ready to collide with Demos and the GOP head to head. The first half of September would have to be devoted to transition, the selection of a running mate and the decision about a national convention. They would have to prepare a platform and get ballot position in the last six states where Wallace was still not on the ballot.

There were two critical months to go, much to be done, and not enough money. Contributions were still coming in, but they needed television exposure badly. It was expensive. The unorthodox methods they had employed so far had indeed brought George Wallace to a position of strength, but it would take more than that to put him in the White House. The pickup truck candidate would have to get a faster-moving vehicle to propel him to the highest office in the land. While he was doing that, he still had to keep the confidence of the little people who had so willingly sent him their egg money out of the sugar bowl. It was going to be a neat trick to play both sides against the middle and never let any of them know exactly what he was doing.

During the hectic month of August, Wallace lost ten pounds. He took a brief vacation in Miami the first week of

September. When he returned with a cold and abruptly cancelled the Washington, D.C., news conference, where he was to have named his running mate, aides refused to say if his illness was the reason for the cancellation. Speculation was that he did not have a running mate. Former Governor A.B. "Happy" Chandler of Kentucky had been picked up, then dropped, as a possible running mate for Wallace. His progressive past got in the way and, according to Chandler's wife, Mildred, "There failed to be a meeting of the minds." The two were scheduled to meet at the D.C. news conference, but it was called off.

Everywhere George Wallace went, hostile signs were raised. Demonstrators carried placards reading "Wallace go home," and "U.S. Racism Kills Here and in Vietnam." In many speaking places, chants would echo through the building, "Soul power, Sieg Heil," and "Kill Wallace." Wallace supporters did all they could to drown out the noise with their own cheers and foot-stomping.

On October 3, 1968, in the Pittsburg Hilton ballroom, General Curtis LeMay (retired) was announced as the American Independent Party Vice Presidential candidate. The sixty-one-year-old officer entered the race lacking experience in the political arena. LeMay's ideas and attitudes reflected those of Wallace in every respect. If George wanted reinforcement from his running mate, he could not have picked a better man. If, however, he wanted a balance of political ideas and someone with name exposure, Curtis LeMay did not fit the picture.

Almost immediately, LeMay made a big faux pas in Columbus, Ohio. He said he advocated using the atom bomb, calling it "Just another weapon in the arsenal." Right then and there, many "on the fence" voters scratched LeMay off their list and Wallace went with him. The influence of "Old Iron

Pants" military background had cost the Wallace-LeMay team votes.

Enemies of Wallace jumped on the opportunity and exploited it for all it was worth. Wallace responded by saying he believed the U.S. could win the war in Vietnam "with conventional weapons," but the egg had been laid and the incident could not be put aside. LeMay's mistake haunted them right to election day.

In the middle of October, plans were made to get LeMay out of the way by sending the former Air Force chief of staff to Vietnam on a four-day fact-finding trip. Meanwhile, George continued his tour, meeting with adversity in Duluth and Peoria.

Wallace had demanded much more than ordinary credentials to aid in weeding out student hecklers. So, the press jumped on him in Peoria. *The Journal Star* did not like Mr. Wallace's demands for what they described as "the life history of newsmen as the price of credentials to cover his activities here." With a number of derogatory remarks and some name-calling. reporters vowed to cover him anyway, saying they figured "it is our job to get the news regardless of what barriers some character puts in the way, and it really isn't that big a deal one way or another." The paper was furious with the ex-governor for inconveniencing them and they did not hesitate to show it.

In Duluth, the third party candidate soft-pedaled his usually fiery speech and assured the audience he would do all he could to end the Vietnam war if elected president. Many people still did not like him, and the Concerned Citizens Committee members were very vocal about saying so. Then Art Seidenbaum really ground it in when he headlined his October 16 column in *The Los Angeles Times*:

"Voting for Wallace—an Act of Political Masochism."

At the rallies, the hecklers kept coming. But half the time George and his staff did not see them; they were too busy trying to raise enough cash to appear on all three national TV networks on election eve. The time was reserved, but they had to take in $63,000 per day in Texas to pay the bill. The team worked out their pitch this way: In the best tradition of an evangelist, Bill Jones would warm up the audience. "How many of you good people want George Wallace elected president?" he would shout. Then he would call for the hand raising. This was repeated, asking who would work.

Next came the request for volunteers to circulate petitions. The petitions had eighty-five blank spaces, and with each signature, the worker asked for a cash contribution. The distributor sent the completed petition and the money to Montgomery and each person who made a donation received a thank you note from Wallace. The personal touch paid off and the money flowed in. One single signature on a petition netted anywhere from one to one thousand dollars. Many fell in the middle category.

In the campaign's final two weeks, the highlight of the tour was the appearance at Madison Square Garden. Seventeen thousand, five hundred people packed the Garden and gave Governor Wallace a twenty-minute standing ovation. Wallace was elated at the response and scoffed at the demonstrators present. "If you come up here after I get through," he said, "I'll autograph your sandals." The ego boost helped erase the memory of unwelcome treatment he had received elsewhere.

Pressure was building. As time closed in on Wallace and his team, speeches became briefer and they moved along even faster. No matter what happened, George just kept digging in. If protesters kept up their noisy chant too long, he would stop his speech, look directly at them and tell them, "If you want to scream and yell, why don't you come over here and pay these people to let you use the facilities tomorrow night? But tonight we rented the hall and I'm tired of your interruption." Sometimes his outspokenness shut them up.

Towards the end of the campaign, with everybody tired out, the group began to move around in an almost mechanical manner. Dave Harwood was still a member of the security force, and he recalls just how strenuous the campaign really was. "With a presidential candidate you are constantly on the move. You get tired, so tired," he said. "You haven't been home. You dress well and look well, but it's just security all the time. Even when the speaker is on the platform, you have to be right there.

"Finally, you ask yourself, 'What am I doing here? I could be home at night. I could be working an eight or nine or ten or twelve hour day.'" He paused and sighed as if just the memory of it exhausted him.

Then brightening suddenly, he explained where his energy came from. "Then that little man [Governor Wallace] comes out on the platform and says, 'I'm gonna give y'all a good speech tonight. You've never heard one like it. I want you to listen close. Before I start, I want to tell you I'm from the South and I represent just as good and fine and intelligent, cultured and self-righteousness people as you or anybody else and don't you forget it!'

"The ten thousand people in Michigan, or wherever we might be, stand up and applaud and I say to myself, 'Dave, I know exactly what you're doing here,' and I wouldn't be anywhere else." Harwood smiled and added, "Now that's the kind of man he is—so magnetic. He is a person who does not demand loyalty but gets it. He does not give you any special attention; he really gives you a good letting alone." And whatever he did give to Dave did not go unappreciated.

The absence of professional campaigners was a burden to

the campaign efforts. Considering that lack and the need for organization, causing too few people to have too much responsibility, the campaign of the American Independent Party had gone very well. But even obtaining information about what needed to be done had been difficult for the workers. Few, if any, comprehensive staff planning meetings were conducted. The staff, which really meant two or three key Wallace people, rather haphazardly decided what was to be done. And, instructions from them had to be painfully extracted. They were doing just about as much wrong as right, but with grueling determination.

The geographic bias which Wallace claimed kept Southerners from winning prior presidential nominations was still the Easterner's way of keeping control. George leaned on that, using it as a pre-planned excuse should he lose the race.

The end was drawing near when Wallace and his colleagues arrived in Norfolk November 1. Claiming the whole South, Wallace gave his forecast of what would happen if he became the next president. "One of the first things I will do," he said, "is ask Congress to repeal the 1968 fair housing law.

"I will return lock, stock and barrel absolute control of your public school system and you can run them any way you want to run them.

"I may bus some of you professional college students to the draft board. I'll grab you college students raising money for the Communists and put you under a good jail, too.

"We're going to change direction in this country and return it to sanity."

Throughout his speech the anti-Wallace people were screaming, "We don't want Wallace."

When Wallace concluded, he responded to the razzing segment of the crowd by shouting back at them, "You're going to get him November 5, whether you want him or not." With

157

that, George directed the cameraman's attention to the hecklers, indicating that he would like to see them picked up on TV.

Meanwhile, the Gallup Poll was showing Nixon as the forerunner with forty-two percent, next came Humphrey with forty percent, Wallace with fourteen percent and four percent undecided. George Wallace frequently asked the audience how many of them had been polled and they would scream back, "None, none, none."

It was almost over. Heckled to the last, George Wallace ended his campaign in Atlanta, making an eleventh-hour appeal to the voters. The Wallace entourage had traveled by DC-6, DC-7 and Electra Turbo Jet well over a hundred-thousand miles.

On November 5, 1968, all the efforts of one year came to a climax in Garrett Coliseum in Montgomery. Hundreds of newsmen came and all the major TV networks were represented. The moment of truth had arrived. Election returns were in and the verdict was pronounced. Wallace had done his best and despite his boast "We gonna win," he got 9,906,473 votes—a little less than nine percent. Richard Milhous Nixon was elected the thirty-seventh President of the United States. Wallace said nonetheless that he considered his presidential campaign a success. "We turned the other two parties in different directions. If we had not been in the race, some of the statements by the other two candidates would never have been made." Attempting to prove a point, he told reporters that "a year ago, if someone asked you whether this movement would get ten million votes, you would have answered in the negative."

Then, in a jocular mood, he denied that he had political plans for the future, saying he was going to "sit around the Confederate monument in Clayton and practice law in

Alabama." Still, reporters knew that they had not heard the last of George Corley Wallace.

CHAPTER TWELVE

A DAY OFF

Once, when the Wallace group was traveling hard and heavy towards the end of the 1968 campaign, George leaned back in the car seat, turned to Judge Glen Curlee and said, "Say, who do I have to see to get a day off?"

Now he had it. The presidential race was over and Alabama had a new governor. Lieutenant Governor Albert Brewer succeeded Lurleen and George relocated his family into the house on Farrar Street. South Central Bell Accounts Manager Roy Dobbs thought that was the way Wallace had truly expected things to turn out. Dobbs had expressed his feelings earlier.

One day, when the 1968 campaign seemed to be going especially well and the reception at the rally was overwhelming, Jack House, a press secretary, barged in and slapped Dobbs on the back. "Well, we're going to walk right into the White House," he said.

Dobbs deflated House's high spirits. "Jack, let me just tell you," he said, "I'm not against it, don't get me wrong. I'm just kind of a third party sitting out here." He stopped and turned towards the whole tour group. "You know folks, everybody says Wallace is going to the White House and they're all giving a hip, hip, hurray—except the governor."

House squared his shoulders. "What the hell do you mean?" he asked.

"You just think about it now. You watch him, knowing all the background," Dobbs said. "This year Governor Wallace knows, I believe, that he is not gonna make it. But there's a lot of things he's gonna do. He's gonna open up the eyes of a lot of people because he is getting on the ballot; he is making a big push in the third party. He's doing something that no one else has ever done; he's making these other parties come around and talk differently. He's getting his story told whether he goes to the White House or not. And this is his objective for 1968."

Dobbs did not think the race was a loss, and he was sure George Wallace did not feel it was either.

So now George, who was perhaps not as deflated as some people thought, returned to the private practice of law. He had time on his hands but not much, for soon the 1970 governor's race would get under way.

George had done a lot for Alabamians, a lot that would win him votes later. During his term as governor, he always encouraged people to come to him with their problems even though many of them had to be directed to specific state agencies. He had helped many a person whose plight had come to his attention. One case involved a backwoods black woman. If the office personnel had paid close attention to their jobs, the letter from her would never have reached the governor's desk. Somehow it did, and it told him that she was concerned because her teenage son could not go to school. She knew that the governor had been on television stressing the importance of getting an education, and she felt he might help her. So she took a chance and wrote to him.

Written in phonics with the words running together, the letter was postmarked Grove Hill, Alabama. But it probably actually came from a shack on a cotton field far removed from that town. She asked for help for her tenth-grade son who wanted to continue school but could not because he lacked decent clothes. With faith and hope she told him that the boy wore "a size fourteen shirt and an eight-and-a-half shoe."

By the time the letter reached the desk of Ben Hill in the Department of Pensions and Securities, Governor Wallace had already taken action. Without saying a word to anybody, he had gone home, boxed up some of George, Jr.'s clothes, and sent them to the boy at Grove Hill.

When the mother's letter of thanks came by return mail, she had another request. This one was easy because she merely asked, "Now what I want is a big picture of you to put in the living room to show all my friends who told me, 'It won't do no good to write the governor.'" A photo was sent by return mail.

Even while George was out of office, people continued to seek his advice and support. He still pulled a lot of weight in Alabama.

In 1969, when the court order came out mandating school zones in Mobile County, Edna Wade discovered that her children could not go to Theodore High School as they had planned. She first attempted to contact Governor Albert Brewer and could not even get to his receptionist. The doors were locked. In desperation, she called Wallace and complained to his secretary about the school situation in Mobile. Within two hours, he called her back and made an appointment for the following week.

By then, three mothers were involved. On the scheduled date, Edna, Millie Hobbs and Evelyn Harding—all from the Mobile area—went to Montgomery to keep the appointment.

When they first entered Wallace's office, he was as apprehensive of them as they were of him, Edna recalls. "Then all of a sudden he popped a big old cigar in his mouth, leaned back and relaxed. All four of us relaxed simultaneously; then we really began to talk."

His advice was simple. He told the three ladies to "do things the right way to sway public opinion to your side." He cautioned them against breaking the law but urged them to do everything possible to bring publicity to bear on the question.

While they talked, three Montgomery businessmen flipped the pages of magazines in the reception room waiting to keep a luncheon date with George. But the housewives were in his office from eleven a.m. until one p.m., instead of the half-hour they expected to be there.

It was time well spent. The ladies filed class action suits locally. Then, in October, 1971, Edna and Millie, joined by two other mothers, Betty Rogers and Betty Livingston, traveled from Mobile to Washington, D.C. They had become involved with Concerned Citizens of America, and they walked two miles in each of fifty cities getting petitions signed to present to President Richard Nixon "proving busing was not beneficial to the children of this country." Mrs. Livingston called it, "A mothers-in-tennis-shoes type action." As George Wallace suggested, their action did not break the law. It was not even militant; they kept it low key. Even though busing continued, the publicity worked for the Mobile mothers. They eventually managed to get their way. Through local pressure, their children were allowed to attend Theodore High School. And their success netted George some loyal campaign workers for his next race.

CHAPTER THIRTEEN

THE MAN WHO IS

George Wallace always had a great need for people. From his college days when he would come home on holidays, dump his clothes, then go to the stores in Clio just to talk, he connived to increase the number of people surrounding him. His "don't leave me alone" attitude was attributed to different things by different people. Albert Brewer said, "George's primary interest is in power and he has to have people around him to be in the limelight."

Bob Vance and Bob Ingram held similar opinions. As detached observers, each has seen Wallace in action many times.

When Bob Ingram was appointed Finance Director for Governor Brewer, he severed his relations with Wallace and since then has looked at Wallace in a little different light, with what he calls "a more objective view." Ingram always knew that Wallace "loves the royal crowd." Now, he sees this mania for attention "like an addiction that George must get out; he's a political animal who loves politics and gets ego-kicks that way. If the crowd does not love him back, it becomes a matter of concern."

Many reported that when George was down and out, there was only one way to revitalize him—stick a microphone in front of his face. One of his colleagues, Executive Assistant Derryl Gordon, described what happens. "He can look like he's feeling bad, and you put a microphone in front of him and give him a crowd, and it's just like giving him a blood transfusion," he said. "He gets his energy off of a crowd and speaking; then his enthusiasm becomes contagious. When George is in the office, there is a feeling of excitement. But things are not the same at the Capitol when the governor is not around."

Gordon continued, "You can come up here on a day when he's not in the office and business goes on as usual but it does not have the air of excitement; you know it hasn't got it. But he can come in that office over there, and it is just like a magnet all over this place. I mean really and truly, there's something going on all the time. You stay busy all the time anyhow, but he radiates excitement." And although he was just talking about it, there was excitement in Gordon's voice.

Being able to stimulate others to action may not have been enough to satisfy other state leaders. The party lord who had irritated Wallace during the 1970 governor's race, Robert Vance, said that although he considers George the "ultimate candidate" for governor, once elected, Wallace "does not administrate to the best of his ability." But Vance gave him credit for having the capability to exert the power of the position expertly. "I don't know that he would lack the skill if he really applied himself," he said. "The day-to-day work of the governor just doesn't interest him." Maybe some people did not like Wallace because they felt he didn't take care of his duties as governor, but those who did like him liked him a lot.

Wallace made people give vent to strong emotions. They hated him or they loved him; there was little middle path. His former confidential secretary, Sara Crumpton, thought it was unfair because "people who look at George Wallace on TV and hear him called a 'bigot' don't know him. I think to myself, 'That's not the man *I* know they're talking about; the man *I* know knocks himself out to help the little person.'"

Bill Sellers, *The Mobile Press Register* political reporter who traveled with Wallace in 1968, remembers an incident which graphically describes the governor. "He's just down-home folks," Sellers began. "One touching moment I recall happened one day when George had some spare time between speeches and he decided to run by government-financed Fitzsimmons Army Hospital (Denver, Colorado) where they had a lot of Vietnam veterans.

"Wallace went through and began chatting with servicemen and others—the hospital was not restricted to veterans. There was a seventy-five-year-old woman in one of the big wards, and when Wallace walked in, she said, 'I'm from Alabama. Is my governor really here to see me?'

"Wallace walked right over to her and said, 'Sure 'nuff, honey. This is your governor come out here to see you.' That woman started crying and all of us did. She said, 'I'm originally from Elba, Alabama. I remember you campaigning back there and you stopped by my cousin's store.'

"George nodded. 'Oh, yeah! You're talking about old George Ezell with the corner store. George was for me all the way.'

"At the governor's memory of George Ezell, that woman lit up like a Christmas tree and I suppose they had to let her out of the hospital the next day."

In his own natural way, Wallace had made the lady feel that she was as important as he was, even if he was the Governor of Alabama and she was merely a private citizen.

But as his opponents will point out, George had plenty of flaws. Numbered among his faults was his inability to make decisions concerning others. His supporters said it was soft-heartedness. He often put off naming cabinet members even when the need became critical. If he could only name one, he hesitated because someone else was likely to get hurt feelings.

George fired only two people during his entire political career. One was Sara Crumpton, his secretary, who was later placed in another state position. Her dismissal was attributed to Cornelia Wallace's jealousy of Sara's standing with the Wallace children. The other was Safety Director W.L. Allen, who was reportedly fired because he missed too many days of work. Problems at home interfered with his attending to the responsibilities of his office.

Alabamians have their own ideas of the assets and liabilities of the governor. He, too, has an opinion. In an interview with a Mobile reporter, the governor tried to be honest about himself.

Adamantly, Wallace insisted he was right and the ideas of the media were wrong. He talked about it, and worked hard not to mention the word "black." "I think that in years past many people and much of the news media misunderstood the position people of our region in general took and made it appear that we were opposed to people because of the way they looked or the way God made them.

"But our objection was always against big government trying to solve every problem that existed in the states and at the local level. This has been misinterpreted as being anti-somebody as was my strong pitch for law and order in 1968 misinterpreted as being aimed at a certain group in our country, which it was not. Now, all take that attitude in campaigns regardless of their race.

"I believe that the people of this state want to see good things happen to all citizens regardless of who they are, but they've always felt that big government could not solve every problem from one thousand miles away and that initiative and solution came at the local level where the problems were better understood and people better understood one another.

"I believe that was misunderstood and I believe it was

shown it was *not* misunderstood when I was so successful in amassing more votes, popular vote, in the primaries in which I contested with the other Democratic contenders. When they [Americans] heard and listened to me they recognized I was not what the media had said I was, that the people of Alabama were not what they had been termed to be. Alabamians really spoke the sentiment of the average citizen in Michigan and throughout the country."

George Wallace Continued to eat his hamburger steaks and listen to Tammy Wynette and other country singers, but he was not too much of a redneck to command attention from top-ranking dignitaries. After he became governor in 1963, members of the senate of both parties, officials from the president's cabinet, the vice-president, and the President of the United States all visited Alabama. This had never happened before. And the backwoods boy from Clio got his share of recognition for this unprecedented attention from the hierarchy.

CHAPTER FOURTEEN

THE SECOND MRS. WALLACE

Just before the inauguration, George gave reporters another tidbit. On January 4, 1971, at Trinity Presbyterian Church in Montgomery, he and Cornelia Ellis Snively were married by Dr. Robert Strong. Cornelia was the niece of one of George's opponents, former Alabama Governor Jim Folsom.

In the mid-fifties, during the term of "Big Jim," Cornelia was a fourteen-year-old girl living in the governor's mansion. One night, she sat crouched on the stairs and peeped through the banisters. The dark-haired man she saw made an impression on her then; he was just a person who had come to visit her Uncle Jim. George Wallace was one of many such men popping in and out of the mansion, and Cornelia Ellis often saw her mother greet them when they arrived.

"Big Ruby," as they called her mother, was divorced. She lived with Governor Folsom, her widowed brother, and was official hostess for the mansion. Flamboyant and colorful, the pair made news in the South. The girl who watched from the shadows was destined to become newsworthy herself when she moved into the mansion a second time.

George C. Wallace was not a man to stay single. His friends suspected he would find someone and remarry as soon as a suitable period of time passed after the death of Lurleen. They thought it would be the best thing for him. For some time, there had been gossip around the Capitol about George's romantic attachments, but the talk was vague and unsupported. Still, many people felt that the best way to stop the gossip and stay out of trouble was for George to get married again.

When George met Cornelia Snively, she was a divorcee with young sons, not exactly a traditional aspirant to be First Lady of Alabama. In Southern politics it was frowned upon to be divorced, and the conservative governor could hardly vary from values of his area. Also, how could the daughter of hard-drinking Ruby Austin and the niece of Barefoot Jim come into the mansion with her tee-totaling husband and take over? Would she accept the stringent rules set by George's example? Her colorful, active past did not indicate that she would be that adaptable to a quiet, serene life. Even if Cornelia could conform, what in the world would they do with Ruby?

Clearly there were problems ahead, but once George made up his mind, nothing was going to change it.

One person heard about the upcoming marriage in December. On Christmas Eve, 1971, Tommy Giles' telephone rang. The voice on the other end asked, "Is this Tommy Giles, the photographer?"

It had been a hard day and Tommy gave a weak, "Yes."

"This is George Wallace," came the reply. "Are you completely tied up with your family tomorrow?"

Giles stammered, "No, no, sir, Governor," and Wallace asked him if he could come to the mansion and take a picture.

When he went to the assignment that Christmas day, the photographer found out the reason for the urgency. The group portrait that he took included George, Peggy Sue, George Wallace, Jr., Cornelia, Josh and Jim Snively. It was to be used as an engagement announcement. Soon there would be a second Mrs. Wallace.

Just two weeks before the inauguration, Cornelia Ellis Snively and George Corley Wallace were wed. This brought the total number of children who would live in the mansion to five. Bobbi Jo was now married; George had three children still at home and Cornelia had two young sons. Again there would be an energetic family living in the governor's mansion.

George was happy. The lean, attractive brunette was just what he needed to fill the gap in his life. He was in high spirits the day he jokingly invited his friend, Glen Curlee, to "come along" on the honeymoon.

Curlee grinned and replied, "Surely you're kidding, Governor."

George quipped back, "No, I don't want to go off to Florida with a woman by myself. People will talk about me."

Another old friend of George's, Ralph Adams, was not surprised when the governor picked a new bride nearly twenty years younger than himself. He was amused at George's account of his trip to the courthouse to get the marriage license. Adams reported what happened. "Some lady in the courthouse kept telling George how lucky he was to find this beautiful girl. That would have been all right, but she was really rubbing it in. In addition to her harping on the subject, George strongly suspected that she had never been one of his supporters. It hit him the wrong way. He tolerated it as long as he could, but finally he had enough. So he told her nonchalantly, 'Oh, I don't know how lucky I am. Really, there's over thirty million women in this country looking for husbands and there's only one single governor.' He got the license—and no more talk."

The two Mrs. Wallaces were so different it was difficult to see how they both married the same man. Lurleen's modest manner had won the heart of George Wallace and the trust of the people of Alabama. Her simplicity in dress and demeanor had drawn the people to her. Cornelia, a ravishing beauty who raced cars and dressed extravagantly, was a much more worldly type. She did not sit in the background but showed a direct interest in politics herself. She appeared with George on TV, sometimes to the embarrassment of Alabamians who were disturbed at her interruptions. They thought she was patronizing the governor.

Some of the people who felt that the match would not work at first later said "Cornelia's been good for George." Even Catherine Steineker, Lurleen's former secretary, expressed this opinion. Prejudice against the new wife dwindled. And some people thought that perhaps George chose Cornelia because, with maturity, his tastes had changed.

Cornelia with George

Cornelia with George in Capital

CHAPTER FIFTEEN

THE THRILL OF THE CHASE

Once again, George finished campaigning and was governor. Once again, he was more concerned about running for president than he was about running Alabama.

But no race lasts forever. Once elected, the candidate was faced with the job. In Alabama, more and more observers began to feel that George only wanted to hold the position of governor, that once he was in office he was unable to tolerate the dull details of everyday work.

One person who saw the problem was Ray Jenkins, Managing Editor of *The Alabama Journal*. He saw the lack of attention to the mechanics of office as a gaping fault. He pointed out how it manifested itself. "He seems to kind of lose interest in government once he gets in there." Jenkins said. "He has no broad programs of philosophy or what have you. What does emerge in his way of service to the people comes in spurts, almost as an afterthought. They'll sit around saying, 'What are we going to do now?' and someone will come up with an idea and they'll take it and run with it. There's no real sustained planning. There has been a rather discernible lack of interest in running the job of governor, in the hard nitty-gritty details of administering the bureaucracy in an efficient way." Jenkins believed that any success of the Wallace administration had happened accidentally.

With a shrug, he said it disappointed him that Wallace's

"sheer love of the campaign does lead him to neglect the duties for which he was elected."

The position Jenkins took was reinforced by Bob Ingram, editor of *The Alabama News Magazine*. "George likes to run for office more than any man I know," he said. "But once he gets in, he lives for the day he runs again. He is not the greatest administrator of state government this state has ever had. He gives a lot of responsibility to other people."

Ingram, as owner of a magazine dealing mainly with politics, observed many Alabama politicians in the previous two decades. He had seen politicians come and go, and he went a step further, saying, "George would go if we lived in a society which did not elect their public officials." If that was the way the Alabama political system operated, Bob Ingram said he felt that "George would never run again."

Members of the governor's cabinet rejected this view. They admitted Wallace "would rather be out in the hall shaking hands," but they did not feel that he was so undisciplined as to let his personal pleasures interfere with his work. They felt that he got a lot done, even when he was not there in person, by delegating authority effectively. Trade schools and junior colleges continued to be built, and new industries and businesses brought their plants to Alabama. Also, the daily flow of paperwork continued to be processed at the Capitol. Besides, when George was away, his watchdogs, like newspaper publisher Jimmy Faulkner and Montgomery businessman Oscar Harper, kept a close eye on activities at the Capitol.

Those who believed in the Wallace platform did not mind if he took time off from being governor to try to spread his message around the nation. They believed in his ideas and ideals and would like to have seen them adopted all over the United States. His loyal Alabama supporters seemed glad to share the governor with other Americans.

For a perennial runner, the timing was just right. Between the inauguration and the beginning of the presidential campaign, George had just enough time to set his house in order and delegate authority to those he considered capable of running the state. In political circles, there was very little doubt that he would run. Everybody knew that George was continuously running or getting ready to. When the signal gun went off indicating the start of the race, George could be expected to be there, crouched in position. His past losses would hardly deter him.

Nor would current scandals. Seymore Trammell had been his trusted advisor, and his second escapade involving income tax evasion might embarrass George, but it wouldn't stop him from seeking the presidency. Even though Trammell was later convicted and sentenced, the Wallace campaign continued. George C. wore it well. His combative spirit constantly led him into, rather than away from, battle. If winning a race had been as simple as putting a name on the ballot, he would have enjoyed no thrill in political victory.

Fortunately, this was not the case. The hurdles were plentiful. The rank and file multitude, whose support George Wallace claimed, did not have the power to make the 1972 race successful. If they—like his financial advisor, Jimmy Faulkner—felt that Wallace was a patriot, a fighter for principles who had been falsely portrayed, then perhaps they also believed that he really wanted to "bring the government back to the people," as Faulkner stated. But they also knew that, in the past, the strength and power of the two major parties prevented this from happening. The power structure could block every move the American Independent Party made.

Before George Wallace announced his 1972 candidacy for

President of the United States, he had to have a cause. The segregation issue was dead. Integration had become law and its enactment was well under way. Southerners still gritted their teeth, but they had to bear it, like it or not. Busing was the new, popular cause, the "in" subject. Alabama's governor could jump on that and expect full support of white citizens. Many of them believed, as he did, in the concept of neighborhood schools. George would receive some support, too, from those who just did not want their children run all over town to get to school, even if they did not care about the racial aspects of it. Even his avid opponent Ben Stokes agreed with Wallace that the neighborhood school concept should be inviolate.

Inspired with this new resolution, the Wallace troops got out the bullet-proof podium, dusted it off, loaded it on the back of the flat-bed truck and went traveling again.

From the sidelines, an interested observer watched the scene closely. National Democratic Party Chairman Robert Vance saw Wallace's running again as the very essence of what drove George Wallace—the thirst for battle.

What he considered unfair, prejudiced descriptions of his motives and behavior did not slow George down. And his friends came to his rescue. State Representative Maurice "Casey" Downing, an orphan boy who had to fight his way to the top, too, defended the governor, saying, "George stands for the basic freedom of all people. The things we fought for all these years—freedom to work to earn a living, to own land, freedom from fear, local rule and diversification of power— that's what he stands for and that's what the people see in George Wallace." Downing added that the United States was "made great by private initiative" and he felt that Wallace, working against a centralization of government, would protect the system by being based on diversity of power.

Major parties kept preaching consolidation, elimination of

unnecessary state authority, and supreme power of the Supreme Court. They had more money to spend, and they got their message to people George could not reach.

There were reasons people voted for, or would not vote for, George Wallace for president.

Albert Brewer conceded that George Wallace "offered to anyone disgruntled or upset about any facet of government or society, a way to cast a protest vote." Then he mentioned the other side of the issue. "Maybe people felt they might be throwing their vote away or perhaps the party structure, Republican and Democrat, was of such strength that when it really began to get in gear, there was no way for an independent movement, lacking the organization of the major parties, to compete." Brewer felt that the integration issue which propelled Wallace to success in Alabama would probably deny him the national office. He may have been right. The public has a very good memory.

Governor Wallace thought differently. Optimistic by nature even when he was called a "caretaker governor," George did not let the nickname disturb him. His former minister challenged him, too, by posing the question, "Is George still running?" and then answering smugly, "He's still alive, isn't he?" If George knew about that, it did not bother him. Neither that, nor anything else, was going to keep him away from the national campaign.

Except for the hand of fate. An abrupt interruption of the 1972 campaign would come. It had been often anticipated and feared, but never really expected.

MARY S. PALMER

CHAPTER SIXTEEN

"GEORGE, HEY GEORGE! LOOK OVER HERE"

Wallace was scheduled to appear in Laurel, Maryland, as a presidential hopeful Monday, May 15, 1972. Ten thousand, five hundred and twenty-five Laurel citizens had shown an interest in his rally. Much of the groundwork was done by people of the area, such as Dora Thompson from Hyattsville. She and many others had worked long and hard. The rally was expected to be a huge success.

The night before, back in Montgomery, Wallace was ill at ease. He called Glen Curlee, an old friend from college days, to come cheer him up.

Outside the white three-story governor's mansion of pressed brick and stone, oak trees swayed in the wind when an Alabama State Trooper opened the Perry Street entrance gate to let Curlee drive in.

In telling about the long talk he and Wallace had that night, Curlee recalled that "George seemed upset. He was subtly leading up to something, but I was not quite sure what." The conversation turned to a discussion about insurance. On the pretense of asking what Glen's insurance included, Wallace revealed facts about his own. It was as if he felt compelled to detail the information.

Near midnight, Wallace suddenly popped out with, "Curlee, do you think they're gonna shoot me up there

181

tomorrow?"

Instead of answering "Yes" or "No," Curlee replied, "Well, Governor, you've been lucky so far."

#

Harry Styne had put in many hours the second week of May preparing for Wallace. As Public Relations Director of the Merchants' Association of the large Laurel Shopping Center, he supervised the construction of a platform in front of the Equitable Trust Bank. He made arrangements for microphones, security, restrooms and electrical power. Since the platform was directly in front of the bank, Barry Bragg, the bank's manager, offered the use of the bank's electricity for loud speakers and gave permission for Wallace aides to use the bank restrooms.

By nine a.m., the Center was ready for George Wallace. Styne called to check on the Laurel police arrangements. Then he dropped by to see the manager of the Hot Shoppe, Barry Bragg at the bank, and other store owners to be sure that everything was as near perfect as possible. On the way, he passed Gary Thorpe, a black janitor at the Webster Men's Store, who was sweeping the sidewalk. And he smiled at the smartly dressed mannequins advertising two-hundred-dollar suits through a clean display window.

On the stage, an electrician tapped the mike with his fingernail. "Checking-one, two, three, four," he said into it. His partner down on the asphalt thirty yards away made a circle with his thumb and index finger. "Loud and clear," he called out.

The seventy-two-degree temperature brought shoppers out in large numbers. During the morning, people wandered in and out of the shopping area enjoying the sunshine. Some made purchases, then left only long enough to have an early lunch and return in time to get a front row view before the anticipated crowd arrived to shut them out. There was plenty of time; Wallace was not scheduled to arrive until one p.m.

Some of the shoppers waited at the Center's Hot Shoppe. Others went below street level to Georgetown Alley and bought magazines in the book store and figurines from the gift shop. The merchants were glad to have the crowd. It was good for business. Even Harry Styne's washateria at the back of the shops was filled with people washing and drying clothes while waiting for Wallace to begin. Those who arrived close to the hour of the rally parked their cars in the underground parking area.

Now, last minute details had to be finished, such as setting up the souvenir stand. It was placed near the platform, and on it were Wallace buttons, hats and other paraphernalia. Every dime they could collect helped. The pre-planning was done. Styne, Bragg and members of the Wallace entourage were satisfied that the day would pass without incident. Emmett Eaton of Montgomery and Dan Ballard, both campaign coordinators, were pleased with the results in Maryland so far. The Laurel stop was drawing a crowd, they were happy about that, too.

An hour before the Wallace group was due in Laurel, Dora and her co-workers set up tables for souvenirs. Dan Ballard helped, hurrying them until he got word Wallace was going to be thirty minutes late.

By noon, the town was buzzing. The Center, which had a good layout, could have accommodated more than the three thousand who showed up. The bank was in the middle of a wide-open parking lot, and because the platform was placed so near the bank building, the crowd looked smaller than it actually was. But it was comfortable in the fresh air and there was no wind. The crowd increased as curious shoppers paused to see what was going on.

The chance listener provided Wallace just the audience he wanted. He had the support of his loyal followers, and he felt he could reach those who attended rallies. But those on the border, who might just happen by, were the ones that he needed to court—those undecided souls who were looking for a man who had ideas compatible with their own. People who wanted a candidate fighting for law and order but those who would not press for heavy sentences for minor crimes might be swayed by hearing his platform. George felt he could convince them he was their man.

Wallace always did everything possible to put things on a "down home" basis. People found something appealing about his "next door neighbor" approach. George knew it, and he always had a directness of action people responded to. State Trooper Dave Harwood said, "George never releases a hand until he has looked its owner straight in the eye." Some people, such as Alabama House Clerk John Pemberton, will swear, "You can put Wallace in a room with his worst enemy and he will convert him in about fifteen minutes."

Shortly before the governor arrived, Secret Service men, who had been to the area three times prior to Wallace's visit to check everything out, positioned themselves in doorways, behind the platform, and at the back of the crowd. They cautioned Barry Bragg to make sure the bank's glass doors were locked. This precaution was taken so no one could sneak up behind the governor while he spoke.

Three rallies were scheduled in Maryland shopping centers. The first was in Capitol Plaza, followed by one in Wheaton. Laurel came next. There had been trouble in Wheaton. The crowd was antagonistic and troublemakers had thrown bars of soap with nails in them. The bad reception there caused the Wallace corps to be late, but they finally got to the Laurel Shopping Center.

In addition, Wallace had experienced throat trouble for several days. His voice was still weak. He arrived at one forty-five p.m., greeted the officials, then reached for the microphone. When he spoke into it, nothing came out. Emmett Eaton sent John Henig for some honey so Cornelia could mix it with lemon juice for George. If George could not speak, Cornelia would replace him. But after George swallowed the honey mixture, his voice returned and he was able to speak for himself.

During the delay, the crowd became restless. Harry Styne had not met Wallace, but they quickly shook hands and George went up onto the bandstand. Styne was immediately impressed with Governor Wallace. He had not expected so straightforward a man.

Mrs. Wallace did not stay for the speech. She looked very smart in the cool-looking yellow summer dress which accentuated her trim figure, but her jet-black hair was rumpled. She wanted to have every strand of it in place, so she went next door to the beauty shop at Montgomery Ward.

Inside the bank, from his desk, Bragg listened to the opening remarks. Tellers peeped out the windows. State police were on one side of the building blocking off exits. Security men were on each side of the stage. Secret Service men were on top of the stair steps, and local police were scattered in the crowd. Approximately forty policemen were guarding the area. Bragg said, "I do not know where they could have given more protection."

Governor Wallace stood behind the six-hundred-pound bullet-proof podium and spoke from beneath a canopy. Usually, he made his speech from an open truck bed, but this time it was set up differently. The Master of Ceremonies,

George Magnum, called out, "Ladies and gentlemen, the next President of the United States—Governor George C. Wallace!"

Over the mike, Wallace's voice came across loud and clear. "I did represent more of the average citizens of this country than did any other candidate, based on the fact that the man who works each day for a living and pays the taxes and holds the country together has been ignored except on election day," he told the crowd and then continued in the same vein as many of his other speeches, hitting hard on the law and order issue. "Police should get more respect," he added. The pro-Wallace crowd applauded loudly at the conclusion of his speech. A few hecklers tried to be disruptive. Some blacks also shouted out in disagreement with George.

"They weren't name-calling," said Bragg. "Wallace was a pretty dynamic speaker who wasn't bothered by the heckling—he acted like he enjoyed the challenge. I guess the surprising thing was there were only six or seven heckling and nobody was really violent. They weren't the kind who have animosity. They just disagreed with him. It's really the type thing you don't mind seeing." It also surprised the banker that no anti-Wallace placards were being waved.

About three-thirty, after Cornelia had her hair done, she returned to the shopping center. She began talking with Harry Styne, standing behind the bandstand. She told him, "Things are very quiet here. In Wheaton, people threw everything but ice cream."

Realizing her husband was nearing the end of his speech, Cornelia asked Styne to direct her to the ladies' room so she could freshen up. He took her to the door of the bank and had a female teller direct her to the restroom. Cornelia made quite an impression as she entered. Girls in the bank enviously ogled and made a number of complimentary remarks when she walked by.

Outside, the crowd cheered and clapped as George concluded. Styne stood on the bank's steps listening and waiting for Mrs. Wallace to return so he could escort her. The area was blocked off, but there were about six steps, and Styne wanted to be sure of Cornelia's safety. When Mrs. Wallace came through the glass doors of the bank, George wound up his speech. It was effective and he got plenty of applause. Just as his wife was being helped down the steps, George left the stage.

As he usually did when security was not a problem, George stepped down into the crowd to shake hands. He had felt a little cheated at Wheaton when he had to rush off, but in Laurel the mood of the people was happy. The band played *Dixie* as the governor moved to his left through the crowd. A female supporter gave him a peck on the cheek. George paused long enough to remove his coat and that gave Laurens Pierce, a Columbia Broadcasting System cameraman, time enough to catch up. He was right behind the governor filming the action from about three feet away.

As George drew near, people eagerly grabbed for his hand. He was all smiles. He listened closely because he was a little deaf and it was hard for him to hear the names of people he was introduced to. The TV cameras carefully skipped around the crowd and focused right on him.

In the audience stood a young white male, waving his arms into X's above his head. His voice rang out once, then again, "George, hey George! Look over here! George, hey George! Come over here and shake my hand!"

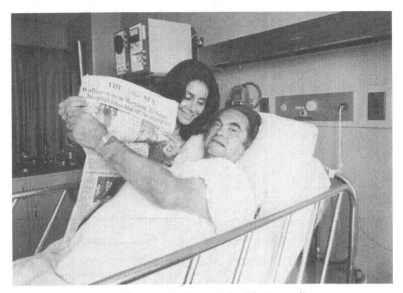

George in Hospital with Cornelia

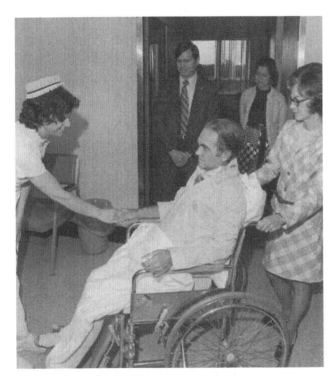

George with Nurse

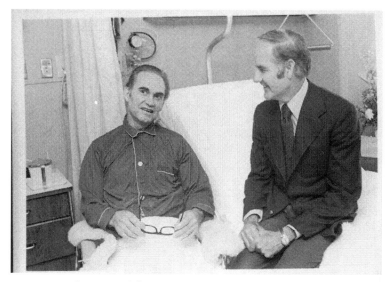

George with Governor George McGovern

George at Mass in Holy Cross

CHAPTER SEVENTEEN

BLOOD-SPLATTERED ASPHALT

In an instant, Wallace was shot and fell to the ground. Mrs. Wallace leaped down the steps and literally jumped on top of him to protect him from further injury. Howard Hendrix, Director of Labor for the State of Alabama, recalls what happened from the moment he saw Arthur Bremer with a gun. "I was ten steps from him, sitting on the tailgate of a trailer. I saw a man I later found out was Bremer rest a gun on a woman's shoulder, then I heard gunfire. Before I got there, Cornelia was already on top of George." The sounds, first thought to be firecrackers, came from a thirty-eight-caliber pistol. It appeared that Wallace had been shot in the chest. But the crowd could not get close enough to tell because the group nearby surrounded him tightly.

The first reaction of people was to duck the bullets. Then screams echoed through the air. Frightened mothers hugged whimpering children close to shield them from harm. People ran. Some headed for the underground shopping area. One young man zigzagged across the parking lot, past Harry Styne's washateria and away from the scene. He knocked a man to the ground and his eyeglasses flew off. They were crushed underfoot before he could retrieve them. The man crawled away on his hands and knees.

Hendrix was appalled at the reaction of their own campaign workers. "They just glared," he said, adding, "I remember seeing nightsticks and knuckles coming into contact with someone's teeth."

Campaign coordinators took over as soon as they composed themselves. They began to plead for help, asking that the crowd move back. When people did not respond, Reverend Magnum pushed his way to the mike. "Move back!" he commanded. Upon hearing his orders, slowly the crowd moved into the vacant space they had left in front of the podium.

Meanwhile, Secret Service agents wrestled the assailant to the ground. Hendrix shoved people out of the way and was one of the first to reach Bremer. Uniformed officers rushed up and held Bremer on the ground. One plainclothesman put handcuffs on his right wrist, and another officer grabbed Bremer's left wrist and snapped the cuffs in place, making sure he could not get away. Others were injured, too. One was Secret Service Agent Nick Zarvos, who clutched his throat.

Captain E.C. Dothard was knocked twenty-five feet backward by a bullet which grazed his stomach, and Dora Thompson's blood oozed through her knee-high boot onto the calf of her leg.

Nobody knew exactly what had happened. Gary Thorpe, a Webster Men's Store employee, was arrested because the police thought he hit a Secret Service man, but he was later released. Bremer was kept in custody.

Before the shooting, only one person even noticed Bremer that day. Around noon, Laurens Pierce, the CBS newsman who had known Wallace twenty-five years, turned his camera in the direction of the audience where the governor was to speak. For the umpteenth time Pierce was there, following Wallace, taking pictures which would go on the news that night. Right then, he was setting up to be sure everything checked out. When he looked in his viewfinder, he saw Bremer in the middle of five or six people in the front. He recognized the man as someone he had seen before so after he completed the shot, he shut off his camera and walked over to Bremer, saying, "I've seen you at previous Wallace rallies."

Pierce was surprised at Bremer's reaction. "He looked embarrassed," Pierce said, "as though he was trying to avoid any notice and he said, 'No, no. Not me,' and turned away." Pierce just nodded and left. He was not too surprised, however, since he recalled from past experience that "people who are members of a group who come to see a luminary like the governor are frequently embarrassed to have attention called to them individually." Although most newsmen were assigned to Wallace for only a limited period of time, Pierce had been with him since 1968 and covered George everywhere he went in the 1972 campaign.

He remembered Arthur Bremer at other rallies because he had been excessively vehement in his applause and acted a "little off balance." Pierce said, "He was the longest and loudest applauder in the group. He had a very glandular exhibition of apparent support for the governor. I wasn't signaled that this man was a possible assassin at all by the snub because this had happened before—people turning away to avoid individual attention being called to them. In retrospect, I expect he was trying to be a little bit less conspicuous."

Bremer had taken a tack which has been successful for others. First, he appeared to support the cause; then, in a turnabout action, he took advantage of his position and moved in close enough to shoot to kill.

When the shooting occurred, Laurens Pierce was one of the persons nearest Wallace. Fortunately his camera was running, covering the events as a presidential candidate should be covered, recording anything the governor said or did, staying right with him the whole time. When George moved out into the crowd, the camera followed him and provided the television audience with the coverage they liked. So when George began handshaking, Laurens moved in close. When the explosion of the gun came, and smoke temporarily marred his vision, Laurens realized at once that he, too, could have been one of the victims. The bullets missed Jim Taylor, head of the Secret Service detail, and they missed Pierce. But they struck four others.

Wallace was like a member of Pierce's family and the newsman's first reaction was to put the camera down. But his training would not let him. The rationale of knowing there were three thousand other people there to help overcame the desire to go to Wallace's aid. "I couldn't turn from it as being distasteful," said Pierce. "But I had to constantly keep wiping my right eye just so I could see through the viewfinder."

He needed to immediately take the film to 2020 M Street in Washington, D.C., where CBS is located, but he couldn't get to his car. He needed a ride. He spotted a truck nearby and knew it was the only vehicle he could commandeer. It was a Singer Sewing Machine truck. He persuaded the driver to drive him to television headquarters.

It was urgent that he get away from the scene with the film so that it would not be confiscated. Laurens feared that government officials might step in and take over. Then the true story might never get told. He did not want that to happen. He wanted the news to be presented to the American public. So he took a wild ride in the Singer truck. "I'll never forget that ride," he said. "For the first two or three miles, I was urging speed. I said, 'Go ahead, ride in the ditch, on the side of the road, go by cars illegally, anything. I'll take care of all tickets involved and I'll see that you're amply repaid. You won't be involved or blamed.'

"At first, the driver was very reluctant, but finally he got his foot on the floorboard and I could hardly get him off. The last several miles into Washington, I thought we'd never make it." Pierce chuckled, recalling his own fear, then continued, "He was dashing through intersections without even a pause, through red lights and the like. By then I was hoping we'd get arrested...it was a wild ride but we arrived at the studio in time. The film was processed and on the Cronkite show that night." History was on the screen for all Americans, and all the world, to see. Laurens Pierce gives credit to the gentleman who drove him in the Singer Sewing Machine truck for helping show history in the making.

Back at the scene of the crime, emergency action was being taken. Governor Wallace lay flat on the ground, critically wounded, the feeling gone from his legs. But he was conscious and he looked up at Howard Hendrix, fixing his gaze on him but saying nothing. Howard thought the governor was focusing on something, anything, and trying to move his legs. There was nothing he could do to help George.

A doctor in the crowd told Jim Taylor that they needed to get Wallace to the hospital right away. An ambulance had been called, but had not arrived. Afraid of waiting too long, they put the governor into a Ford station wagon. Dothard was lying on the ground and when they tried to put him in beside Wallace, he objected. "No, no," he said. "Leave me alone. Get the governor to a hospital."

Just as they were moving through the crowd in the Ford, the Laurel Rescue Squad ambulance arrived. The award-winning volunteer group actually arrived in "four or five minutes," according to Styne, but in this critical situation time seemed endless. The area was blocked off and Wallace, with fingernails digging into the palms of his hands, was transferred to the ambulance. Dothard, objecting, was put in the ambulance, too. In addition to the attendants, several passengers climbed into the ambulance: Mrs. Wallace, Emmett Eaton, Billy Joe Camp, Byron Prescott, and David Golden. They would hardly fit, but they all went to the hospital.

When Dothard was shot, he thought somebody had thrown a firecracker, he said later. The second shot "made me feel like I was kicked by a mule," he added.

With Wallace, it was different; he knew he was hit immediately. Later, Wallace spoke of his feeling at that moment. "Well, of course, I heard the shots and I knew I was hit because I was spun around and then I was shot several times as I was falling and, of course, the first thought was 'It's fatal' and I always thought when people passed away they, slowly, you know, just slowly, faded out, like maybe going to sleep and I, of course, asked God to let me live if it was His will, but if not, that I not suffer.

"All of this happened in the twinkling of an eye. Then, immediately, I looked for Cornelia because I thought I would never see her again. But before I could see her, she was down, of course, on top of me. Then I told her 'I can't move; I'm paralyzed.'

"I still hadn't faded away but I tried to move my legs because I instinctively thought I was paralyzed because for some reason I just thought I was hit in the spine.

"I began to have excruciating pain. I was in pain all the way to the hospital and never went out until I was put to sleep. I was conscious until I was put to sleep and very much aware. I never went into shock, and all the way to the hospital in the ambulance I knew every turn and move and everything that was said. But I kept asking them to give me something to knock me out as I was hurting so badly, and I couldn't do anything about it because I was in terrible pain."

As the ambulance sped down the Beltway to Holy Cross Hospital in Silver Spring, the blood on the asphalt in front of the Equitable Trust Bank was beginning to dry. A few people still milled around the area in disbelief. Others came to view the scene of the shooting. The stores remained open but were not doing any business; shopkeepers were too shocked to transact sales.

CHAPTER EIGHTEEN

FROM MONTGOMERY TO MONTGOMERY

Whenever a candidate goes to a new area, his people scout out the hospitals before the event. They make a dry run to those nearby. Then, if an emergency arises, no time will be lost getting to the best health care facility available. Although Holy Cross Hospital in Silver Spring, Maryland, was not the closest one to Laurel, the Wallace people chose it as being the best equipped. They picked out a route, determined the distance as twenty miles, and estimated travel time at thirty minutes. Campaign workers never intended to use this information.

As the ambulance carrying Wallace rushed down Highway One, a couple of young service station attendants, Richard Reed and Skeet Newlan, realized something was terribly wrong. A solid line of police cars passed by, and helicopters purred overhead. Traffic was pushed aside to make room for emergency vehicles. The boys could not believe the number of police cars and ambulances speeding on the road. Nobody stopped to tell them what was wrong, but they soon heard it on the radio.

Perhaps the course of history had been changed by what occurred that day in the town in Maryland.

On the drive to the hospital, Wallace remained alert. Staying awake was extremely painful, but it proved helpful to the doctors. Emmett Eaton kept reassuring the governor and trying to console him. "Governor, it's just a nick," he said.

"You're going to be okay." Every time George winced, Emmett repeated the statement that was far from true.

George was not convinced. "Emmett, I'm not too sure about that," he replied. "I think you'd better take a second look and see if you're not wrong about that.'' George knew that his condition was serious.

Ironically, when they arrived at the hospital, they were in Montgomery County. It had not been in the plans, but George Wallace had gone from one Montgomery to another.

Certainly Wallace had not really anticipated any dreadful occurrence on this trip. True, he had talked about the risk and danger with Glen Curlee the night before the shooting. But if he had really believed something would happen, he would surely have acted on his premonition and cancelled the trip.

Indeed, things had looked good. On the way to Laurel, George and his traveling companions discussed the fact that everything was shaping up. The campaign was drawing good crowds and contributions. There were problems in Wheaton but, all in all, there was a solid balance and the plus side showed more than the minus.

Wallace workers were getting support from the average man, the man George was trying to help by getting elected. Those blue-collar workers had come forward with contributions and volunteer work. George and his associates were pleased. They believed people interested enough to become involved would develop a missionary complex and convince their friends. The movement could snowball.

People who attend rallies are not always sincere supporters. Some worm their way into the group to find out how best to discredit and disrupt the campaign's forward progress.

At the Wheaton rally, three hours before Laurel, a group of militants were present. When the governor did not arrive on time, the crowd grew impatient. People were pacing up and down and getting right up against the platform. Somebody had failed to tie the rope tightly around the telephone pole to keep the crowd back. When it became slack, the people moved in. The situation was not safe. Emmett Eaton knew what to do. He had been an advance organizer and had been around rallies a long time, beginning in 1958 when he worked with the governor in labor relations as a steelworker in Birmingham. He got involved in the campaigns in what he called "a leaner era when we didn't have any resources." Now they had come up in the world, and Eaton was still around, one of the old regulars with George.

Eaton found the security man. Together, they moved the crowd back and Eaton moved ahead. He asked people to hold the rope so they could retie it. A man standing by a lady with a small child was asked to help. Eaton picked him because he was "clean-cut looking." But the day after the shooting this judgment proved wrong. When he saw the photographs taken at Wheaton, Eaton recognized the shooter as the man he had asked to hold the rope. He'd been identified as Arthur Bremer. The irony of it all appalled him.

It set Eaton to thinking. Although he had not seen Bremer before, it was possible that he had talked to him on the phone. Usually the regular campaign workers took telephone calls, but if a caller was especially persistent, the call was turned over to Emmett. While they were in Maryland, someone kept calling and saying he wanted "one minute with the governor to take his picture" and he insisted "it will only take a minute." He would not take "No" for an answer and called again and again. Finally, they gave the phone to Eaton. He always exercised extreme caution before introducing anyone to the governor. So he offered to meet the caller, but whoever it was refused to set a time. As Eaton recalls, the man said, "No, not you. I have to see the governor. I only want to see the governor." Eaton considered it too risky, so the caller's wish was not granted. With hindsight, Eaton thinks "there's a good possibility it was Bremer."

Eaton might have made a mistake about something else. He had turned down a Rockville rally "because it was out in a field and you couldn't get vehicles out where the governor would be speaking. Besides, the bad entrances and many trees made it a security risk." So Eaton chose Laurel. Bremer was there, but he could have been anywhere with his gun. He could have followed the campaign crowd wherever they went, and he probably would have. If they'd gone to Rockville instead of Laurel, it might have made no difference at all.

One thing Emmett Eaton could not put out of his mind about Laurel. He could still hear the guy yelling, "Hey George, hey George," from behind some people. All Eaton could see was one hand out—his left hand. Eaton felt that the governor probably saved his own life because when the man would not put out his right hand, the governor moved on—just a little distance away from the bullets.

In the ambulance, Eaton absent-mindedly fingered the tie clasp he had pulled from George's bloody shirt and stuffed it in his pocket. He had George's billfold and glasses, too. George's ripped-off shirt was thrown on the floor beside them and his worst wound lay bared. It was on the right side of the chest, near the armpit.

The nurse and Eaton were pressing the wound to stop the bleeding while another attendant gave oxygen. They checked his heartbeat constantly. Everything possible was being done to save his life. George kept asking, "How far? How far?" And he asked his friend to be sure they gave something to knock him out when he got to the hospital because he was in such terrific pain.

There are many "ifs" in such situations. If Wallace had been on time in Wheaton, would it have happened there? If they had gone to Rockville instead, would George have been safer? If he had not stepped down to shake hands, would Bremer have left? If-if-if—but from all indications Bremer had done his stalking well, and nothing would have stopped him short of his being found out and arrested before he had a chance to shoot Wallace. Regardless, the assassination attempt had happened and the victims were on their way to seek treatment.

As they sped down the interstate, Cornelia was crying. She repressed the sobs, but tears streamed down her cheeks. She had no way of knowing the extent of the injuries of her husband or whether they would be fatal. But she controlled herself and said, "Take your oxygen, George," and with much effort regained her composure.

When the ambulance drove down Forest Glen Road and pulled into the Emergency Entrance of Holy Cross Hospital, help was ready and waiting.

CHAPTER NINETEEN

A STEP BACK

Other things were happening on Forest Glen Road in Silver Spring, across from Holy Cross Hospital in a private residence. May 15 was the Ryans' twenty-fourth wedding anniversary. They had invited two couples over for cocktails, then they were going out for dinner.

Mrs. Ryan, a gracious, easy-going mother of four, emptied the ashtrays and took out the garbage. She looked across the street at the hospital and thought how neat the well-kept lawn looked. A blue jay pecked away at a single blade of grass, and a nun in her habit strolled slowly down the path. Even though an occasional ambulance siren shattered the silence, it was a quiet neighborhood which suited the Ryan family fine. Mrs. Ryan enjoyed entertaining and was looking forward to seeing her guests that evening.

But the Ryans' plans for that night never materialized. They did have company, though, a whole lot of company. Most of their neighbors brought lawn chairs, placed them on the freshly-cut grass and sat right in front of the Ryans' house. Their yard became the bleachers.

Across the street, Tom Burke, the hospital's public relations man, had just walked down the corridor to the Assistant Administrator's office to tell Herbert Bell he thought that he would "leave a little bit early," since his work was caught up and not much was going on. As Burke turned to leave, the Assistant Head Nurse burst into the office and yelled out in a high-pitched voice, "Governor Wallace has been shot!"

Burke, disbelieving, said, "Say it again."

She repeated, "Governor Wallace has been shot, and he's on his way to the hospital. Some other people were shot, too."

As Burke and Bell headed for the emergency room, they ran into Sister Helen Marie, the Hospital Administrator, an RN who had been in charge of the surgery suite for six years. She knew what had happened. Fingering her rosary, she told the two men, "If it was a gunshot, we'd better page and see if there is a surgeon in the hospital."

The action began.

Burke put out the call, and immediately seven physicians appeared. Only five were needed. They were: Dr. Joseph Schanno, vascular surgeon, who became chief on the case; Dr. Herman Maganzini, cardiologist and internist; Dr. John Haberlin, general surgeon; Dr. Eugene Libre, hematologist, and Dr. Joseph Peabody, thoracic surgeon. In addition to these, one other doctor responded to the call.

Dr. Marvin Kolkin was a patient on the fifth floor in a room overlooking the parking lot adjoining the emergency room. His wife was visiting him when she heard all the commotion down below. She ran to the window to see what caused so many sirens, slamming doors and loud voices. Looking out, she said to her husband, "It must be terrible down there. Something terrible must have happened, Marvin. It's awful."

Then Dr. Kolkin heard the page, "Any surgeon in the hospital report to the emergency room." He picked up the bedside phone, dialed the emergency room number and asked, "This is Dr. Kolkin, do you need help?"

The clerk on the other end did not know that he was a patient. She answered, "Oh, yes, Dr. Kolkin. If you're in the building, please come here."

The doctor undid his I.V., slipped a robe over his pajamas and appeared in the emergency room in a couple of minutes.

"Dr. Kolkin," a shocked nurse chided, "You're in no shape to help. What are you doing out of bed? Get back upstairs." He nodded and followed her orders.

The injured governor arrived at Holy Cross. The minute the ambulance pulled up, the door opened and in came the stretcher bearing Governor Wallace. People began scurrying around. There was total confusion in the emergency room and throughout the hospital.

Dazed, but still conscious, George looked around. He saw Bell, Burke, and Sister Helen standing in the doorway like an honor guard awaiting a festive occasion. But it was far from that. Once past the door, they rushed him back to a Code Blue room with all the security men, a couple of nurses and four doctors following right along with the stretcher. When they arrived at the special room equipped with cardiac and pulmonary resuscitation machines, one of the Secret Service agents tried to force the door open and get inside where they were working on Wallace. He knew Wallace was still alive, and he did not know any of these people. The agent felt it was his job to stay with the governor. Burke pleaded with him and the other security men to stay away and not hinder the hospital personnel because "these people are taking care of Governor Wallace." Reluctantly, they backed off. But the group clustered together and remained right outside the door.

Inside the room, six pairs of hands worked furiously. The flow of blood was thick and steady, and it had to be stopped before they could find what was wrong. Dr. Schanno asked George, "What hurts? How do you feel?" Luckily, he could answer. "Just the fact that we could discuss with him the lack of feeling in his legs aided us greatly. We could make tests to find out where the numbness was and what it meant," Schanno said.

Because of internal bleeding, exploratory surgery was necessary. They knew that there was at least one bullet, and possibly several, in his body. Therefore, they had to assess the extent of the damage causing the numbness. They summoned a neurologist, Dr. Baltazar E. Perez. By then, the physicians felt certain that there was spinal cord involvement.

Out in the hall standing guard were twenty-five Secret Service men, a dozen Prince Georges County police, three FBI agents, half-a-dozen Maryland State Troopers, four Alabama State Troopers and twenty Montgomery County police. Each group was determined to do its job. They leaned against the walls shifting from one foot to another, chain-smoking and waiting for someone to come out of that room and tell them what was happening. In about twenty minutes, the different agencies were given their assignments. Most were sent to other parts of the hospital. Only the Alabama State Troopers were allowed to stay with the governor.

Back at the Holiday Inn campaign headquarters, Executive Secretary Derryl Gordon and his volunteer help waited. Everybody wanted to go to the hospital, but Gordon took his people back to the motel to call their families and let them know that they were all right. The telephone began ringing incessantly. Before the day was over, they had received eight or nine hundred phone calls from all over the United States. One was from a Catholic nun in California. Acting as their spokesman, she wanted the governor to know that her community of black nuns was offering prayers for his recovery.

The only news Gordon and his group got was second-hand information from the telephone calls. They could not get away from the phones long enough to find out anything for themselves.

But the Ryans, across the street from the hospital, were getting their information first-hand.

It started the minute George Wallace arrived at Holy Cross.

#

Earlier, when her preparations for the evening were complete, Mrs. Ryan decided to relax a few minutes before her four school-aged children came home looking for dinner. So she took a good book into the sunroom to spend the peaceful afternoon reading. She had only been there ten minutes when two ambulances, half-a-dozen Prince Georges County police and motorcycles, ten Maryland State Troopers and a car full of Alabama State Troopers tore into the Holy Cross Emergency Entrance. Through the big windows she could see all the turmoil. Hopping off the couch, she dashed to the front door and heard voices shouting in staccato-like chants, "Governor Wallace has been shot!"

In the ten-year history of the hospital, there had never been anything like this. The entire area was a bevy of noisy confusion. Sirens roared as more ambulances and police cars screeched to a stop outside their emergency room. Two minutes later, helicopters landed on a never-before-used helicopter pad in front of the hospital.

In a few minutes, the Ryans' yard looked like a school campus between classes, except the people cutting across it were running, not walking. Everyone rushed toward the hospital.

At five p.m., the four Ryan boys came home from school, but thirty minutes later, their father could not get up the street. By that time, the area was blocked off. Finally, after Frank

Ryan identified himself as District Director of Family and Child Services in Washington, D.C., and showed the officials an ID card, they let him go home. Some neighbors were not so lucky. They had to leave cars a quarter mile from their homes and walk the rest of the way. At that time, the authorities did not know whether some of the people milling around might have been involved in the assassination attempt and, thinking it unsuccessful, might try to finish the job.

One false report came out saying the governor had died, but it was quickly corrected, so few people heard it. The hospital received a bomb threat, too.

The whole section surrounding the hospital was incredibly busy. Newsmen tromped through the Ryans' yard urgently canvassing the neighborhood, waving hundred-dollar bills and trying to buy telephones. Some people may have taken the money but Colonel Ryan refused. He told them they were welcome to the use of his phone, but he would "never take anything for something like this."

They took up his offer and came inside in droves. The line formed to the right, went through the living room and the hallway to the side room where the phone was located. It stretched the width of the house and out the front door. Very shortly, the bottom floor of the two-story dwelling was completely occupied with people who had flown in from all over the United States. Reporters had to go somewhere; the one pay station in the hospital lobby was not sufficient.

The bathroom was being used constantly, and the men began asking for coffee. They were thirsty and beginning to get hungry. They had been on the road all evening long and had no time or way to get anything to eat. Out came a roast Mrs. Ryan had cooked and put in her refrigerator. It was slivered as thin as possible and rationed out in one-hundred sandwiches.

A worker in the McGovern camp asked to buy food. He

had had a sandwich and wanted to know if he could get something for his five buddies outside. But Mrs. Ryan had to tell him she was not really prepared for that. Feeding those inside the house was all she could manage.

Before the rest of the world knew, the Ryans were finding out about Wallace's condition. One Washington radio reporter, making live reports via the phone, was being picked up on a radio in the next room. Some of the inside information and the terrible reports, such as "He'll never make it" were never on the air at all.

About eleven p.m., the neighborhood Boys' Club opened their facilities to the newsmen, providing a place for them to get a late evening briefing on the condition of Wallace. Relieved of the burden of caring for a houseful of news people, Mrs. Ryan went to the kitchen to get a much-needed cocktail from the shaker she had made for her expected guests. When she opened the kitchen door, a German Shepherd looked up at her with soulful eyes. He was steadily gnawing on the big bone which was all that remained of the roast. In all the confusion, he had wandered into her kitchen and made himself at home. She sat down on the floor beside him and cried.

At Holy Cross, doctors began treatment. During the first medical attention Governor Wallace received, Dr. Bill Lukas, President Nixon's physician, looked over the shoulder of Dr. Joseph Schanno. Living so close to Washington, Schanno was used to treating senators and diplomats, but having the president's doctor watching his every move made Schanno triple-check each instrument before he used it. It was slowing him down. Finally, Schanno turned to Lukas and said, "If you see me make a mistake, for God's sake, tell me."

Elsewhere in the hospital, the other three victims were being tended to. A team of medical people were brought in by helicopter. Every window in the hospital had a light on all night long. The helicopter landing pad was turned into a muddy pathway because so many people had come in. TV trucks pulled in and put up lights. The major traffic tie-up caused sixty thousand people to be stuck in their cars on Georgia Avenue, the main street, during the rush hour. Nobody could move. When traffic finally cleared about midnight, a whole new crop of people came—the curiosity seekers. With the inevitable engine failures, flat tires, and fender-bending accidents, they caused another traffic jam. Once again, area residents were plagued with people using their phones and bathrooms. The let-up had been brief.

Other problems developed. Over at the hospital, many patients did not get dinner that night.

Every available employee was working either directly or indirectly on the Wallace case. Side chores, like verifying identification, took hours. At that time, hospital employees had no ID cards, so each new shift had to be screened. Newsmen were all over the place and consequently had to be constantly checked. Members of the Wallace staff hung around waiting to hear news, and dignitaries kept arriving one by one.

The first limousine to come roaring in was that of Senator Hubert Humphrey, who happened to be in the area. He was closely followed by Governor Marvin Mandel. The shooting had happened in Mandel's state and he came offering any kind of medical assistance possible.

Governor Mandel was in his office in Annapolis when he first got the call that Wallace was shot. The Security Detail had called the State Police, and they relayed the news to the governor's office. Nobody knew the extent of the injury, and there was still some confusion about which hospital the Alabama governor would be taken to. Mandel instructed his aides to get his car out and keep checking to see where to go. Not wanting to waste any time, they left before receiving the information. On the way, they got the word it would be Holy Cross. They arrived at the hospital only five minutes after Wallace.

The first person Mandel ran into was Wallace's Press Secretary, Billy Joe Camp. He shook hands limply but his eyes were focused on the door behind them where Wallace was being treated. Frank diPhillipo, Governor Mandel's Press Secretary, saw what the situation was and took over.

"Reporters, television crews and everybody was wandering through the hospital," diPhillipo recalled. "So I instantly went to the Hospital Administrator and said, 'Show me the largest room you have.' They showed me their meeting room on the second floor. I went down to the lobby where most of the press was centered and told them we would all go upstairs and try to organize a news conference and give them information as fast as we could. That involved a statement by Governor Mandel, a statement by the Colonel of Police on what information they had gotten about Bremer from the FBI and from other State Police, one from the Lieutenant of the Prince Georges County Police in whose jurisdiction it had happened, one from the spokesman for the hospital on the condition of the patient, one from Billy Joe Camp speaking for Wallace, and one from a doctor."

That was not all that had to be done. Mandel said in the meantime, he "called the telephone company and asked them to please get out a special unit to install some phones." He was impressed that within an hour a battery of phones had been installed. Then there was a need for a pressroom. The room at the Boys' Club became a press center with more telephones available there. Removing the press people from the hospital helped thin the crowd.

Next, Mandel spoke to the doctors and called the University of Maryland and had the shock-trauma unit doctors flown down by chopper in case there was any special treatment needed. Then he and diPhillipo spoke to Cornelia. Mandel put his arm around her shoulders, but all he could say was "I'm sorry." He made sure she was set up in a motel close to the hospital and asked diPhillipo to get her a sandwich and a cup of coffee.

With these things taken care of, the governor's group commandeered a doctor's office and made it their headquarters. Fortunately for Mandel, it belonged to a division head who was Chief of Radiology and who also was a pipe smoker. Mandel, who usually had a Meerschaum pipe on his lower lip, laughed about it later, saying, "Yeah, we even used his tobacco."

But the petty grievances Mandel and his staff had to put up with were not so funny. The conflict between the local police, who had Bremer in custody, and the FBI who wanted to take charge, continued. The president had called L. Patrick Gray (then head of the FBI) and had told him to have the FBI take over but the Prince Georges County Police had Bremer and did not want to turn him loose. "The question was who would have custody of Bremer?" said Mandel.

So Pat Gray called Governor Mandel and asked him to intercede with the local police. "I told them if he was going to get killed or shot or anything else," said Mandel, "I would rather it be done under the FBI custody than ours." They agreed to forfeit their authority.

When the FBI agents were driving Arthur Bremer to the Baltimore County jail, the first question he asked was, "How much do you think I can get for my autobiography?"

The Governor of Maryland never met Bremer. "No, I've never seen him," he said later. "I didn't want to get near him. I might have shot him." His main consideration at the time was to see that Wallace got all available treatment which might help him recover from the wounds. Second, he wanted to see that Mrs. Wallace and the family were taken care of.

An interesting sidelight is that it was Mandel who had pushed a tough gun law through the Maryland legislature. Bremer was later indicted and convicted on that new law— possession of a weapon without a license. Moreover, having bought the gun in Wisconsin, he had compounded the difficulty by transporting it over several state lines. But the law had not prevented George Wallace's being shot.

The act repelled the people of Maryland. Mandel told of it with deep remorse. "The whole thing was such a total tragedy; an almost unanimous reaction of shock was shown by the people of Maryland. It was a total abhorrence of what happened," he reported. "Many believed that such a thing could not happen."

Bremer had been a campaign worker with the Wallace forces for over a month. He just walked in the Detroit headquarters one day and signed up—number thirteen on the list. Day after day, he would come to the Holiday Inn headquarters, pick up literature, then go over to the plants at shift-changing time to pass out material to the workers. During the whole Northeast tour, Bremer asked crazy questions like, "Who do I give these pamphlets to?" and he wore clothes that looked as if they had been slept in. He fooled a few people. By giving a pitiful story, he talked an influential campaign boss— Grey Hodges—into letting him spend the night in a room stacked with papers. They had rented an extra room at the Holiday Inn in Minneapolis for storage, and they told Bremer he could sleep there if he had no place to stay. The campaign coordinators knew that part of the game was to provide meals and quarters for many of the transient workers. If they were hard up, they even got a little cash. Once Hodges handed Brewer a twenty-dollar bill. Bremer was treated no differently than any other worker. As long as they were reasonably sure that he did his share, they would carry him along.

Earlier in the campaign, a movie about Martin Luther King was shown on Milwaukee TV at campaign headquarters. Wallace supporters felt that it was probably arranged by Humphrey supporter Loren Green in an effort to hurt Wallace's chances in the state. Out of curiosity, all the campaign workers were together watching the show. Arthur Bremer sat on the floor near the doorway reading a book. People had to step over him to get in because he had his feet stretched out across the entranceway. Hodges, a gruff, impatient man, came in and, perturbed by Bremer's blocking the doorway, he barked at him, "Get the hell out of the way!" With that, Bremer jumped up and the book fell from his hands. Hodges picked it up and read the title: *The Assassination of Robert F. Kennedy.*

This did not really tip Hodges off. Another event had happened during the campaign which was much more suspect. A Holiday Inn switchboard operator was under suspicion. Jim Golden, head of the Secret Service, had been listening in on conversations coming in to the motel. At times, he thought that someone else was plugged into the calls directed to Wallace headquarters. More than once when Jack and Artice Poulsen walked their two boxer dogs early in the morning, they saw that same switchboard operator, a hippie-type female, talking with Bremer, who was lying across the counter. On her lapel she wore a lady-lib button and a hammer and sickle pin. Whenever she got a chance, she chose a table near Wallace people at lunchtime. That was not the extent of her anti-Wallace activities; once she was photographed in Racine, Michigan, with a friend at a Wallace rally. Both were putting thumbs down.

Bremer had been accepted as "just quiet." He was a loner and did not leave himself open to many questions. When the

Wallace group was moving on, Bremer asked Hodges if he could go along into Indiana with them, but Hodges said, "I could see something just wasn't right with him and I answered, 'No, fellow. We're just done with you.'" By then they felt that his appearance, the way he acted when he did speak, and his strange, unbelievable stories, bragging outlandishly of past accomplishments, betrayed him as a man who could cause problems.

"But how're you gonna know?" Poulsen asked later. "I had suspected other people in the campaign—if you're gonna think everyone is suspicious, well, we wouldn't get anywhere." All charges against Bremer could have applied to some other workers, as well. The one thing which might have clued someone in was that Bremer constantly asked Hodges about the governor's plans. "Where is he going today?" he would ask. "Will he come out through here? What door is he going out?" It seemed obvious that Bremer had an excessive interest in the details of George Wallace's comings and goings. But he could have just been nosey.

#

During George's seven-and-a-half weeks in the hospital, visitors came in droves. Some got in, some did not. For the first few days, all the limousines came bringing dignitaries to visit Wallace.

Mrs. Humphrey came with Mrs. McGovern, Joan and Ted Kennedy came. Vice President Spiro Agnew arrived. Ethel Kennedy, her leg in a cast from a skiing accident, encouraged George, telling him, "As you go down, you have to come back up."

By the time President Richard Nixon arrived, hospital workers were so accustomed to seeing high-ranking officials in the corridors that one nurse, talking on the phone, glanced up, then said to the caller, "Oh, that's just the president passing by."

Nevertheless, Dr. Joseph Schanno took the president seriously when he shook his finger at him and said, "You better be the best. I've told the world you're the best."

Ordinary people also knew that Wallace was in the hospital. Other patients were very much aware of his presence, so was the hospital personnel.

During his stay, one hospital nun got to know George Wallace well. Sister Maurita, Assistant Administrator of Holy Cross Hospital, was the image of what an Irish nun is expected to be like. Her accent was not too noticeable until she talked a few minutes, got excited, and sped up her speech. The day Governor Wallace was brought in, County Limerick could have claimed Sister Maurita unquestionably. Just telling about it later thickened her accent. In a heavy Irish brogue she said, "It just came over the screen that he had been shot, and we had heard that he was going over to Leland in Laurel. The next thing was a Code Blue for the emergency room, but I was not thinking it was going to be Wallace. I went down to answer and Sister Helen told me Wallace was coming." She made the Sign of the Cross.

From that day until Wallace left the hospital, Sister Maurita was always conscious that the Governor of Alabama was in their care. She said, "He was treated as a patient and nothing else as far as that goes." But the governor was bound to get some special attention. His personality would have brought him a little extra notice, too, even if he had not been a dignitary. When he went back and forth to therapy, Sister Maurita and everybody on the floor "just seemed to think he was a very kind, warm person." On television he had been the big, bad bear who hated Negroes, but in person they saw a different man, one Sister Maurita called "a gentleman." She especially liked it when Governor Wallace said, "I hope you're all praying for me."

During those two months, the stereotyped ideas about him had changed. Before Wallace came to Holy Cross, Sister Maurita said that he was thought of as "just another political figure who said things our staff might not go along with. But now, he certainly showed his kindness and his courtesy, his confidence." Wallace grew in their esteem. Even here, a seriously ill George Wallace had made his mark.

On July 7, 1972, after fifty-three days, the governor left the hospital to start over. He accepted the disability from which Dr. Schanno said he could not be healed. Father Roger Fortin, the hospital chaplain who had constantly been at Cornelia's side, planned a Mass of Thanksgiving. Much had happened since May 15, some of it irreversible, but now God was to be thanked, not only for what He had done, but for what He had not done. George Wallace's life had been spared. Religious hospital staff members took the reverent view that Wallace had "walked through the valley of the shadow of death" and had come out on the other side.

On the eve of his departure from Holy Cross, George came down from Room 716 where he had spent many weeks suffering but improving. Now he read a part of the Catholic "Mass of Praise and Thanksgiving" celebrated in his honor. Once again, the voice of George Wallace would be heard on the air, but this time openly praying while reading the twenty-third psalm in a dramatic, emotional fashion. The weak voice was hardly recognizable to those who heard it say, "The Lord is my shepherd, I shall not want..."

His voice lacked force, but the words were brave and strong, and the people of the nation began to believe that George Wallace would get well. As a fighter, he had used a system of doing things which someone once described as "inch by inch, it's a cinch; mile by mile, it's not worthwhile."

On July 7, at 9 a.m. Governor George Wallace was ready to leave the hospital. But before he did so, he read a statement to those who had so diligently cared for him:

"On the occasion of my departure from Holy Cross Hospital, my family and I express our heartfelt gratitude and thanks to the many fine citizens of the state of Maryland for the tremendous courtesies extended to us during our stay here. We especially thank Governor Marvin Mandel and his staff, the county and municipal officials, state troopers and other policemen who endured long hours to help at the hospital.

"Sister Helen Marie, the doctors, sisters and staff of the hospital will always hold a very dear place in my heart. They saved my life and I wish God's blessings to them all."

The hospital ordeal was over, thanksgivings were said, a banquet had been held commemorating the Alabama governor's departure, and now he would be sent back to the world. He could no longer "Stand Up for America" as his slogan stated. From now on, whatever George Wallace did, he would do sitting in a chair.

CHAPTER TWENTY

RESPECT FOR THE PRESIDENCY

When George arrived at Dannelly Field in Montgomery on July 7, his mother saw him for the first time since he had been shot. Because Mozelle Wallace had had brain surgery for the removal of a tumor, she was unable to go to Maryland to see her injured son. The last time she had seen him was when he visited in Montgomery on Mother's Day. When he left that day, she cautioned him, as she always did, to "be careful."

He hugged her and said, "Don't worry 'bout me. I'll be all right. You take care of yourself now, y'hear?"

When she was told of her son's critical injury, Mrs. Wallace shed many tears, but she knew that was not going to help George. What George needed most was encouragement and faith that he could get well. "The only consolation I had was that I always felt—well, if he is shot, he's doing what he wants to do," she told her friends.

Now, almost two months after the injury, George was returning home, and his mother had to face seeing him in a wheelchair. She and her daughter, Marianne, went to Dannelly Field together. Marianne had not seen her brother after he was shot, either, and she hoped she would be able to recognize him. In newspaper pictures he had looked so thin and as if he had aged ten years. But when the plane landed and the governor was wheeled off, both his mother and sister were surprised and pleased.

"We were amazed at the way he looked," said Marianne. "We thought he looked good and his spirits were good." George had regained some of his weight, and his arms were strong as he pulled his mother towards him for a peck on the cheek.

George was always a fighter. He was a champion boxer in the thirties, and he had cultivated those gifts in the political arena. Now he was going to need all the fight he could muster. He prepared himself by acting as if everything were normal all during his hospital stay. He had kept active and in touch with the world. George visited other patients, including Dora Thompson, who was recovering nicely from the bullet she took, and he read the papers.

Another event which occurred while George was incapacitated was the Watergate break-in June 17, 1972. The bizarre burglary which seemed so insignificant at its beginning, soon took over all the prime time on TV and radio. Two years later, it would climax in the resignation of President Nixon. It might also lead George Wallace to think about running for the presidency again in 1976. He read about it with much interest and followed the unfolding plot with an ear tuned to how it would affect him.

Though George came to doubt Nixon's personal integrity, he still had great respect for the office of the presidency. When he was ill, President Nixon kept insisting on seeing the Alabama governor. Each time Dr. Schanno told George the president wanted to visit him, George refused. Finally, late in June, the day before Nixon was to leave for Russia, Schanno told the governor, "Now look, the president is putting the pressure on. He really is insisting on seeing you before he leaves." And he added, "You really don't have any excuses."

He remembers George's answer. "You know what he said to me? He said, 'I just feel so bad to have the president come and see a sick man like me and not be in my best physical shape.' He felt bashful and humble that the president should come and see him in his present physical status and that only somebody who's really up and good should be seen. That's the way he feels about the presidential office—an Eagle-Scout type of attitude."

The politics on a national level worried George, however. He had profound feelings about Watergate and he made a long statement regarding it to an interviewer. "I hope that the president is certainly not involved because of the interest I have for the presidency and the respect for that office and the hope for stability in our country," he said. "I would hope that any president, when elected, would have a successful tenure of service because that is in the interest of our country on the domestic and on the foreign scene. But this country is strong and viable and able to withstand any happening of this sort and will weather this storm and will continue its greatness. And I believe it will even be a greater country because those in positions of responsibility now realize that the attitude of the average citizen has been really the attitude that ought to prevail in government because they, in the final analysis, are the ones who have brought stability and power and compassion. It hasn't come from the exotic noisemakers who want to destroy our society.

"We have defects in our society because we're human, and human beings administer it. But in this country, there are more opportunities for people of all groups than in any other country in the world. Any change that ought to be brought about can be brought about within the constitutional context—that is, peacefully, through the election process. Therefore, I think any happening like Watergate will be overcome by this country, which is too big to succumb to any one happening in government."

As the governor continued to talk, his rhetorical pattern became complex.

"I have a lot of faith in the people. I have been often very critical of actions of those in government, of the courts, of the Congress, of the president, but that's the American way. I would preface any criticism I make about things we can change through the political context that in spite of the bumps and in spite of the defects in administration and laws, for instance— which I've talked about which levies too heavy a burden of taxation on the average citizen while exempting some that ought not to be exempt. In spite of all this, our country's still the greatest and finest and strongest. There are more opportunities here than anyplace else."

Watergate disturbed Governor Wallace, but it did not destroy his faith in the United States as a nation. He continued to serve as governor and kept on speaking out. He made preparations to go to the Democratic National Convention in a wheelchair.

The Convention was held in July in Miami, and the Governor of Alabama and his group were present. So were the minority groups with each different segment of the population carefully balanced to make all equal. While such special attention was being paid to youth, women and blacks, Governor Wallace and his people were being snubbed. Even though he attended, Wallace did not take an active part in convention activities. Meetings would be set, and the Wallace group would not be notified. Chairman Larry O'Brien's people would make excuses, saying, "Oh, you didn't know about that? Somebody was supposed to tell you." But they never said who.

CHAPTER TWENTY-ONE

STYLE AND PHILOSOPHY

Back in Alabama after the 1972 campaign, George Wallace and his workers had a pause in activity which gave him and them a little time to think about goals and values.

Whether the Democrats liked it or not, Wallace had achieved a measure of success. Wherever he went, nobody asked, "Who is that?" By now he was well-known and people clamored to get near him, to shake his hand. He had planned it this way, but he did not take full credit for the results.

Repeating that his family set the example for his success, he said, "My family wanted us to be educated and go to school and not be dependent. My mother worked for thirty years when she retired. So I would attribute our drive and push to the fact that my family wanted us to accomplish something and not remain status quo." To this, he added that when he is known, Alabama is known and that the success came about as a result of the "people giving me the opportunity as governor of this state to talk not only about affairs purely domestic but about those affairs that are happening in Washington that affected us at the domestic level. I believe our success came in expressing the viewpoint that was my viewpoint and was also the viewpoint of the great majority of the people in our country for the first time on the national scene."

If being ignored by party leaders upset George, his discouragement never lasted long.

225

People invigorated him. All it took to bring George out of a moody spell was, as Jimmy Faulkner recalls, "a little old lady to shake his hand; this puts him back on top of the world once again." A lot of people got the impression that George would help them if they got in trouble. They did not seem to believe that George Corley Wallace would ever let them down.

Whether sick or well, George was noted for meeting commitments. His National Campaign Director Charles Snider often heard him say while on the road rushing from one speaking engagement to the next, "I'm supposed to be there to speak and those people are looking for me. I can't let them down." And on they pushed to the next town where the crowd waited.

Snider also was impressed by the way George showed his consideration for the average man. Once, when they were on the campaign trail, an Alabama State Trooper pulled over the car in which Wallace was riding. Distraught when he saw the governor, the trooper said, "Oh, Governor Wallace, I didn't know that was you."

Wallace did not say, "You can't give me a ticket." He allowed the man to save face by saying, "I told that fellow to slow down."

Whenever it was possible to avoid hurt feelings, George did it, even if this meant he would have to hedge a question or not answer it. The loyalty of his friends was important to him, so when they asked him to attend the opening of a flower show or do something else he preferred not to do, he did not like to decline directly.

One morning a Montgomery businessman, who had worked in Wallace's campaigns and contributed hefty sums, came to his office asking him to attend a Lions' Club meeting. George said his work was piled up and the legislature was in session, but the man insisted. After all other excuses failed,

George came up with the answer known around the Capitol as "the final resort." It involves no commitment because it is simply, "I will, (then in a lower tone) if I can, (then in a whisper) if I feel like it." And the governor was off the hook.

Some problems could not be solved so easily. Then George had to analyze issues and offer solutions. Some people think he offered solutions where there were none. "To George, no problem was unsolvable. He always had a solution," said Robert Vance, who did not intend the statement to be a compliment. Other political adversaries also saw George as "flexible." They say he had "gone the full circle of friends" because he changed friends according to their usefulness. Vance admitted, however, this was not always duplicity. He claimed Wallace has changed his approach rather than his position as he evolved. Undisputed, though, was George's ability to sense the concern of the electorate. In that, his opponents as well as his constituents called him a "genius."

Some said George was naïve because he often let anyone into his camp. Friends, not necessarily the best managers, often got into positions of authority. Even though he constantly complained, "The press is against me," he still welcomed them, saying, "Maybe this time it'll be different." But callousness and ossification which overcome many a politician had not reached George. He was still much influenced by the tide of popular opinion.

In 1963, when George was first inaugurated, black was black and white was white in the South. In the interim, numerous changes were made, and equal rights had become a part of everyday American life. George made it his business to stand up for Alabamians; now, if he still wanted to take their side, he had to decide first what it was, at a particular time, that they wanted. He toned down his segregation cry until it was barely audible. Even the busing issue used in the 1972 campaign was not solely based on color. It was, as much as anything else, a plea for neighborhood schools.

Wallace backed down carefully, still trying to appease his white supremacy supporters while building a whole new base, including any blacks who could forget that Wallace ever called for "segregation forever," or who could believe that he had changed. This group had grown immensely in Alabama and he wanted their vote. Wallace still claimed he was for all the people, that what he tried to stop was "big government interference."

During his illness he had plenty of time to think about his own goals. He gave a clear picture of what his motives were, saying, "I suppose maybe I've had more time to reflect upon my general philosophy of life since I almost lost it and was, in effect, snatched from the jaws of death. I look back and see where maybe I could have done things differently. Maybe I wasted some time, but I think my general philosophy of life is that you ought to try to leave this life better than you found it. You should make some contribution to the betterment of humanity because the only way that you can serve God is to serve your fellow man." He said he would do this by bringing about a change in peoples' attitudes if he could. In his rambling, conversational style, he told an interviewer, "The one change that I think would help us more than anything else is the realization of how dependent we are upon nature, which is God. If we would rekindle our faith and really have a religious revival in the sense in this country of being more aware of the problems of other people, especially the unfortunate, even though we are that way anyway, I believe maybe that one great change would be that people would have a little more religious impetus." Such a change was beyond George's power.

But from his place at the top as a state ruler, the governor did try to reinforce his own principles. He stated that "All people who occupy positions in the governorship of a state, or as a president or senator, sometimes feel lonely." He clearly understood that people in leadership positions could not permit themselves the luxury of spending too much time with any group or individual. They must restrict themselves and ration their hours. Consequently, they do not receive the constant support of their family and friends, which would ordinarily sustain them in difficult situations. To deal with this, sometimes George boosted his spirits by going back home.

He said to the interviewer, "All of us are human, and we become sometimes frustrated and tired, and going home does refresh and aid you. In fact, up until I was hurt, I frequently visited my county of Barbour and my hometown originally of Clio and the town of Clayton, where I was living when I was elected governor, to see local people and people that I sprang from and to see people who are the salt of the earth that I know well. It was always refreshing and always helped overcome the loneliness that this position sometimes places a person in because there are so many occasions in which the final decision on important matters of a state has to be made by the governor. He has no one to pass the buck to. Sometimes this puts you in a lonely position because many times we are torn between what position we should take, in the sense of what is best for our people." The burden of making difficult, far-reaching decisions often fell heavily on the shoulders of George Wallace. The weight could be staggering and depressing.

Others recognized the fact that Governor Wallace had sacrificed personal comfort in accepting responsibility and pushing programs beneficial to the Southeast. Georgia's Governor Jimmy Carter, who became president in 1977, praised Wallace's effectiveness in aiding the image of the

South by saying, "He's done a great deal to bring to our region of the country the attention of political observers from throughout the nation and the world." Whether the attention was good or bad, that statement was true.

CHAPTER TWENTY-TWO

RUNNING UP THE FIFTY CAPITOL STEPS

Barring a miracle, George would never again run up the fifty white Capitol steps in Montgomery as he had done so often when he was a young legislator. But his mind kept going full speed. It had not been affected at all by his "accident," as he called the attempt to assassinate him. He felt fine and believed he was once again in good physical shape. But before he ran for re-election as governor in 1974, he had to be sure.

So he called in a new friend.

When George was a patient in Holy Cross, he and Dr. Joe Schanno became close. Before Schanno even met Wallace, he was a supporter; and one day he came to the hospital with a Wallace button pinned to the underside of his coat lapel. Some of George's friends asked him, "How lucky can you get? All the doctors in Maryland and you got one of your backers." During his hospital stay, Wallace and Schanno developed a personal as well as professional relationship.

So when it came time to see how Wallace would do out of the hospital, Dr. Schanno took him over to his house for a Fourth of July picnic. The trouble was, he did not tell anybody, not even Holy Cross Public Relations Director Tom Burke. George disappeared all of a sudden, and no one knew where he had gone. When the press got wind of it, they went to Burke. All the newspaper knew was that the governor had left.

Burke called the doctor. But Schanno was not concerned

231

when Burke told him the press wanted to know where Wallace was. He even sent a message to the Washington Post. "Tell them it's none of their damn business." He felt there had already been too much intrusion on the governor's privacy. Then he softened up a bit and said, "Send the press on over. They can join the party."

When Wallace decided to seek the governorship again, he called Dr. Schanno down to Montgomery to see if he was fit. In August of 1973, almost a year in advance of the election, the doctor was summoned to Alabama to check Wallace over. Schanno reported, "He's very conscientious about whether he's capable of carrying on in office. He asked me, 'Do you think I can make it and do my job as governor and whatever political future I have?' and I reassured him, 'Look, there isn't a thing you can't do physically that any other person can do as far as political life is concerned.' George Wallace is in excellent physical shape. Before the accident, he kept himself in training. In fact, if he had not been in good shape, he never would have made it. He looks like he accepted the fact that he's got to be a paraplegic. He can do anything except walk." Schanno concluded, "'George,' I told him, 'I can't see any reason at all you can't run for any political office.'" The doctor assured him that all the surgical problems and all the problems with his bladder had been corrected.

While Dr. Schanno, his wife, and their eight children visited in Montgomery, they learned a little about Alabama. As they sat on the back porch of the mansion drinking tea, Cornelia's boys, Josh and Jim, ran through the yard playing catch with a black boy who lived behind them. When Josh asked his mother if Jesse could spend the night and reminded her that "his cot's still made upstairs," Schanno thought how much that scene would shake up the Northern liberals if they knew about it. But they probably did not even know the

Alabama governor's mansion is in an integrated neighborhood.

By the time George's fifty-fourth birthday rolled around, he was doing extremely well and was ready to get back in the limelight. Since the shooting, he had survived minor surgery several times and looked and acted as if he were back to normal, as normal as life in a wheelchair could be. A tremendous party was planned for August 25, 1973, at the Coliseum in Montgomery. It would feature a country band and all the festive trimmings. The day was a gala occasion. Paper hats saying "Happy Birthday, Governor Wallace," and decorated with a red picture in the shape of Alabama were passed out. Ten thousand people came and most of Alabama's sixty-seven counties participated by bringing beautifully decorated cakes. Outside the Coliseum, barbecued chicken dinners were served.

Inside, there was cake and punch. Everything was free.

The most beautiful cake of all almost did not make it to the party. The Mobile Shriners had a twelve-hundred-pound cake to send to Montgomery. But the state trooper assigned to deliver it did not want the job. He was afraid something would happen to it on the way, since it was so large. At the last minute, he agreed to take it, but said he would not be responsible. However, it arrived intact and received a place of honor at the party.

George was only one year removed from his near-fatal accident, but he had come a long way. On his birthday, he was back full-swing at handshaking. People crowded around and lined up as he was wheeled up the ramp to the stage. Many who once thought they would never see the governor alive again were thrilled to feel the firmness of his grip.

#

At the same time, back in Maryland, the man responsible for the shooting was brought to trial. Dora Thompson was called as a witness. She was surprised to see Arthur Bremer, bearded, wearing glasses and appearing quite different from before. Dressed for the trial, he looked much more respectable. Mrs. Speigel, the lady on whose shoulder he had steadied the gun when he shot Wallace, identified Bremer in court.

Dora's second surprise came when the defense attorney asked her only a couple of questions. Oddly enough, both were only indirectly related to what happened. He asked, "How long were you in a cast?" and "Didn't you go to Alabama after the shooting?"

Dora was still on crutches from her injury, and she had to hobble down the aisle. By that time, she was scared and angry because the "protection they gave Bremer was hard to believe!" she said. Bremer was flanked on both sides by policemen. She added, "It was fantastic! You'd think we were the criminals." Mrs. Thompson resented the way courts make witnesses nervous.

Bremer's father fully supported him. Not long after the trial, he was in a bar above Don Stricther's gun shop in Milwaukee where Bremer bought the weapon he used to shoot Wallace. From the target range adjoining, Howard Hendrix, Alabama State Director of Labor, and his friend Dave Crossland overheard Bremer's father raising hell to Stricther, yelling angrily, "If it wasn't for S.O.B.'s like you selling pistols, my boy wouldn't be in trouble." A six-foot-three, two-hundred pound Stricther threw him out of the bar.

Convicted and sent to jail for fifty-three years, Arthur Bremer wrote a book in the form of a diary. It was published in a six-part series in Harper's Bazaar. He faced a suit filed by Dora Thompson in the amount of six hundred thousand dollars, now pending. If Mrs. Thompson wins her suit in court, he will not profit at all from his book.

As for Bremer, until his release from prison November 9, 2007, he stayed in solitary much of the time since he could not get along with other prisoners. By contrast, George's celebration of his fifty-fourth birthday saw him surrounded by thousands of friends and supporters in Montgomery's spacious Coliseum.

CHAPTER TWENTY-THREE

STILL THE SAME GEORGE C.

Four tragedies occurred in the life of George Wallace. His father, George Wallace, Sr., died during George's first semester in college; his wife, Lurleen, was taken with cancer; he was struck down in an attempted assassination; and he had failed in his efforts to be president. He refused to allow any of those things to break his spirit.

He learned, and learned fast, ways of retaining his independence even in a wheelchair. He was determined not to let his disability restrict him.

Once he was well enough to begin speaking again, a way was devised to allow George to do it standing up. At the opening legislative session on May 1, 1973, his aides helped lift him to a standing position behind the podium. Then they fastened a strap around the center of his back from one side of the podium to the other. This permitted him to rest his arms on the top of the bullet-proof dais and gave him necessary support. The system worked perfectly, and George used it every time he spoke.

The support which enabled George to speak from a standing position was a great morale booster. By putting him back at a higher level than the audience, people could forget about the wheelchair, and concentrate on what the man had to say. And George could tell them what he had always told them—about "Congress proposing and executing programs of spending that take money out of the average citizen's pockets and spend it on programs that leave those it was intended to help in the same condition they were in when the program started," and the "foreign aid to countries opposing the United States" and the "welfare mess" and "national offensive and defensive posture." He blamed most of these tendencies on the "exotic left" who drifted away from "what the average citizen wants."

If he spoke about segregation, he still maintained he had not changed. He told an interviewer, "This is something that existed in our part of the country by custom for many years and was sanctioned by the courts, and it was the feeling of the people that it was in the best interests of all concerned. It really was not in the minds and hearts of anybody who practiced it by law or otherwise that it was aimed at being against anybody. So a man's true feeling emanates from his heart. If he is for something because he dislikes someone, then that's one motive; if he is for something because he genuinely believes that it's in the best interest of all concerned, then that is not bad.

"But, of course, the courts have stricken down that which they once upheld, and the people of our state and the other states affected have accepted the theory of so-called non-discrimination. I don't believe the people, when they practiced this practice, felt they were discriminating against anybody; they felt they were doing what was in the best interest of everyone. Even in those times, the people in government were working trying to bring more industry and better facilities for people of all races. I feel that every citizen should have an opportunity, an equal opportunity, to make a living based on his ability and what he can do. I believe that's the majority attitude in this state and in the country.

"But we do object vigorously to the artificial and theoretical means of arriving at certain goals that certain liberal ivory-towered thinkers have thought up, such as destruction of neighborhood schools; busing here and yon of people of both races across cities and towns and counties in order to bring about quotas and balances which is so artificial and unreal that it has created much chaos in local educational systems. The people of this state and other states in the region adopted the so-called freedom-of-choice plan, allowing people to go to the school of their choice regardless of who they happen to be, and the courts agreed to it.

"Then they came back the next year and said, 'It's not working because not enough people transferred from this section of town to another section and vice versa.' Of course the answer we gave was, 'They could if they wanted to.'

"They replied, 'Well, that's your problem.' So, really, they were not after non-discrimination. They were after something else and that's what the people object to, not only in this state but throughout the country. So, I would say that the people of this state want to see all the people prosper and realize the American dream regardless of their race or color. They do feel that local democratic institutions such as schools ought to be allowed to be controlled more than they are by local people with the idea that the law is, and has been, accepted, that it be done on a non-discriminatory basis."

Those words notwithstanding, even his most outspoken critics will admit that Wallace had changed. Some of them considered him more acceptable. Ben Stokes, a Mobile lawyer, reflected the attitude of many Alabamians. He said he never before cast a vote for George Wallace, but he admitted voting for him in May of 1974 for re-election as governor. And why did Stokes then decide to vote for a man that he had strongly opposed in the past? Because he felt that Wallace had changed his attitude.

Stokes told an interviewer about it. "I don't think that

there's anything about the governor's views or program or what-have-you which is racist-oriented now," he said. "I think that, except for past conduct, he would be acceptable to the black community now, pretty much. There are some blacks with whom he could never be acceptable. In his public speeches and in his public position and everything, he has not had any anti-black attitude. This endured up through 1971, well '72 to a degree. He was storming about the country speaking about the busing." Stokes saw a mellowed Wallace who knew enough to recognize when the fight was lost.

Ben Stokes knew that Wallace used what he had to use to achieve his political goals. He understood that George seized issues to command the response of the people. But Stokes did not advocate breaking laws to reach these goals. He thought with the mind of a lawyer: he wanted to preserve the law and to have respect for it. Stokes saw that in former years, George, a judge with a law degree, had acted in an irresponsible and indefensible manner. He was repelled by Wallace's actions because he felt that "George ought to know better."

He expressed those feelings very frankly, saying, "I think the actions of Wallace during those years helped set the pattern of disobedience to the law and disrespect for the law. I feel very strongly about that. It's for that reason I never considered myself a Wallace ally."

Now that Wallace had changed, Stokes was ready to forgive and forget. Even when they differed politically, Stokes personally liked Wallace. It always pleased him when George took the time to meet a page Stokes took unannounced to his office. He admired the governor's unpretentiousness, too. "Once you get into his office, he is so warm, friendly, ingratiating, he's just homespun and down to earth, no pretense or artifice at all about him," Stokes said. "This I admire. He's got the common touch, there's no question about that."

He also admired the strength of Wallace and attributed it to an upbringing which, while not in poverty, certainly was not in the land of plenty. "He really scratched and worked. He developed a sense of real competition and battle because of his pugilistic career and the work and scratch and struggle to get where he is. Plus, I'm sure that Wallace's size has something to do with his bellicose nature. Like Napoleon, Stalin or Hitler, it's sort of a compensatory reaction, I think." Stokes felt that George had to have a louder mouth than most just to prove himself.

Ben felt that whatever reasons lay deep behind the actions of George Wallace, he always knew what would be beneficial to himself. When he saw many young liberal governors getting elected, he recognized the development of the new South. In the last five years, Ruben Askew of Florida, Jimmy Carter of Georgia, and others have been put into office, proving that citizens now advocated equal rights for all. Stokes felt that "George sees that this is popular now, but it hasn't been that way long. He recognized the new trend and adapted to it."

Stokes said, "George swings with the tide of public opinion rather than lead the public into new positions by leadership. It's an after-the-fact type thing instead of before-the-fact." If particular issues are George's "thing," Stokes felt that he should immediately champion them and not wait to see what the popular course of action will be.

A period of social unrest which launched a rural black-belt populist into a political career had subsided, and the fire had gone out of the controversy. So, George, with his accurate political antennae, tuned in to see how to change his approach. In so doing, he may have come back closer to where he started from. However he arrived at his current position, he was now there.

George kept his interest in living by constantly stimulating it. Watergate had become a big flood. He read about it and studied it. American servicemen had moved out of Vietnam, and for all practical purposes, as far as the United States was concerned, the Asian war was over. Prisoners of war returned to the United States and a heroic Alabamian was the first off the plane. Jeremiah Denton's words, "God Bless America," went down in history, and Mobilians, proud of their fellow citizen, feted him when he returned to town in April of 1973. Governor George C. Wallace and his family participated in the ceremony in historic Bienville Square. Wallace also entertained fourteen returned prisoners of war at the mansion and expressed gratitude to them from one former serviceman to another.

In these ways, George kept himself occupied. He had no time to dwell on his disability. When the Southern Governor's Conference came up in September of 1973, Governor George Wallace was chairman. The event was hosted at Point Clear, Alabama, at the Grand Hotel, a quiet spot with magnificent oaks hanging out over Mobile Bay and decorating and shading the grounds. The exclusive facility was secluded and guarded. Other governors, and their wives, welcomed the privacy and especially appreciated the fact that guards were unnecessary outside rooms. The peaceful setting was appealing and, even though the conference was work for George Wallace, he and Cornelia still had time to relax and enjoy themselves. But George had never been one to relax too much.

In addition to his duties as governor, personal activities also kept George occupied. The Wallaces were having a wedding. Peggy Sue Wallace and Mark Kennedy were wed December 15, 1973, at St. James Methodist Church in Montgomery. Lurleen had been buried from there, and Bobbi Jo had been married there. The wedding was an elaborate affair befitting a governor's daughter. The Reverend John Vickers performed the ceremony and, as everybody expected, no liquor was served at the reception. But the wedding cake and other refreshments were ample to serve the three thousand guests. At Derryl Gordon's suggestion, chairs were removed "so the guests won't stay too long." But many were enjoying themselves so much they did not take the hint.

With that done, George got back to business. He was a shoo-in for the 1974 campaign, his only serious competitor being Senator Gene McLain of Huntsville. The campaign saw some mud-slinging, but not enough to dirty the ballot. McLain had no real following, and his only recourse was to find something to pick at. He leaned heavily on the fact that he could offer fresh blood, that George had been in office too long. He did not unsettle the governor, who had other things on his mind. At the time, George was busy taking acupuncture treatments from Doctor Chu, a native of mainland China who came to Montgomery from New York every Monday. Although Dr. Chu claimed that he could help Wallace, results were disappointing and finally treatments were terminated.

Governor Wallace kept active. When he was invited to a Clio homecoming held in his honor on November 10, 1973, he was elated. The ceremony began with a colorful parade. There were at least a thousand people lining the main street. Following the parade, the assemblage went to the field where George once played quarterback for Barbour County High. There, they heard a concert by Troy State University's band.

The real thrill of the day for George was seeing and talking with his former classmates. The class of 1937 was well represented. Roscoe French had come from New York City, and Elton Stephens, now a millionaire, had come from Birmingham to give a brief biography of Governor Wallace. Most of Clio's one-thousand citizens also turned out.

Mildred Laird was instrumental in the planning of the

event. She had not been in the same class with George, but she had known him well. Since she still taught school in Clio, she had kept up with everyone in town. One such person was Ethelene Galloway, niece of the woman who worked for the Wallaces when George was born. She was the one selected to make the presentation of a gift to the governor's mother. Barbour County High School's Alma Mater was sung, bringing memories long forgotten.

And brand new signs were erected at both ends of town. They read:

"Welcome to CLIO Native Home of GEORGE C. WALLACE"

CHAPTER TWENTY-FOUR

MAKING MORE MARKS

George was on the move again.

In the front yard of the house where George C. Wallace was born stood a huge oak. He played under its limbs as a child. A couple of days after Wallace was shot, a bank employee, Catherine Easterling, passed the tree on her way to work. She noticed that some of its limbs were wilting. It had started so quickly that she mentioned it to her brother-in-law Dan Easterling, Clio's mayor. He, too, recalled that the tree had always seemed healthy before. In the next few days it suddenly began to droop, and within a month the tree was completely dead. Since there was no one else to do it, Dan had to cut it down. Clio citizens speculated. Whether it was a mysterious coincidence was left to their imagination, but even stranger happenings concerning the huge oak were the subject of Mayor Easterling's talk at the Clio Homecoming. He revealed that not only was George Wallace on the mend but the giant oak had once again sprouted from its center. Little shoots were coming up in the middle of the stump, and the tree, too, was coming back.

George kept getting better and going full speed as if nothing had happened. His associates had a hard time keeping up with him. Now, with his eyes on the presidency, he was still leaving them behind.

While Charles Snider, National Campaign Director, kept

245

the machinery oiled in the American Independent Party National Headquarters, the governor once more entered the national race. His schedule, as he went from state to state, would have made a lazy man cringe. In March of 1973, he was in Dallas, Texas, attempting to raise money to pay off the $200,000 debts incurred after he was shot. He told three thousand fans present, "Let's keep on keeping on and someday we'll see real restoration of constitutional government." And if Bruce Biossat of Washington did not see the November, 1972, issue of *Life Magazine* displaying the Alabama governor batting a tennis ball from his wheel chair and showing he was able to function well, he might have had some excuse for his remark in April that Wallace would have to take "the test of fire when the Alabama Legislature convenes in May."

In April, the 1972 vice presidential nominee, Sergeant Shriver, came to Montgomery to visit Wallace, who was not too sick to spend one hour and forty-five minutes talking with him. In June, the governor traveled to Florida to receive the Freedom Heritage Award from the Florida Academy of Family Physicians. On the second of July, he was in Flomaton for a Governor's Appreciation Day. For the Fourth of July, a historic meeting was planned. The Independence Day Celebration in Decatur, Alabama, would bring liberal Ted Kennedy to Alabama to share the platform with George Wallace.

Although the meeting was viewed with scorn by Wallace's more conservative supporters, they had already seen changes in a liberal direction in the administration of George Wallace. Back in May, he had appointed two blacks and a woman to the supervisory board of the Alabama Law Enforcement Planning Agency. Dr. Garrick Hardy of Montgomery and Jessie Lewis of Birmingham were the first two Negro appointees. Ruby Noonan, the wife of State Senator Lionel "Red" Noonan, was the woman. Even before that, two blacks, Oscar Kyles and

Leonard James, became rookie State Troopers, an unheard of occurrence in Alabama. Not much static was heard about these appointments, but when Alabamians learned that Ted Kennedy was coming to their state, speculation began about a possible Wallace-Kennedy, or worse yet, Kennedy-Wallace ticket in 1976. Immediately, Southerners were upset.

Peter Lisagor of the *Chicago Daily News Service* made light of the visit, saying, "Only an orator born in the wings of excess would brand Senator Edward M. Kennedy's Fourth of July sortie into Alabama as an historical moment. It was so branded, of course, even though neither logic nor the objective evidence sustained that judgment." Ligasor's opinion did not keep Alabamians from worrying. They would not accept his idea that Kennedy's trip was designed "to do homage to the crippled little Alabama governor, who was being given a patriotic award by the civic boosters." Even when Winifred Turner, assistant managing editor of *The Decatur Daily*, tried to take the blame for bringing Kennedy to Wallace country, citizens refused to believe that it began as a joke. They saw it as a political mistake.

Veteran black leader in Mobile, John Leflore, and a political newcomer, Mayor A.J. Cooper of Prichard, both spoke out. Cooper said, "This was no political marriage we saw in Decatur. It wasn't even an engagement. But it was the first date, and it went well." And Leflore attributed Wallace's mellowing to his health, saying the governor seemed willing "to bend a little." John Dillin of *The Christian Science Monitor* agreed but asked, "As his health gets better, will he be willing to continue to mellow?"

In Decatur, Kennedy called for the South to "surmount the injustices of the present and the divisions of the past," to help restore constitutional principles "trampled upon" by the Nixon administration. In the eloquent oratory of his brother, the late president, he outlined what had to be done by the South to fulfill its future promise. While response to his speech was not overwhelming, it could be described as affirmative.

Kennedy had effectively appealed to the people by sounding a little like Wallace. He said that the current administration denied Americans fair taxation. He praised the potential of the South, "the Southern virtues," which he said, "may enrich and even save the Union."

Wallace sat beside him and listened. He accepted the "Audie Murphy Award" when Kennedy made the presentation. But he declined to comment on what the meeting meant. Nor would he discuss the possibility of a 1976 Kennedy-Wallace ticket. "I'm not even thinking of running in 1976 at this time," he said. "It is highly hypothetical to talk about me on a ticket." But he added that the Democratic Party should go back to middle-of-the-road positions. "If not," he said, "it will never be successful during the next election or so."

No one could deny, however, that the possibility of a Kennedy-Wallace collaboration showed promise. Civil rights groups would accept Kennedy even if they had to take Wallace to get him. Kennedy had favor with the national news media, and the Wallace image as a racist could be toned down to make George acceptable. At the same time, moral judgments levied against Ted Kennedy for his actions and statements at Chappaquiddick could be smoothed over with help from "the friend of the people." The arrangement could have been beneficial to both men. But despite the urging of Richard Godwin, former top aide and advisor to the late President Kennedy, and Alabama Senator Pierre Pelham, political advisor to Wallace, a coalition did not materialize.

Wallace stood alone and kept on making his mark in and out of the state. He attended the July 29 Fleet Blessing in Bayou La Batre, the Southern Governors' Conference at Point

Clear in September, and the Clio Homecoming in November. He met various other commitments and was scarcely still a minute.

All that summer, media attention focused on a wealthy Wallace financial supporter. James H. Faulkner, a newspaper publisher, had always given Wallace good press reports, too. Now, Faulkner and David G. Volkert, president of a Virginia engineering firm, were indicted on charges of alleged payments in connection with construction of the second span of the world's longest bridge, the Lake Pontchartrain Causeway in New Orleans. Faulkner and Volkert both pled innocent before U.S. District Court Judge R. Blake West in May. The indictment stated that Faulkner received $400,000 in the scheme. Others were named, too, but many observers thought that the Nixon administration was out to embarrass George Wallace by the prosecution of his friend. The governor was embarrassed and so was the state, but all this was soon overshadowed by the developing scandal on the national scene. That was so grave that the media paid little attention to the internal problems of Alabama.

Vice President Spiro Agnew was on his way out. As Governor of Maryland, Agnew had allegedly profited from cash payoffs made by engineering firms in line for state contracts. He was allowed to settle for a charge of income tax evasion and to resign. On a Thursday night in October, 1973, Gerald Ford was sworn in as the fortieth Vice President of the United States.

President Nixon was right behind him watching. He saw impeachment coming and realized that his turn to step down would soon follow.

In Alabama, Governor Wallace kept moving. He continued to make speeches but had to take time out in the early part of October to spend a couple of days in the hospital for his seventh operation; this was necessary to improve bladder function.

As soon as he recovered, he attended a meeting of the Southern Conference of Black Mayors held in Tuskegee. Under heavy security, he spoke to the group, telling them he was "for all the people of Alabama." His statement had a little more credence than it had in the past. The Saturday before, he had crowned Miss Terri Points of Birmingham as Homecoming Queen of the University of Alabama. She was the first black girl to receive the honor.

At the end of the month, however, more trouble was brewing. An alleged fraud in Highway Department purchases was causing a furor. Wallace was outraged. He said, "I've built a good record and paid a high price for it. I don't want anybody tampering with it." He called for a complete investigation. The State Examiner had charged that ninety-three thousand dollars was paid for automotive parts never delivered, and Ruby Lee Latham, treasurer of Machinery and Supplies, Inc., was charged with false pretense and grand larceny. Supplies ordered from her company supposedly were never received by state offices. A Highway Department employee, Robert O. Wilson, accounting equipment maintenance director, answered questions concerning transactions, saying he "took orders from Gerald Wallace and Richard Stone." (Stone was assistant state finance director.) A third person, Billy R. Ballard, maintenance superintendent at Decatur, was suspended from his job. In January, Miss Latham was convicted. The governor's brother claimed no involvement in the highway conspiracy and somehow was kept out of it.

In December of 1973, George made his first appearance in the North since he was shot. He went to the Waldorf-Astoria in New York to accept the Order of Lafayette Freedom Award and was gratified by the enthusiastic reception he received. He had been to the Midwest to the 46th Meeting of the Future Farmers of America and had received the expected welcome there, but he was not quite as confident about the attitude of sophisticated Easterners.

Generally, things seemed to be going well. But in some quarters, there was talk of a lifetime pension for the governor by those who felt that his disability hampered his administration. The governor, who had checked again with his doctor, had reassurance that this was not so. He planned to continue as governor and to run again for president

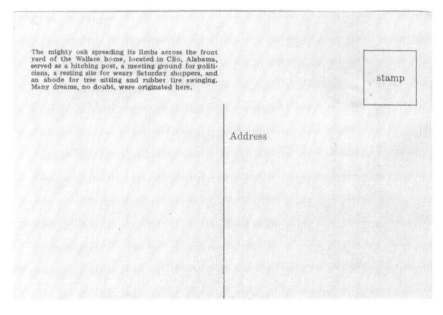

The mighty oak spreading its limbs across the front yard of the Wallace home, located in Clio, Alabama, served as a hitching post, a meeting ground for politicians, a resting site for weary Saturday shoppers, and an abode for tree sitting and rubber tire swinging. Many dreams, no doubt, were originated here.

stamp

Address

Back of Campaign Postcard

Front of postcard

Clio Sign dedication

Clio sign erected 1973

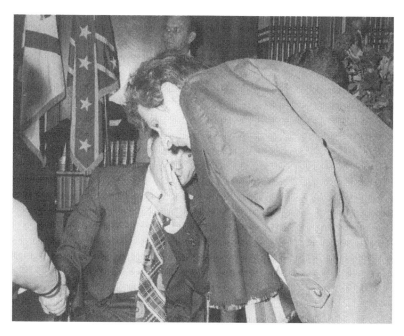

George with Milo Howard

CHAPTER TWENTY-FIVE

HITTING THE ROAD AGAIN

W allace prepared to run again.

Friends that George Wallace made during his fifty-three-day stay in Holy Cross Hospital came to Alabama to see him. Sister Helen, the hospital administrator, visited twice, once when she made a speech to the Birmingham Heart Association and before then in October of 1972.

That fall, Sister Helen and Sister Maurita went on vacation in the Virgin Islands. When they returned to Jacksonville, Florida, they remembered Governor Wallace had said, "Come see me." Being fairly close to Montgomery, they called him. He sent a plane to pick them up, and they were brought to the mansion for lunch. The two nuns were invited to spend the night, but since it was the day Vice President Spiro Agnew was scheduled to arrive in Montgomery, they declined.

Dora Thompson, also shot by Bremer, had recovered and she, too, came to Alabama. She had a short visit with George and talked on the telephone with Cornelia, who had impressed Dora as being "very thoughtful." She brought beautiful bouquets of flowers to Dora during her stay in Holy Cross. But Mrs. Thompson did not see Ruby Austin this time. The last she had seen of the First Lady's mother was when she barged into Dora's hospital room, told her how sorry she was that she had been hurt, then blurted out, "I'm hoping that George can get elected president. I'm ready to move out of the governor's mansion and into the White House."

George had also returned to Maryland. He went to help raise money for Holy Cross Hospital. While there, he used the opportunity to renew all his old acquaintances.

With the worst of the ordeal behind him, Wallace again began to do what he knew how to do best—run for office. He dropped the acupuncture treatments in January, uncertain of the results. He tried other things to alleviate his pain, including seeing a mysterious Mr. "A" who George said "was not a psychic healer because I would not see a psychic healer." And he had visits from a man named "Mr. Kory." Both men had promised dramatic cures but had given nothing. Now, resigned to his fate, George got busy campaigning for the upcoming governor's race.

He announced his candidacy for re-election on February 25, 1974, but did not officially open his campaign until March 22 in Birmingham. As an incumbent, George did not need to do much campaigning, but he engaged in the contest with the same intensity he put into any endeavor he undertook.

He was no longer just a "race" candidate. He had already named blacks to state positions. Now, Taylor Hodge, president of the Allied Funeral Council Association, received a post on the Southern Board of Embalmers. This put another black man on a board. N.A.A.C.P. official treasurer emeritus Alfred Baker Lewis admitted that Wallace was changing his image. Nevertheless, the Southern Poverty Law Center was suing the governor for discrimination in appointing board and commission members.

More visitors came to Alabama to see the governor. J.S.F. Botha, South African ambassador, paid a courtesy call in Montgomery. And George had a boost from the press, too. In *Parade Magazine*, Professor Warren Miller of the University of Michigan claimed Wallace would benefit from Watergate.

He said the American Independent Party could "surpass the Republican Party and become the number two party in the nation." *The Mobile Press Register* also came forward on March 29 endorsing Wallace as the "best bet" for governor. And when Wallace went to Mobile on March 29, five hundred persons packed Sage Armory and heard him say, "You made me what I am and, good or bad, I am proud of it."

In the governor's race were former Governor Jim Folsom and perennial candidate "Shorty" Price. The other two contenders were Gene McLain and Thomas Wesley Robinson. The Republican candidate was State Senator Elvin McCary of Anniston. McLain was the most vocal and kept accusing Governor Wallace of involvement in the State Highway Department fraud. He also promised that if he were elected, he would do all in his power to fight the succession bill. McLain did not want any governor to succeed himself.

Then Wallace picked up the support of Tuskegee's black mayor, Johnny Ford, and the endorsement of the Ozark Voters League, a black group of several hundred members. They said, "We sincerely feel Governor Wallace will do his best to help all citizens of the State of Alabama and their communities."

That was a big help. Next, a segment of labor who had not backed Wallace before gave its endorsement. The Alabama State Council of Carpenters came over to his side.

While Gene McLain was proclaiming that Alabama had its own Watergate and that George was using state people to campaign, the Democratic Conference—predominantly black—met in Birmingham and agreed to support George. Even though Robert Ingram, editor of *The Alabama News,* said George had "peaked out politically," it certainly did not look that way.

To stay in office, the governor had to keep the state going and make sure the people were satisfied. So following a riot involving forty prisoners in Atmore Prison, George took steps towards prison reform. Two guards had been killed in the uprising, and the legislature had been severely criticized by the Escambia County Grand Jury. A few days later, $150,000 was made available to upgrade the prison. Only then did the people calm down.

In May, the primary told the story. George Wallace would go back in office. Even though he still had to face Republican Elvin McCary and Prohibition Party candidate Jim Partin in the general election, it was no challenge. Actually, McCary had little support, even among Republicans. In November, George won, capturing eighty-five percent of the vote.

Beginning a third term, George faced a tottering economy which had been hindered rather than helped by the weird wage-and-price control. These had been imposed from Washington, then removed. The fluctuating market contributed to inflation and recession while the mid-East problem reduced the fuel supply and raised prices. The issue on the minds of most Americans and most Alabamians was clearly inflation. The high standard of living which had so long been a way of American life appeared to be on the decline. As prices soared on grocery store shelves, Alabama citizens began to tighten their belts.

Wallace continued to travel. He shared a platform with Ralph Abernathy, Martin Luther King, Jr.'s successor, while receiving an honorary degree from predominantly black Alabama State University. In July, he told an American Legion Convention in Mobile that the United States "needs military support to bring peace to the world." In August, he was in Albuquerque, New Mexico, blasting the federal bureaucracy.

By September, George had appointed seven more blacks to state boards and had Civil Rights leader Charles Evers, now Mayor of Fayette, Mississippi, on his side. Evers said, "I think

Wallace realizes his way has been wrong." This gave him a few more points with black citizens who valued Evers' opinion and reinforced his black support.

If Wallace was looking toward the 1976 presidential race, the Washington situation would help his candidacy. The Harris polls reported that he had risen in American esteem, but said he would still be weak against a Republican candidate.

Nixon, however, was rapidly losing ground. On August 9, 1974, he made an unprecedented move for a United States president by resigning from office. Gerald Ford took the Oath of Office the same day and later asked Governor Rockefeller of New York to serve as vice president. The country, tired and disheartened because of the national scandal which disturbed and confused its citizens, was glad relief had finally come. Most Americans were sad, too. It was not a victory to see the president finally step down. For the first time in its history, this country had a president and a vice president, neither of whom had been elected to office.

But life and politics go on. Labor Day, 1974, found candidate Wallace talking about a "new, rising South" to people in Saraland. Later, at the Southern Governors' Conference in Austin, Texas, he said the same thing.

Meanwhile, Ted Kennedy had significant problems—a sick wife, a son with cancer, and the shadow of Chappaquiddick still hanging over him. He refused to be nominated or drafted for president. He said his "prime responsibility" was at home.

Kennedy would not support Wallace either for president or vice president, and all Wallace would say about the matter was that Kennedy was entitled to his opinions.

After a head-on collision with Alabama Democratic party chairman Bob Vance in June, one which Wallace lost, George played down the mid-term convention of the Democratic Party to be held in Kansas City. When the December 6 event came up, Wallace attended but kept a low profile. Charles Snider, Wallace's National Campaign Director, said the governor told him there was no point to the convention anyway. Still, if the governor did not think it was important, he did not have to go. He could have stayed home and counted the two million dollars Snider and his group raised for the campaign between August of 1973 and August of 1974.

Some months before, a senate leader, majority whip Robert C. Byrd (D-West Virginia), said Governor George C. Wallace should have a say in the Democratic Party's selection of its next presidential candidate. This occurred before Kennedy had withdrawn, and he was the leader as a Democratic hopeful. The Gallup Poll placed Wallace second with twenty percent, Muskie with seventeen percent, McGovern with sixteen percent, and there were several names with under ten percent each. Wallace's popularity had not increased by chance. He had been doing advance campaigning for over a year. In fact, his headquarters had gone non-stop since 1972. The election looked great for him now, especially when, two weeks later, Kennedy dropped out of the race.

Not everybody agreed with his platform. That did not matter to George Wallace. Even if he could not move into the White House in 1976, his job in Alabama was good for another four years.

CHAPTER TWENTY-SIX

ONCE MORE 'ROUND THE BLOCK

The Inauguration Ceremony was held on January 20, 1975. It lacked the pomp and ceremony of previous inaugurations, and there was no parade at all.

This time, George Wallace, who was now in a wheelchair, could not stand on the spot where Jefferson Davis took the Oath of Office, so the ceremony was held at the foot of the Capitol steps. The weather was overcast and dreary with a thirty-two-degree temperature; nevertheless, many state dignitaries were there shivering in the cold. Mississippi's Bill Waller was the only out-of-state governor to attend, but former Alabama governors Patterson and Folsom were present. In the crowd of three-thousand faces, old-time Wallace supporters and youthful new recruits smiled and applauded.

Cornelia wore an outfit made of the Wallace clan plaid with a tam to match. Lee, Josh and Jim were also dressed in Scottish attire.

George was grim as he took the Oath of Office from his brother, Jack, but his mood changed the moment he entered the Capitol and began greeting well-wishers. He smiled as he watched Scottish dancers decked out in colorful plaids perform for the pleasure of the guests. He glanced once at a sculpture of Lurleen, but quickly turned his attention back to Cornelia.

After the performance, the governor was wheeled to his office, where he welcomed the long line of people extending down the hallway to the rotunda. They chatted with each other while waiting to shake his hand. It took hours. As one lady from Enterprise stood in line, she motioned to Charles Clark, the state photographer, to take her picture greeting the governor. She wanted it for evidence to show those people at home who told her she should stay home and watch it on television. They insisted that she would "never get to see the governor anyway, much less get close enough to shake his hand."

But she did see the governor because he sat right there until the last person went through the line. When Seymore Trammell came up, George greeted his former colleague warmly and looked him straight in the eye just as if his earlier escapades had never embarrassed the governor.

After the inauguration, national Democrats began to worry. They knew George. He was governor, but he did not intend to stop there. They anticipated his fourth attempt to finagle his way around the block of party leaders and capture the presidential nomination. Wallace was a master politician, one they feared more than they would admit out loud.

This time, too, George had to fight to gain recognition.

Once more, he claimed that he was motivated by a desire to reach a position from which he could help those with whom he identified. He had grown mentally and politically and had varied his tactics and responded to the need for change. Still, George looked at things cautiously because he felt that there had "always been honest differences of opinions in legislative bodies, among governors, congressmen or presidents who come from one particular section or another." He often said that "the great majority feel basically the same about the basic issues because, communication-wise, we are a closely-knit country." George Wallace felt that many people were trying to get to the same place by different routes.

Wallace had changed. Much of his understanding of the feelings of black people had deepened since his own stand-off with death in Maryland in 1972. If Wallace thought he had survived the attempt on his life because he still had something to do, he was certainly making the most of the second chance.

For someone who wanted to change the politics of the United States, the timing was perfect. People suffering from a failing economy were frantically looking for a suitable candidate to revive the country. After the sad reign of President Nixon and Vice President Agnew, a search was on to find a man who could lift the United States out of the past and give it new meaning. Many were looking for a hero.

There was no proof that Wallace or anyone else could meet their requirements. No one could argue George was perfect. His enemies still felt that he was power-hungry. Other governors found a weakness in his abrupt approach to the resolution of problems. They thought George was too arrogant and impulsive.

But in the overall picture, how was he viewed as a potential candidate? Had he changed sufficiently to make him all the things Americans wanted in their next president? Many saw Gerald Ford as inadequate, too. But did George have what Ford lacked? The people expected a great deal of their candidate. What they wanted was a savior.

Wallace had made his promises: "to lean heavily on the Joint Chiefs of Staff for military advice" and "to try to stop those Washington bureaucrats from trying to tell New York, California, Alabama, Georgia or any other state how to run the schools." He also promised to protect the rights of labor, saying, "I'd stop high government officials from interfering with labor unions—people's business." Added to that list were his promises of "carefully appointing Supreme Court justices." Some of his solutions were vague or ambiguous. He promised to fight inflation, saying, "We're gonna cut prices and increase profits."

If having name identification would capture the nomination, he had a good chance. An incident which happened in Rotterdam, Holland, tells how far-reaching his fame was.

An Alabama couple was traveling through Europe by train and made a stop in Rotterdam. It stopped to take on passengers and they leaned out the window and started a conversation with a young, hippie-type man standing on the platform. The man asked where they were from in the United States. When they answered "Alabama," he straightened up, pulled at the sleeves of the U.S. Army jacket he was wearing and said in precise English, "Ahh-George Wallace. Did you vote for him?" He was proud that he knew something about their country.

All over Europe the couple found the same thing. Brazilian engineers visiting the Coliseum and railroad agents working for the Dutch government were opposed to Wallace, but they knew of him. People in England, unassuming peasant girls and high-ranking officials, common British laborers and a Scottish plasterer, all knew about Wallace and Alabama. Both Communist Italian university students and a Dutch university student responded to the name "George Wallace." The Italian student called him "very much a capitalist, not a good man." Shaking his head, the Dutch student said, "I can't believe he'd be any different in person." Mention Alabama abroad and the name "Wallace" popped out. It seemed that the name and the state were synonymous.

Back in Alabama, except for being unable to walk, the governor received a clean bill of health. He was not wearing himself out with thoughts of revenge on Bremer. In fact, he claimed he had forgiven and forgotten him.

George was now serving as governor. He had shown his

interest in the 1976 presidential race and said that "the people I represent will be very much involved." Without fully committing himself, he gave every sign that he would run. "GCW Candidacy Seen by This Summer" came out as headlines on February 2, 1975, in *The Mobile Press Register* bearing a Washington dateline. To seasoned political observers, it was virtually certain that Wallace would seek the Democratic nomination and, failing that, he would run as a candidate of the American Independent Party.

For Wallace, the race to win the highest office in the land was important, but so was something else—he had to have something going all the time. In his life, no dull moments were allowed; his every waking minute had to be lived in a room with the air full of electricity.

George Corley Wallace—the enigmatic but undeniably charismatic individual—was trying to identify with average U.S. citizens, possibly for their advantage and certainly for his own.

CHAPTER TWENTY-SEVEN

A TIP OF THE SCALES

Wallace made a great effort in the 1976 presidential campaign, but by the Florida Primary it became clear that he was not going to win. Nevertheless, Wallace staff were pleased with the influence he had.

But he was not going to be elected President of the United States. As former Alabama legislator Ben Stokes predicted, the same thing that propelled George Wallace to undreamed of heights brought about his downfall in 1976. Now, his stand on segregation was no longer popular, even in the South. Besides that, he was so determined to help "little people" that he sometimes gave them jobs they could not handle, often in his own campaign organization. It hurt them and it hurt George.

The fact is that the Wallace group operated a loosely organized, haphazard campaign which had to fail. From the beginning, newcomers to the Wallace corps took over the campaign and refused to rely on "old heads" and thereby receive the benefit of their experience. On at least one occasion, Micky Griffin, a top aide, publicly denounced seasoned members of the Wallace force. He wanted to bring in a group of younger people to give new impetus to the campaign. It is hard for a candidate to succeed if his forces are not united.

Perhaps George did not want to win after all. The competition, the excitement, the challenges were really his

267

meat. A psychiatrist might argue that he had no true aspirations to the top position in the land. He might have even feared and subconsciously suppressed his own movement by hiring incompetent persons. But probably he did not. Maybe he just jumped in and hired whoever spoke up and said he wanted the job.

No matter what George Wallace's expectations actually were, many things worked against him. He tried three times to be the Democratic nominee and also ran as an American Independent Party candidate. Now, running during the Bicentennial Year, George found his popularity declined. There were several reasons for this. Perhaps it was due in part to the failure of his campaign people, and the news media's determination to include his wheelchair in every photograph.

Now big contributors, who always want to go with a winner, shied away. As the media repeatedly condemned George and showed him as a cripple (they made much of the time he was dropped by an aide), members of the press forgot that nobody liked George Wallace but the people. They portrayed him as a sick man who would be unable to carry out the duties of the presidency. Contributions fell sharply.

Then Cornelia made a disastrous appearance on national TV. She said George cried like a baby following the assassination attempt. Members of the Wallace camp said that Cornelia was disgruntled because George refused to let her run for governor in 1978. They claimed that she was getting revenge. Whatever the cause, her remarks were demeaning and hurt George's campaign. Added to this, reliable sources reported that Cornelia was partying around with a Montgomery doctor. They said George was distressed when he had to exert time and energy calling people in an effort to locate his wife. If George did not have trouble enough with his political life, his wife added to his problems.

His campaign staff hurt him, too. The game was lost in Florida. Micky Griffin, one of the Florida campaign workers, struck out at longtime members of the Wallace corps, saying they "were not needed." He claimed it was "all wrapped up in Florida." National Campaign Director Charles Snider did not interfere. That turned out to be a huge, overconfident misstatement. Like football, politics is a game of inches; when the votes were counted, it showed that old standby workers should have been transported to the Sunshine State to help the cause. George Wallace was down by only three percent, but he had lost to Jimmy Carter. In so doing, many observers agree, he had lost his chance to become President of the United States.

By the time Alabama supporters were flown to North Carolina to try to pull it out, it was too late there, too. People saw Wallace as a loser. No matter how hard his people pushed, it could not be changed. Heartbreak for Wallace, elation for Georgia's Jimmy Carter.

But the whole effort was not wasted. The Wallace movement did do something for the cause of conservative government. The McGovern group did not have the power and the influence so predominant four years before. A turn-around could be seen, and those who followed Alabama's governor for over a decade were not displeased at the results. In the long run, it will have to be acknowledged that George Wallace played a big part in the making of a president. In the 1976 campaign, the three competing candidates all turned out to be middle-of-the-road candidates echoing some of Wallace's ideas. Wallace followers felt their mission had been accomplished.

If their man could not win the nomination and have a chance at the presidency, the next best thing happened. The people had candidates who reflected George Wallace's ideas and ideals—not in their entirety, but to a far greater degree than during the 1972 election. George Wallace had made his mark.

CHAPTER TWENTY-EIGHT

A DIME'S WORTH OF DIFFERENCE

Wallace finished his term as governor in January, 1979, and was not eligible for re-election. He resumed his private law practice at One Court Street in Montgomery and accepted an appointment as Director of the Office of Rehabilitation Resources at the University of Alabama in Birmingham.

Fob James became Governor of Alabama. Except for Lurleen's administration in 1966 and Brewer's takeover to finish her term, the period from 1978 to 1982 was the first time since 1946 that George Wallace did not hold a political office. He kept a relatively low profile. It was probably the only time in his adult life that he was not in the public eye.

He announced in March, 1981, at age sixty-one, that he and Linda Lee "Lisa" Taylor, age thirty-two, were engaged. Cornelia did not like the news at all. In fact, she said she spent several hours at Wallace's home conferring about a reconciliation. But George and Cornelia had been divorced three years, and the talk did no good. Sometime between July and September, 1981, George and Lisa were married, but they would not say exactly when. They did say it was a small ceremony in Autauga County officiated by Wallace's friend, Probate Judge Jim Corley. It was her second and his third marriage. Many of George's friends advised against the union. They remembered Lisa as a country-and-western singer who performed in Wallace's 1968 rallies. With her showgirl background, she was too much like Cornelia to suit them.

In 1979, George had strongly indicated he was through with politics forever. He seemed weak and tired and he told his friends, "I'm through." But when 1982 rolled around, although he at first denied he would enter the governor's race, George Wallace was ready to go again. At age sixty-two, he said he was a new man because his wife, Lisa, had renewed his interest in politics. Lisa was very quiet, but she did support his running.

With his excellent sense of timing, he began a rigorous speaking schedule. In April, 1982, at an Alabama League of Municipalities Convention, he admitted to toying with the idea of running. Kathy Jumper of *The Mobile Press Register* reported Wallace bragged about having new political support. He said, "About seven of the groups who opposed me running in 1970 are now urging me to run." Perhaps this was because George Wallace had changed.

The most convincing proof that Wallace had changed was that despite his old segregationist image, he was getting the support of more and more blacks. They could relate to his new position. They saw he turned his attention to more timely issues—the economy, unemployment, and crime.

When he announced his candidacy for an unprecedented fourth term as Alabama governor, George Wallace courted blacks. And the black vote was expected to be the deciding factor in the race.

The primary was where the contest was really fought. George Wallace and outgoing Lt. Governor George McMillan, who served with Fob James, were the two main contenders. Others included the Speaker of the House Joe McCorquodale, former Governor James Folsom, and Reuben McKinley. All claimed victory, but when the primary was held September 7, 1982, McMillan and Wallace ended up in the run-off. On

September 28, 1982, in a close race, Wallace beat McMillan. With over ninety-nine percent of the boxes reporting, Wallace had 506,305 votes. He had fifty-one percent of the vote and McMillan had 487,144, or forty-nine percent of the vote. McCorquodale was extremely upset and claimed that Wallace had told him that he was not going to enter the race. He blamed Wallace for his failure. Seeking revenge, he threw his support to Republican Emory Folmar.

But it did not help the Republican cause at all. In the general election on November 2, 1982, Wallace received 552,520 votes to 350,892 for Folmar. He had sixty-one percent to Folmar's thirty-nine percent.

People were worried about whether Wallace would be able to fulfill the duties as governor. On TV, he often hesitated when he spoke. When the cameras focused in close, bags showed under his eyes. But he was not hospitalized during the campaign—his health was okay.

Despite remarks floating around during the campaign such as "he's too sick" or "his speech is slurred" or "he won't be able to fulfill the duties of the office" and even a very convinced "he'll never win this time," George won.

Early on in the campaign, before the general election, things had not looked promising. Wallace campaigners themselves seemed to lack confidence. Then, the night before the election, there was an upswing, and supporters were elated. Response to telephone calls from campaign headquarters began to evoke a strong, affirmative response. Instead of "I'm sorry, I'm voting for Folmar" or a cut-off, callers began to hear, "You bet I'm voting for Wallace." The workers' spirits were lifted. Somehow things had changed.

The phenomenal achievement was that Wallace had won the blacks over. In the run-off, where the black vote was critical, he won heavily in mostly black counties. He led in fifty-three of the state's sixty-seven counties.

Before the general election, more blacks switched to Wallace. On October 11, 1982, Alabama Democratic Conference chairman Joe Reed announced that his most influential black political group was casting their lot with Wallace. He admitted that he was not comfortable with the decision but said, "It's all I have in front of me." With McMillan out of the race, the ADC said, "The party is more important than the personalities." In a unanimous vote, they found Wallace preferable to Emory Folmar. Reed added that Wallace promised "he would not let black folks down." When asked if Wallace had changed, Reed said time would tell and that it was up to Wallace to prove that he cares about blacks.

Some observers thought this trust was justified. One supporter said blacks saw Wallace as "basically a religious man who loves everybody, regardless of race or creed." He added, "Wallace didn't hate Negroes; I don't think he would have liked Martin Luther King if he'd have been white."

Another observer, who admitted to voting for Wallace in 1982, said that she felt that Wallace got the black vote "by convincing those people he's going to help them, get jobs for them. Before, when he was governor, times were prosperous." They figured they could bring back old times.

Wallace had taken great pains to do what was politically prudent. He had promised blacks appointments to commissions. He brought more of them into the mainstream of Alabama government. James C. White was named head of the State Department of Revenue. A campaign worker said that Wallace went a step further. "He could have stopped the appointment of black Yvonne Kennedy as president of Bishop State Junior College in Mobile, too. But he didn't." The observer said one reason Wallace made concessions to the blacks was that he feared things had grown away from him in his four-year absence. He also said, "Wallace overestimated Folmar's strength, so he made deals with blacks he normally wouldn't have."

Some Alabamians felt Wallace was the lesser of two evils. One Mobilian expressed the opinion that "In the primary, McMillan lost the run-off because Alabamians resented Coretta King and Jesse Jackson being brought in from out-of-state to act as agitators." He added, "Democrats traditionally go Democrat. What they saw in Folmar was big business breathing down their neck and stepping on them. The average black wants results, not promises."

Arthur Roach, a long-time supporter, agreed that Folmar lost to Wallace for the same reason. "When Folmar ran for Mayor of Montgomery, he made wild promises. But when they weren't kept, he had problems, especially with black officials and black police officers."

By 1982, Wallace's black following had increased in number and dedication. Mike Royko was astounded. It was especially difficult for him to believe Wallace's showing in Lowndes Country. He wrote in his column, "If there was one place in this country where I would have thought George Wallace would not have received even one percent of the black vote—or even one solitary black vote—it would have been in Selma and the surrounding farmlands."

In March, 1965, Selma had been the site of a dramatic Civil Rights movement confrontation. Royko was utterly baffled by the turn-around. Wallace had gotten about forty-five percent of the black vote. He said, "I wouldn't try to explain it, because I can't. Black political analysts will have to try—although it will probably confuse them, too." He called it incredible that only eighteen years after Wallace called for "Segregation today, tomorrow and forever," black voters were going to "put him back in the state mansion." But he could not resist speculating on the reason, saying it could be because, "Wallace campaigned on the bread and butter issues of today—jobs and the economy" or that Southern blacks felt that Wallace might never have been as bad as he appeared but was "just playing the political opportunist all those years." Royko saw a possibility of empathy for a man in a wheelchair. All he could really be sure of was that black voter opinions had changed and, as he remarked, "Whatever the reason, Wallace has obviously been forgiven by thousands upon thousands of Alabama blacks he once treated like sub-humans. Why, they say that during his campaign he even sang, *We Shall Overcome*."

One factor was bound to make Wallace more acceptable to blacks even if they did not consciously realize it. As a handicapped person, he was now a member of a minority group, too. In that light, they were able to relate to him. Probably this worked in both directions. Being in a wheelchair better enabled George Wallace to understand compassionately how it felt to be a minority. Like it or not, he had joined their ranks.

Regardless of how, George had won blacks over. He had come a long way from the die-hard segregationist who stood in the schoolhouse door at the University of Alabama in 1963.

He also managed to keep the support of most of his long-time conservative followers.

On January 17, 1983, with three thousand people watching, George Wallace became the Governor of Alabama for the fourth time. Red, white and blue banners speckled with white stars decked the platform. The crowd lined Dexter Avenue in front of the Capitol.

After being presented by his son, George Corley Wallace took the Oath of Office from his brother, Jack, at the foot of the Capitol steps, saying, "I do solemnly swear to support the

Constitution of the State of Alabama so long as I continue a citizen thereof and to faithfully and honestly discharge the duties of the office on which I am about to enter."

The speech which followed was concerned with unemployment and his sympathy for farmers, expressing the fear that farmers, "might be extinct, which would be a great tragedy." He called on TVA to help by lowering their rates and restoring "affordable service." He also struck out at bankers, asking them to "be compassionate" regarding mortgages. He said, "Governments shouldn't let food pile up while people go hungry. As governor, I shall call for relief again and again. Any nation that forgets its poor will lose its soul."

Wallace also reaffirmed a statement made many times before that "The great mass of middle-class of America gives it stability and order." Once more he cited his promise that "What we're going to do in Alabama is to try to preserve the middle-class."

He addressed the fact that "the crime rate is higher than is acceptable to a God-fearing society," promising it "must, and will be, corrected." He ended with a slogan made famous by his adversary Martin Luther King, Jr., "We will call on persons of all races, creeds, color and religious persuasions. And we will overcome our problems."

CHAPTER TWENTY-NINE

THE LAST HURRAH

Despite a failed marriage to Cornelia, failed political campaigns, and failing health, George Wallace continued to pursue his interests. Politically, he may not have been in the forefront in 1983; nevertheless, as Alabama's governor, he met frequently with high-ranking politicians. If his ideas on segregation had not changed, he fooled the public into believing they had. On May 23, 1983, the Rev. Jesse Jackson, founder and director of the Chicago-based operation People United to Serve Humanity (PUSH) came to the executive mansion in Montgomery, Alabama. Although Jackson had urged blacks to vote against Wallace as a fourth-term gubernatorial candidate the year before, at this summit meeting, he asked that they forget differences and unite.

Jackson was in the capital city to promote the registration of black voters. It was ironic that he shook hands with the man who once wanted Negroes relegated to sit on the back of the bus and who also refused them entrance to a state university. But, all that was in the past. Things had changed, and possibly George Wallace had changed with the times. Perhaps Jesse Jackson had changed, too. He was considering entering the race for President of the United States and maybe his motivation was to get the support of any dignitary. If Wallace could help, it seemed Jackson was willing to accept. In any event, among those who knew both men, few were truly surprised at this meeting. Though they were different in color and political persuasions, they were alike in one way—both would do whatever was politically expedient.

On its twentieth anniversary, while newspapers were recounting George Wallace's June 11, 1963 University of Alabama faceoff with U.S. Deputy Attorney General Nicholas Katzenbach, Wallace was acting more concerned with race relations in the present. Five days later, on June 16, 1983, his photo was spread all over the papers shaking hands with black recording artist Joe Simon as Tuskegee Mayor Johnny Ford, also black, looked on. Simon had Wallace sign a proclamation endorsing a state campaign against illiteracy, a move beneficial to all races.

Wallace might have been in a wheelchair, but he was not devoid of power. Many other politicians sought his endorsement. For example, Democratic presidential hopeful Alan Cranston met with Wallace in June, 1983, claiming afterward the two saw eye-to-eye on a nuclear arms freeze with the Soviets if it was "verifiable and balanced" and both wanted peace and jobs for Americans. Possibly, those were the only points they agreed on. Still, the Californian must have thought Wallace's support in any degree was important. It didn't work, though. Cranston lost his bid for the nomination.

The governor did not stop exerting his influence in other ways. He kept his stand on getting tough with criminals, promoting his anti-crime bills relentlessly. Even when crime got worse, Wallace kept trying, coming up with new laws making insanity pleas harder, requiring parole boards to notify victims when criminals were released, and even making it a felony to possess food stamps illegally. Unfortunately, nothing seemed to help.

All these things didn't break the spirit of Wallace, however. During the summer of 1983, although he was hospitalized three times in five months, he rose from depression over health problems and improved. He seemed to have a renewed vigor and the determination to serve out his term as governor. Earlier in the year, he had seemed despondent and concerned over his ability to continue as Alabama's highest executive. But his lifelong dedication to duty persevered and he focused on his job and attempted to forget his pain. His change of attitude actually seemed to improve his condition.

This sixty-three-year-old man in a wheelchair wasn't ready to stop, so he kept on going. It was ironic, though, that some things were happening in Alabama that were exactly what George Wallace said he wanted to stop on a federal level. While campaigning for president, Wallace had said that he was against big bureaucracy in the United States. Yet, in the first six months of 1983, with Wallace as governor, state employees had increased in number by more than seven hundred. Their total had reached over thirty thousand. Alabama had a bureaucracy of its own.

Other problems plagued the governor. An ethics violator, Michael Arban, was hired for a high-level state job. George Wallace, Jr., said his father didn't know it had happened. Billy Joe Camp, Wallace's press secretary, said he did. Regardless, it did not make for good press and it was just another difficult situation that Wallace had to deal with. While opponents used every opportunity to criticize him, others gave him hope. Jeanne Dixon, a well-known astrologer, predicted that the governor would "receive great recognition" in 1983 and that "It will be a time for reconciliation and renewal, as the state of Alabama looks ahead to the future.''

Certain problems, Governor Wallace had some control over; others, he did not. A major example of an area where he was helpless was his health. He could do little to alleviate the pain he suffered daily from the senseless assassination attempt in 1972. If it taught him anything, however, it was how to understand other people's suffering and to have compassion. He realized that he had more, and probably better, medical attention as governor than he would have had otherwise. And, he seemed to appreciate that fact. None of that really did much to improve him physically. To a large degree, this once totally independent man was dependent on others. Because of a madman's bullet, he was now, and always would be, confined to live the rest of his life in a wheelchair.

Regardless of his physical condition, Wallace kept carrying out his duties as governor. In the summer of 1983, he attended the National Governors' Conference in Portland, Maine. He greeted former astronaut and Ohio Senator John Glenn who visited Montgomery as a presidential candidate. In the fall of 1983, he made a ninety-thousand-dollar industry-hunting trip to the Far East on a chartered jet, meeting with business leaders in Korea, Japan, and Taiwan. At home, he spoke at many functions, such as the annual banquet of the Alabama State Building and Construction Trade Council, held at Gulf Shores, Alabama, and the ground-breaking on the multi-million dollar complex of the Alabama Shakespeare Festival in Montgomery. At that event, he said he hoped the new theater would change Alabama's cultural image. Bragging about his state, he claimed that Alabamians were already more cultural than they got credit for. "Alabama has more interest in the arts than *The New York Times* sometimes implies," Wallace said. "We have a great culture in our region and we're also interested in the arts in all forms." The governor didn't miss a chance to rebut a paper he considered his adversary. He also went to Washington, D.C., to the International Platform Association's convention and used that opportunity to harp on his favorite political themes—the evils of big government and the federal courts. In an unprepared twelve-minute speech, he told the thousand delegates that the Supreme Court should abolish the death penalty or proceed with scheduled executions. "Do one or the other and get it over with," Wallace said.

Meanwhile, back in the state capital, integration was slowly, but surely, on the move. A black politician from Mobile, Senator Michael Figures, already held a position of power. Now, George Wallace was allowed to make two appointments to the new five-person state Personnel Board and he chose Norman Figures, Michael Figures' brother, to fill one of those slots. Perhaps receiving this honor was almost as rewarding to the black graduate of Alabama State University as being named one of the Outstanding Young Men of America had been.

On August 24, 1983, the grandfather of Wallace's children died. Henry Burns, father of Alabama's only woman governor, Lurleen Burns Wallace, died from natural causes at age eighty-three. Outliving his daughter by seventeen years, he left behind his wife, Savannah; a son, Cecil; and five grandchildren, including the three Wallace children. Losing their mother at a young age was worse, but, no doubt, the Wallace siblings would also grieve this loss. Since George's father had died before they were born, Henry Burns was the only grandfather they had ever known.

Life continued, though, with George, Jr., trying to shake the image of being "Little George." Although he denied it, people close to him seemed to think that he really preferred a career other than politics. He had tried to be a rock musician. From appearances, though, his family loyalty won out. George, Jr., was gradually stepping to his famous father's side with politics as his career goal. His wife, Kelly, was expecting a baby early in 1984, so he said he wasn't in a big hurry to get into politics. However, with both parents having been governor, it seemed inevitable that he would someday enter the political arena. Odds of success in politics were extremely weighted in his favor. He looked like his mother and spoke like his father, and he had been involved in campaigns since he was seven years old. With good looks, charisma, and experience, he had many advantages over his opponents. Name identification didn't hurt a bit, either.

Later, when George, Jr., did enter the field of politics in 1986, all those things paid off. He was elected Treasurer of the State of Alabama on his first try, and he served two terms. He did lose a close congressional race in 1992 and he lost a bid for Lieutenant Governor to Don Siegelman in 1993, however. Whether he'd admit it or not, that loss may have been a relief.

In spite of many improvements in Alabama, negative events of the past kept getting headlines. "Church bombing still not forgotten" reminded *Mobile Press Register* readers that four little girls had been killed twenty years earlier in the Sixteenth Street Baptist Church in Birmingham, Alabama, during Wallace's first term as governor. The Sunday, September 11, 1983, edition recounted the entire story in a three-column article on page 13-C. The man who was pastor of the church at the time, Rev. John H. Cross, said he had "compassion and pity" for the man convicted of the crime, but the mother of victim Denise McNair pleaded with the black community not to forget, causing some Alabamians to wonder if race relations would be helped or hindered by her admonition.

Even with unfavorable press stirring up reminders of a tragedy that had happened during Wallace's reign, he was able to get enough support from his constituents to improve the state's economy. Although Alabama had been put in proration by the previous administration, now, the legislature managed to create a better cash flow and bring in more funds, enabling Finance Director Henry Stegall, III, to announce that the budget was balanced. There were even enough funds to appropriate money to other areas, such as $450,000 to the Alabama Crippled Children's Service for University Hospitals in Birmingham and the University of South Alabama Medical Center.

While George Wallace was saving money, his third wife, Lisa, was busy spending it. And she was severely criticized for doing so, especially making pleasure trips at the state's expense. Even though her predecessor, Bobbie James, used state planes for pleasure saying it was perfectly legal because an ethics ruling to that effect had been issued, Alabamians complained when Lisa used them twelve times in three months. She protested that other first ladies had used state aircraft just as much, and, although she did fill in for her husband at a public function on one occasion, not being able to justify the rest of the trips caused angry citizens to protest. There was nothing in the law to prevent it, so Lisa continued to fly at taxpayers' expense.

George Corley Wallace had other things to contend with, too. The University of South Alabama President Fred Whiddon was miffed at Wallace's backing legislation abolishing his board of trustees; Alabama citizens were angry that he was reneging on a promise to oppose new taxes; and his brother, Gerald Wallace, was accused of getting contracts with state government agencies and of being a power broker in the Wallace administration. Governor Wallace denied the accusations against his brother, and claimed he had no choice as far as raising taxes went because the state needed the money. The rift with Whiddon continued. If those problems weren't enough, George's political power was diluted at another level. He was replaced as a delegate to the Democratic

National Convention by State Representative Alvin Holmes, a black legislator.

No matter what happened, though, some people remained faithful to Alabama's governor. They respected the fact that George Wallace supported working people. One such man celebrating one hundred and two years of life even called Wallace his hero. In fact, on his birthday he read a letter of congratulations from the governor and proudly showed guests a signed photograph that accompanied it. This man, Will "Nick" Hodges, who had been a farmer, part owner of a blacksmith shop, and a county health department worker, felt a kinship with the governor because he thought a certain respect was exchanged.

In 1984, Governor Wallace was earning $63,838.80 a year, while the University of South Alabama paid its president, Fred Whiddon, $92,500 a year. Both men received fringe benefits, too. This difference in salary didn't bother George Wallace. He said, "I'm satisfied and feel my salary is adequate." His response didn't surprise people who knew him. Wallace may have been consumed with power in politics, but being wealthy wasn't his top priority. In his lifetime, he had lived on a lot less than he had now. Perhaps he would have to do so again. Even though some people expected him to run for governor again, this term would soon be over, and he couldn't be governor forever. His income from a future job might be considerably lower.

In any event, at least his mounting medical expenses were covered, and George had a lot to cover. His problems ranged from heart palpitations to urinary tract infections and he was in and out of the hospital several times. The doctors did what they could, but the urinary infections kept causing him to run a fever up to a hundred and two degrees. And the pain wouldn't stop. Much of the time he pressed his side, wincing.

Regretfully, he could not make his customary trip to his Alma Mater for the University of Alabama's homecoming in September, 1984; instead, he watched the football game from Birmingham's University Hospital. He might get better, but he was resigned to the fact that he wouldn't get well.

No matter what, each time George got out of the hospital, he went right back to his Capitol office. Four times in the hospital for a total of fifty days in under two years did not prevent him from attending to state business. Even when a house he owned burned one week and he had to go to Colorado for surgery the next, he didn't give up. Although he slowed down, there was no stopping George Wallace. He ignored the pain and showed up for work on a regular basis.

In addition to physical limitations, George had to contend with unpleasant incidents related to his second wife, Cornelia. Even though they had been divorced since 1978, it was a bit embarrassing when, in January, 1985, she was committed to Searcy, a state mental hospital in Mount Vernon, Alabama. Almost worse, though, was her arrest in 1981 in Opp, Alabama. That time, she was driving a truck that was reported stolen in Elba. Her uncle, former Governor "Big Jim" Folsom, blamed it on a "nervous spell." She said she had borrowed the vehicle. At any rate, despite the fact that George wasn't responsible for Cornelia's escapades or her mental problems, he still worried that, because she was once his wife, her actions might reflect on him, even if indirectly.

If some things disturbed George, other things pleased him. He was especially happy that his efforts to improve education were recognized and appreciated. A comment by Representative Mike Onderdonk, from Washington and Clarke counties, in February, 1985, indicated understanding. He said it seemed that Wallace "wants history to remember him, not as the governor who stood in the schoolhouse door...but as the governor who lifted Alabama's educational standards from the bottom of the national average to a position at the top," even though that statement was hyperbole. Also, Representative Taylor Harper of Grand Bay praised him for proposing that extra money be spent on school libraries and computers. Wallace was elated; finally, somebody understood his true intentions.

To top this off, a black leader complimented him. The Rev. Jesse Jackson said Wallace had a new, more favorable attitude towards blacks, illustrated by the fact that he had put blacks on state boards and appointed black judges. All African-Americans didn't agree. Some voiced their disapproval. In fact, Jackson's praise angered State Representative Alvin Holmes so much that he sent a letter of protest.

Lisa Wallace didn't make things any easier for her husband. She was headstrong and independent, resentful of restrictions placed on her, and disturbed by the fact that she didn't get a chance to pursue her singing career and get on the television show Hee Haw as she had hoped. She also said that she felt neglected. Concerns about his wife did nothing to help George. In fact, they may have even contributed to his poor health. Yet, despite rumors that he would resign his office, in May, 1985, he said he would finish out his term which would end in January, 1987. Quit was a word that wasn't in his vocabulary.

Then came the time when the man who put him in such bad shape physically was up for parole. Even though Arthur Bremer admitted in his own diary that he planned to kill either Wallace or Richard Nixon, George vowed that he had no ill feelings against Bremer. He even said that he wouldn't object to his assailant's parole if that was the decision reached at the June hearing. Wallace's attitude of not wanting revenge was taken into consideration by the parole board, but that didn't help. Bremer had to stay in prison and serve out his fifty-three-year sentence.

By summertime in 1985, a newspaper poll showed that sixty-eight percent of Alabamians did not want to see Wallace seek another term. It seemed that they wanted someone younger and more physically fit. The governor himself said that he would not run for a fifth term unless he could win. After a very long and successful career, George had a big decision to make—to run or not to run. He was determined not to go out of politics a loser.

Towards the end of his fourth term as governor, Wallace was bent on justifying his past actions, probably hoping to regain popularity. Telling people he was no longer a segregationist, he reiterated that, even at the time when he blocked the door at the University of Alabama, he wasn't against black students. What he said he was against was the "omnipotent federal government setting the timetable." He claimed that the University was scheduled for integration in 1964 anyway.

When Wallace went on another industry-hunting trip to the Orient on October 1, 1985, Lisa did not go along; she stayed in Alabama with her hospitalized father. If this made people suspect that the marriage was in trouble, not much was said then or later, when George did not appear at her father's funeral. Another thing people were wondering about was what George was going to do about the upcoming election. Even though he had hinted that he might not run for re-election, he left his options open and kept them guessing. Also, he didn't seem to mind that this $250,000 trip seeking industry for Alabama kept him in the news daily. Running or not, George was the consummate politician; he just had to stay in the public eye.

In a firm but respectful way, newspaper editorials urged

George not to seek re-election. Both *The Huntsville Times* and *The Dothan Eagle* asked that he not try for a fifth term. Although they admitted that their main reason was that they felt George's bad health was causing the state government to disintegrate, they also expressed concern for the man himself, saying they felt he was further damaging his health by trying to perform his duties as governor. Furthermore, they asked that he announce publicly that he would not run. By the end of January, 1986, even though his press secretary, Billy Joe Camp, resigned to seek the office of governor, Wallace still floundered. He would wait until two days before the deadline, at one p.m. on April 4, to decide not to file for the primary.

Throwing kisses to the crowd, a teary-eyed Wallace gave a rare prepared speech, which lasted only five minutes, to announce his retirement. The man who had spent seventeen years in the governor's mansion said it was "time to pass the rope and to pick another climber who can climb to higher heights." Members of the audience did not try to hold back their tears. The man who had moved in mind and spirit from the Old South to the new, now was stepping down, even if his legs couldn't physically allow him to do that. After so many years, George Wallace would no longer hold a political office. With his timing right on target, he knew when to run and he knew when to stop. Nobody expected him to stop being a politician, though. As long as Wallace had a breath in him, he'd be involved politically.

Later, when asked about his proudest accomplishments, he cited the establishment of junior colleges and technical schools, planning a super computer in Huntsville, and being influential in helping conservatize the nation during his four presidential campaigns. He did refer to his regrets, especially the cry, "Segregation now, segregation tomorrow and segregation forever." Ironically, it was that statement that propelled him into the limelight and boosted his political career, and that statement which haunted him forever after.

George insisted, however, that he really did not want to be remembered for his segregationist stand. Regardless of that cry, he made efforts to shake that racist image. Later in his life, George turned things around and convinced many blacks that he was on their side. He was proud of the fact that some former black opponents now had great respect for him. He even received an honorary doctorate from predominantly-black Tuskegee University.

In the middle of all this turmoil, George had to adjust to another change in his life. In February, 1987, his marriage to Lisa ended in divorce. This was not unexpected since Lisa had moved out of the governor's mansion a year before. For a while, she lived in Wallace's private home in East Montgomery with her twelve year-old son, Taylor Gordon. Her excuse for moving was that her son was uncomfortable living in the mansion. Since the marriage had seemed doomed almost from the start, nobody was very surprised at the break-up, not even George. It wasn't a first for him; he'd lived through one divorce. As a survivor, George would get over this one, too.

With retirement, his health seemed to improve. He began work as a fund-raiser for Troy State University on their Montgomery campus, got new glasses and new hearing aids, and took time to visit old friends in Clayton and Clio on weekends. Without political pressures, the sixty-eight-year-old man who had dominated politics since 1963 finally seemed to be relaxing and enjoying himself.

CHAPTER THIRTY

KEEP ON

Another chapter in George Wallace's life had closed. The glory days were over. No longer would he be in the news almost daily. Now, a new governor's picture would be on page one of Alabama papers. It was doubtful, though, that the next chief executives of the State of Alabama would get much national press coverage. It was highly unlikely that any would be as high-profile as George had been. Nobody was before; probably nobody would be in the future.

Nevertheless, the life of the man who experienced so many different things and had such a huge impact on the politics of his state and his nation was going to change. A metamorphosis was about to take place. George did have a job; he had worked at the University of Alabama in Birmingham from 1979-1982, lecturing occasionally and raising funds. That experience led him to a similar job. In January, 1987, he took another fund-raising position as Troy State University's Director of Development in Montgomery. Because of his health, however, he couldn't work long hours.

So, from his wheelchair, out of the limelight and alone, Wallace had plenty of time to think. He mused over race relations and how they had changed in Alabama and in the nation. He didn't mind expressing his thoughts on the subject. In a recent interview, his response to the question of whether race relations were better or worse was, "I think they're better in Alabama; more blacks are elected to office and more are appointed to office." Then, he reminisced a bit, saying this began during his wife's term as governor. "Lurleen got some of the first black registrars. And, during my last term, Frank Mastin was the first black Press Secretary." In a raspy voice caused by Parkinson's disease, he added, "The number of black appointments tripled during that term. Dr. Leon Frazier was head of Human Resources; Hezekiah Wagstaff was Assistant Press Secretary—" the governor paused as a spasm contorted his body for an instant, then he continued, "and we [the royal 'we' frequently used by politicians such as Wallace] had one black appointed to every college board as a trustee—except Alabama—Dr. Bessie May Hollaway was at Auburn."

While the governor thought race relations were better in Alabama, he was quick to point out that he didn't see as much improvement in big cities like Detroit. "They still have trouble in hotels and restaurants," he said, without offering examples to prove his point. Because he obviously wanted to change the subject, his Executive Assistant Charles Carr explained that Wallace cringed at the thought of just being identified with race. Yet, Wallace did make one further statement that was interesting. He made a perceptive distinction between tolerance and acceptance. "Tolerance," he said, "doesn't really mean you like somebody or something, you just tolerate." His once-powerful voice broke and he didn't finish the thought. But the fine points of difference between the two words was there. The implication was clear that while tolerance was merely putting up with something or somebody, acceptance went a step further, into the area of understanding and approval.

It seemed that Wallace had learned acceptance of people of a different color. He had mellowed in his views of those he once considered radical. Jesse Jackson was one such person. Surprisingly, he said of his one-time adversary, "We're good friends. He's visited me and prayed with me and for me." Wallace nodded approval. "He's all right." That was quite a turnaround for a man who once seemed to dislike the black leader and all that he stood for. Wallace had admitted to Jesse Jackson, and to others, that he was wrong in his segregation stance. He sought, and apparently got, forgiveness.

As he had in the past, George Wallace used his charisma and his uncanny ability to equate to others, to reach them on their level, to convince the influential black leader that he was sincere in his remorse. The man who had done all he could to thwart Jesse Jackson's efforts to bring about integration now reversed his position and publicly apologized for his past actions.

The way this happened was interesting. One day Wallace showed up, unannounced, at the Dexter Avenue Baptist Church, admitting that he had caused blacks pain in the past and asking their forgiveness. Oddly, it was not at a time when he was campaigning, and no members of the press were present. Also, when George metaphorically stepped out of the schoolhouse door and apologized to Vivian Malone and James Hood, that unprecedented action received minimal mention in the press. All three accepted his apology. Their response showed magnanimity, especially on the part of Jackson; he chose to accept and forgive, though it was doubtful that he could forget.

Would integration ever have come about naturally? Was forced integration better or worse for both sides—blacks and whites? In response to these questions, Wallace acknowledged that he doesn't know. "Nobody knows," he said, without volunteering a guess or making any speculations. While his statement is true, experts agree that Wallace knew all along that he'd never be successful in stopping integration.

The issue was not moot. Since only forced integration

would work, at least in the South and probably in other parts of the country, it was certainly better for blacks. Now, they had new job opportunities, and they could drink from public water fountains, use any restrooms, and shop anywhere they pleased. As for whites, it may have been better for them, too. In the past, especially in small businesses, many white shop owners did not hire blacks or solicit their business. Sometimes this was simply because of fear of reprisal from their racist white brethren. With integration, however, they no longer had that fear; they just followed the law, hiring anyone they chose and accepting as customers whomever sought their services or purchased their wares. Economically, it gave shop owners a boost and they were quick to take advantage of that fact.

In the long run, both races benefitted. Through interaction, fears were alleviated, barriers came down as people had the opportunity to get to know one another, and inroads were made in tolerance and understanding. It provided a chance for blacks and whites to broaden their horizons and let the United States become the melting pot it was designed to be.

If George Corley Wallace had his life to live over, what would he do? Would his life experiences have made him take a different tack? George had several brushes with death—spinal meningitis, close calls in World War II, and an almost fatal injury from a would-be assassin's bullet. He admitted that he had learned from those experiences, especially being shot. "After that," he said, biting his lower lip, "I got more compassionate for the less fortunate." His eyes glistened as he reflected, "I used to be able to shower, and shave, and dress in fifteen minutes. Now—" his voice drifted off, "I think more about others with handicaps." Losing the governor's race to John Patterson in 1958 might have been disappointing, and ending his political career in 1987 must have been traumatic. It was easy to see, though, that losing his independence was the hardest thing George Wallace ever had to endure.

No matter how hard biographers may try, it is difficult to unravel the enigma of the man once dubbed "The Fighting Little Judge." Can George Wallace the politician be separated from George Wallace the man? That's unlikely. His entire life—in youth, in maturity, and even as a senior citizen—has been focused on politics. Although in public he was surrounded by people and able to respond to their desires and their needs almost to the point of reading their minds, in private, he seemed to shy away from highly personal contacts. Sometimes, this caused family unity to be lacking. The consummate politician always put politics first. In some ways, George was a loner, a man who walked to the beat of his own drummer. Now, he's still a loner; in addition, his deafness isolates him. Even with others around him, he's often alone.

Still, he was not unbending. After careful consideration of a stand, anytime it was politically expedient, George changed. When a certain course of action was in order, George adjusted. This was evidenced on March 10, 1995, commemorating the anniversary of the infamous Selma to Montgomery March thirty years earlier. That time, Wallace was adamant about keeping Negroes from voting. Ironically, Vivian Malone had helped change that. The black student Wallace had attempted to bar from the University of Alabama with his famous stand in the schoolhouse door had not only graduated from the school, but she had become responsible for getting many Southern blacks registered to vote. As executive director of the Voter Education Project, that was her job.

This time, thirty years later, any blacks who wanted to vote had long-since made themselves eligible; registrars' lists were filled with their names. Also, on this 1995 commemorative occasion, there were no Billy clubs or beatings. In fact, Wallace himself met Joseph Lowery, the same man who led the marchers in 1965, and was now president of the Southern Christian Leadership Conference. The two shook hands at the City of St. Jude on West Fairview Avenue and Wallace welcomed Lowery and his followers warmly. Martin Luther King, Jr., probably would have been shocked, but he would have been gratified to see such unprecedented racial unity in Montgomery, Alabama. At least some aspects of the dream he gave his life for had come true.

Regardless of the fact that George Wallace did not accomplish all that he wanted during his four terms as governor (five, including Lurleen's), he was proud that during his last term he persuaded large industry to locate in the state. He also bragged there was "no scandal in my administration. I want to be remembered as a passionate leader, the Education Governor; I established a Medical School in Mobile at the University of South Alabama; a super computer in Huntsville—all four-year public colleges tie into it—and a two-year college system. Also," he moved back in time, "free textbooks for those who couldn't afford them." (This referred to high schools and elementary schools). Wallace was quick to add that, without free textbooks, many disadvantaged children, both black and white, might never have gotten an education.

While Wallace touted his own accomplishments, he did not criticize his successors, even though Guy Hunt was removed from the governor's office in disgrace and jailed, and Jim Folsom's honesty was questionable. George's charitable evaluation of the leadership in Alabama since he left office was that "Good men do their best." Despite all the current political problems, Wallace said there are still honest politicians and he remained optimistic about the future of the state and the country.

In his waning years, some of the former governor's time was spent doting on his children and grandchildren: his only son George, Jr., who was elected Alabama State Treasurer in 1987 on his first try and served two terms; his second child, Peggy, married to Alabama Supreme Court Judge Mark Kennedy; Bobbie Parsons, his oldest daughter; and Lee, his youngest child.

Recently, Wallace did something family-oriented that he rarely took time to do when his own children were growing up. In April, 1995, he went to St. James School to visit Peggy's son, Burns, on Grandparent's Day. Lurleen would be happy to know that. She loved children and, as governor, she worked very hard to help those who were physically challenged. She'd be especially pleased about her accomplishments in that regard now, too. Sadly, one of her own grandchildren, Lee's six-year-old son, Bryan, has Down's Syndrome. Lee cares for him at home.

Another way George spent his time was going back to where they still call him George C. On weekends, he traveled to Blue Springs, a site bearing happy childhood memories of his first dive in a swimming hole at age six, of picnicking, swimming, and horsing around with friends. In spring, summer, and early fall, in Blue Springs State Park somebody is generally having a family reunion. Since George C. knew almost all of the people in Barbour County, he felt comfortable joining any group he found there. It is there that George C. comes alive, especially when he finds a former campaigner among the celebrants. This happened recently when a man from North Carolina said he worked in Wallace's 1972 campaign. George's eyes lit up as they discussed what had happened over twenty years before. The interplay between them was exactly what Wallace needed to forget his problems. Being with people and going back to his roots never failed to refresh him.

Even when he was in his seventy-fifth year, wheelchair-bound, deaf, suffering with pain, Parkinson's disease, and failing eyesight, George Wallace still kept on keeping on. With longtime aide Elvin Stanton at his side, he continued to serve as Director of Development for Troy State University at its Montgomery campus. Accompanied by his bodyguard, Benny Maynor, who's worked for the governor since 1983, and his black companion/assistant, Eddie Holcey, who's been with him for twenty-two years, he usually spent his weekday mornings at Troy State and his afternoons at what was then the newly established Lurleen Wallace Foundation. It was a part of the George and Lurleen Wallace Center for the Study of Southern Politics in the Lurleen Wallace Office Building one block from the capitol in Montgomery. This facility, which opened May 22, 1995, has collected much memorabilia which provided a journey into the past for Alabama's former governor. On the wall was an old poster with the caption, "Keep old age pensions high, health benefits up" and "Stand up for Alabama."

Wallace was revitalized as he'd go through old photographs or the mixture of artifacts that arrived daily, ranging from a campaign button collection to a silver Aladdin's lamp cigarette lighter that belonged to Lurleen. Once concerned that all the remnants of his political career might be lost after he is gone, Wallace gloried in the fact that, thanks to the efforts of his children and his cohorts, it would be preserved for posterity. His office was recreated; his desk and chair sat in one corner and an emblematic University of Alabama elephant sat on the desk. A pair of old-fashioned boxing gloves hung behind the chair bearing a barely visible Alabama Seal. Lurleen's desk, a gift of First Lady Bobbie James, sat in an opposite corner, but the Seal on her chair, not as much used as George's, was still intact. A third corner was a recreation of the Wallace living room in Clayton. It had a claw-footed Empire style sofa upholstered in multi-striped green, red, and yellow velour. Family photos, and a pen and ink sketch of that home, hung on the wall behind. Most donations were items connected to past campaigns like buttons, photographs, and posters.

One day, though, George got a surprise when he saw something he had not seen in years, something he thought was lost. There on a side wall, hanging behind glass, was his old Army uniform from World War II. He thought it had long since been disposed of, so he was extremely pleased to discover that it had been saved.

Although space was insufficient, Director Pat Gallagher said a huge complex was in the planning stages. "The new facility, to be located on the Alabama River in the downtown business district of Montgomery, will accommodate many more exhibits in addition to information on George and Lurleen Wallace," he said. "It is also designed to be an educational facility for research in the areas of political studies, social sciences, and Southern history, all projects which warm the heart of Governor Wallace."

Unfortunately, due to inadequate funding, those plans didn't come to fruition. The facility closed in 1997. The Alabama Department of Archives and History got some of the material. What they couldn't keep was returned to the family and they offered the rest to a couple of smaller museums in Clayton and in Greenville at the Lurleen B. Wallace Community College campus. George Wallace was sorely disappointed. One of his admonitions to future generations was "Get all the education you can." Now, the Foundation wouldn't be there to help them understand the history of his reign.

Vaclav Havel, a former president of the Czech Republic, said in a Harvard commencement speech that "individual responsibility" is necessary "to safeguard democracy through active citizenship." George Wallace echoed his philosophy by advising young people to "Be good, involved citizens" and, unconcerned with political correctness, he did not hesitate to add, "Following the Lord's commandments is one way to do so." Claiming to always have had a belief in God and in the hereafter, he said being shot made him consider his beliefs more deeply. "It was a Damascus experience," he explained, "one of being born again."

Did it bring him to a true change of heart? Did he really repent his opinionated stands in the past? Does anyone know the true answers to those questions? Did George Wallace himself even know? Perhaps, not. Perhaps the focus should be on the future and the past should be forgotten.

In the end of Shakespeare's Othello, written over four centuries ago, the black Moor of Venice admits jealousy blinded him and that he did murder his wife, but he also reminds his contemporaries he is not all bad, expressing the hope that they remember that he did do some good for the state.

No man is all good or all bad. Perhaps historians of the twenty-first century and beyond would be wise, and fair, to acknowledge that, like Othello, Wallace did do some good for the state. Then, his lifelong efforts will not have been in vain.

CHAPTER THIRTY-ONE

KEEPING ON

George Wallace may not have gotten the cowboy suit and the ten-gallon hat he wanted so badly as a preschooler, but he had worn many other hats in his time, at least figuratively. It all began when he was an Alabama Senate Page. Next, he wore the cap of a high school, college and law school graduate. He had served in the U. S. Army Air Corps, been a state legislator, a judge, a father and a grandfather. And, four times as a presidential candidate, he wore the hat of a representative of conservative U.S. citizens who felt they had lost their voice. Furthermore, although opponents might find it far-fetched, had he not been shot some avid supporters believe he may have worn one more hat—the hat of the presidency.

Later, the hat he wore was one of a sick man remembering his long, controversial political career. Even with his multiple infirmities, he kept giving interviews. George Wallace, the vortical pugilist, may have been down for the count, but he wasn't out. With much difficulty he managed to communicate and purport his ideology.

One recent interview, he began with a groan, "I'm in terrible pain today; my health's not good," but he kept talking. He spent the early afternoon in his doctor's office, getting treatment for one of his frequent urinary tract infections. Yet, his eyes were bright and clear as he looked up from his custom-designed hospital bed in the master bedroom of his home. Acutely aware of his surroundings, he acknowledged every person in the room with his still strong grip of their hand. Although he answered questions cordially, at first, he couldn't concentrate. Instead, he kept asking his Executive Assistant Charles Carr to check on his net worth. He wanted his nurse, Linda Russell, right by his side. Also, he was concerned about an aide that he'd fired the day before with no provocation; apparently, he had regrets and wanted to get the man back. It was obvious that George Wallace thought he was going to die.

But he didn't. Instead, he pulled himself to an upright position and took two puffs on his Garcia Y Vega Gran Premio two-dollar cigar. Then he justified his indulgence by saying that Billy Graham, a famous evangelist he admires, told him smoking was no sin, that "God doesn't worry about things like that." After flicking ashes in a ceramic ashtray, he began vocalizing responses to written questions.

Especially at first, he gave many one or two word answers, frequently grabbing his lower right side, saying, "I'm in constant pain." Even though he can't feel below the navel and it must have been phantom pain, it was obvious that his hurting was real. As it eased up, though, he began to reply to questions in a little more detail.

Discussing the governorship, he said that trying to meet all the people's requests was one difficult part of being governor; deciding which ones should be honored was hard. But the biggest decision he had to make was whether to run for a fourth term as governor. It was easy to see why that was a problem. George Wallace had been in office a long time, he was getting older, and his health was not good. At that point, stepping aside might have been appealing. However, George was not known to take the easy way out. He did run and he won.

On some subjects, he had a lot to say. On others, he

cautiously declined comment saying, "I can't read the newspaper, only the headlines."

Although his eyesight was not good, Benny Maynor, an aide, claimed that both George's eyesight and hearing weren't as bad as he led people to believe. He illustrated his point by telling of one night he went into George's bedroom and saw him scanning the newspaper and heard his mumbled comments on its content. "He read it, all right," Maynor said. "Every section of that paper had been handled."

Another incident happened later that same night when Maynor checked on his boss about ten p.m. Since the bedroom door handle stuck, Maynor had to rattle the knob to get it to open. When he did, he found George sound asleep, or so he thought. The next day he discovered he was mistaken when George asked him, "Was that you coming into my room last night?" George was not only not asleep, but he heard the door rattling and he saw Maynor enter his room. "He's foxy," Maynor says, "he can hear and see a little; he just uses his sight and hearing selectively."

When asked about current events, George Wallace expressed definite opinions. Reflecting stands he held in the past, he said that those who were responsible for the Oklahoma City bombing "should be executed," upholding his belief in the death penalty. He also stated emphatically that he feels O.J. Simpson was "Guilty," and that chain gangs, recently reinstated in Alabama, are justified. Also, he was adamant in his approval of the recent ruling against gays in the military, calling their lifestyle "Sinful." Even though his firm stands may appear harsh to some people, his angry image is no longer prevalent. The trademark sneer wa gone; his facial expression seemed to have softened.

His expression softened even more when he spoke of Lurleen, especially when he referred to her untimely death, at age forty-three in the middle of her term as Alabama's governor, as "the biggest disappointment in my life." His eyes welled-up as he said, "She was a good governor" and called her the "best mother I ever saw at the age of eighteen." He said his fondest memories were of the birth of his children.

Yet it's unfortunate that late in life he claimed to be only "fairly close" to his family. George, Jr., who followed a political career but didn't really seem content, sometimes came to watch the ten p.m. news with his father; Lee had recently moved to Atlanta with her husband, Hugh Dye, so she wasn't around much; Peggy, married to Judge Mark Kennedy, seemed to be the closest to her father. She been instrumental in seeing that the Foundation prospered, even though the project failed. Bobbie, who may have benefited from her father's position as governor since her husband, Jim Parsons, reportedly became wealthy through investments in connection with the Emelle Toxic Waste Disposal, seemed less involved than her brother and sisters. She did visit her father occasionally, though. At any rate, all family members tend to stay away when Wallace is in a bad mood.

Because of his physical limitations, George couldn't pass the time with hobbies. In fact, Jimmy Dallas, his aide, patted the TV saying, "This is his hobby." Then he pointed to the cigar lying in the ashtray by Wallace's bed. "This and them cigars," he adds. Yet, even though restricted, George Wallace has a routine and his days are full. He awakens about eight a.m. With help, he showered, shaved, and dressed. Sometimes an interview was scheduled at nine. Following that and a light breakfast, maybe cold cereal or oatmeal, he went to Troy State University downtown. While there, he dictated fund-raising letters or chatted with faculty and honor students brought in by the college president. He said his interest there motivated him.

By 11:30, George was ready for his main meal of the day,

306

lunch. It wasn't just a meal, though. George wanted to satisfy his hunger for more than food. So, he went to places where he could be in the middle of a crowd, like Quincy's or Morrison's. Often, though, he went to Country's Barbecue, where the food is good and where he had his own table and his favorite waitress. There, the crowd was just the mixture he liked, young and old, civilian and military, rich and poor. He also liked the loud country music that livened things up. To be right in the hub of activity, George would eat the potato salad, beans, and bar-b-que and wait until another day to get other of his favorite foods—prime rib, or simply a hamburger doused with ketchup, and side dishes such as snap beans and beets.

If he was recognized and restaurant patrons came over to his table, George was sure to linger long enough for dessert— egg custard pie. Lunch might take an hour and a half. If other diners didn't stop by, he just settled for the attention of the manager and he and his aides left soon after eating.

Next on the agenda was going to another place that George said gave him motivation. His afternoon stop, where he usually spent from one to three p.m., was The George and Lurleen Wallace Center for the Study of Southern Politics. Although he liked viewing all the artifacts reminding him of the past, especially the wallet with the photo of Lurleen that he carried through two other marriages, he really perked up when he had an interview, and many were scheduled at the museum. Oddly, whether his interviewer was friend or foe, he seemed to respond and enjoy talking about politics. With his good memory, he could argue issues point for point. He didn't seem to mind the bantering; in fact, such disagreements obliviously invigorated him. In any case, George Wallace said that it was Troy State and the museum that kept him going.

What else keeps him going? Wallace said it was his faith. What are his religious beliefs? Who does he say that he is? He says that he sees himself as a man who was an honest governor who advises young politicians to "Be sober and honest." He calls himself "a born-again Christian" citing unusual things that happened to him that influenced his life such as "being shot, being elected governor, and surviving World War II," in that order. When asked if he had any dark secrets, however, he didn't reply. In fact, he refused to tell anything that nobody knows about him. He simply said, "God knows my sins."

After he leaves the museum, George frequently visits Lurleen's grave in Greenwood Cemetery, not far from Hank Williams' grave in Oakwood Cemetery. Although it's an emotional experience, it's probably also a catharsis for him, the one place where he feels regret for any real or imagined neglect of Lurleen. Maybe in the stillness of the graveyard he can admit his human failings and, in his own way, say that he's sorry.

Next, George may go home. Sometimes he'll stay there and settle for a light snack at night. One thing that's interesting is that he often has food sent by friends and neighbors, especially cakes, pies, and other desserts, but he will never eat it. Instead, he just tells his staff members, "Put that in the kitchen; I'll eat it later." Unless they eat the food, it goes to waste.

According to Maynor, they once tried hiring a cook and that didn't work, either. Wallace just looked at the well-presented plate of carefully prepared chicken, market-fresh vegetables, and potatoes au gratin garnished with a sprig of parsley, shoved it aside, and said, "Let's go get a hamburger from Hardees," and out they went.

Other times, they no sooner get home than George gets restless and wants to go get a hot dog and a Coke. In fact, Eddie tells of one time that they had just eaten and, although it was seven p.m. on Friday and the hot dog stand he liked,

Chris's in downtown Montgomery, was in a section of town winos frequent on weekend nights, Wallace insisted.

"He wanted to go and he was going." Maynor shook his head. "He has a set mind." The loyalty of his aide gave way to honest criticism. "He wants to go to be in the middle and once he gets talking with folks, it's hard to get him to leave. He can sit there an hour just sipping on a Coke," Maynor said.

Such stubbornness testifies to the fact that George Wallace can be hard to deal with, so much so that several of Wallace's aides find it difficult to remain as a member of his staff. Although he may be incapacitated, George is clearly still in charge.

If it's true that Wallace is in charge of his staff, it's even more true that he is in charge of any statements attributed to him—personal or political. Although interviewers' questions are written, in letters large enough for him to read, answers are always verbal. George responds in a cracked but strong voice. Nobody answers for him. He needs no prompting; the words he chooses are his own. He's clear and straightforward in his opinions, too. For example, he sees the moral decline in this country as serious and says the only way to change moral values is "to have a spiritual revival." Maybe his favorite Bible verse, John 3: 16, "For God so loved the world that he gave His only begotten Son," illustrates to him that God can save the world, and that a spiritual revival is possible.

Politically, George believes that nowadays all candidates are running on his 1968 platform espousing what he proposed almost thirty years ago. He sees his ideas reflected in the Contract with America; the stand against crime; welfare reform; and a general shift to the right philosophically. Proof of this can be seen in many of Wallace's past speeches, too.

As for politics in Alabama, Wallace feels that the Democrat Party is weak now and he says, "It looks like the state's going Republican." In fact, George himself said if no other candidate is acceptable to him, he would vote Republican in 1996, if Robert Dole is their choice for president. His son, George, Jr., also indicated that he might change parties. He said in July, 1995, that if he ran for office again it would probably be on the Republican ticket.

George Wallace also said that all politicians are now held to higher standards than they were in the past because "people are tired of dishonesty in government." If that statement is true, newcomers to the political scene may have to redirect their priorities.

Now, George's days are usually filled with activity, unless he does not feel well enough to go out. Then he spends his time in a bed that cost thirty thousand dollars and is supposed to have adjustments that make him more comfortable but often is of no help. If he's up and about, he wanders through a house that's clean but uncared for in that its rooms need painting and the furniture needs repair. In his den for instance, a badly tattered green, blue, and tan sofa is backed up to a wall with bookshelves that have paint peeling off them. In the kitchen, the round Formica table is a remnant of a past era.

One wall in an office next to his bedroom gives a touch of warmth to the house, though. It is filled with photographs of Wallace with dignitaries, such as Wallace posing with several presidents—Nixon, Ford, and Kennedy. Also, there is a picture with Wallace and Pope Paul II. In the center of this wall is a sentimental letter from Lee, when she was about seven years old, telling her father that one day she plans to follow in her parents' footsteps and be governor.

Also, in the hallway are many photos of his family that add a homey touch. No matter what is, or isn't, in the house, though, George probably doesn't notice its austereness. Anyhow, he never did worry about things; if he does notice that his home has no frills and could stand refurbishing, he probably doesn't care.

His unconcern with his home's appearance is reflected in the fact that he doesn't mind having interviewers come there. Sometimes he has one-that he really doesn't want, too. That happened recently. It seems that Wallace's aide, Jimmy Dallas, who had been with the governor three years, may have felt he had earned a little authority. So, one day, he responded to a telephone call from Cibacuyo Agueybana, a man who said he was making a documentary movie on Wallace's shooting, by granting the man an interview. Maynor was befuddled about the incident because, although he had called and cancelled the interview, the man and a female companion still showed up at 9 a.m. on a Saturday morning and parked their beat-up car bearing a New York license tag right in front of the house. Wallace was upset and grumbled that he didn't want to do the interview.

Maynor said, "It's up to you, Governor. Do you want me to send him away?"

Evidently, Southern hospitality made the governor feel guilty about not honoring the promise, so he let him in. He didn't stay more than fifteen minutes, though, exiting with the heavy-set blonde beside him. The bearded man left in his car full of suitcases, with caps on the dash and in the back window, loudly proclaiming, "I'll be back."

Even though Wallace spent a quarter of an hour that day for a project that may go nowhere, he does seem to be conscious of time. Although he wears a nice wrist watch, he frequently asks, "What time is it?" Perhaps the gold face of the watch makes the dial hard to read or he might just be accustomed to having others keep track of time for him. On the other hand, after years of having every minute scheduled in order to fulfill the rigorous demands of a governor's life, slackening his pace is almost impossible. It's probably hard for him to realize that now his time is his own and he can go where he pleases and do what he wants.

He did say that if he had his life to live over there would be one thing he'd do differently.

There is somewhere that he would not go—to Maryland.

Where he would or would not go is one thing. What he would still like to do is another. People considering what George Wallace, an individual who has been both hated and revered, would want to do in his final years on earth might come to a wrong conclusion. The answer he gives could be surprising.

The man who once screamed, "Segregation now; segregation tomorrow; and segregation forever, and later regretted it; the man who was a Democrat but saw not "a dime's worth of difference" between Democrats and Republicans, and now admitted that, under certain circumstances, he'd vote Republican; the man who vowed to "Stand up for America," and now is physically unable to do so, said in July of 1995 that there was only one simple thing he still wanted to do.

"I want to live a little longer."

George Corley Wallace left this world for the next September 13, 1998, a few weeks after his seventy-ninth birthday and thirty years after his wife Lurleen succumbed to cancer. The man whose name stood for segregation and racial hatred at one time had recreated himself and, in death, was lauded as a political legend who had overcome prejudices and redeemed his past.

Although his role in politics faded in his declining health and retirement, his career symbolized some of the most turbulent days in United States history. Ironically, his stand in

312

GEORGE WALLACE: AN ENIGMA

the schoolhouse door boomeranged. It angered black citizens and the U.S. government to the point of taking action to achieve equal rights. It sparked a fire that could not be put out, causing an immediate and intense push for integration. Had Wallace not taken the stance he did, integration may have been delayed for decades. As he was forced to stop blocking the entrance to the University of Alabama, all he could do was watch as his efforts to prevent Vivian Malone and James Hood from entering produced the exact opposite of the results he intended. The white-dominated Old South bent to racial integration.

Wallace's defense was that he did what he believed to be right at the time. However, he changed with the times. He had the courage to admit when he was wrong and to give a message of reconciliation, a characteristic of a statesman, rather than one of a politician.

Governor Fob James honored his passing with a state holiday. In the Capitol building, Wallace, in a gray suit and red tie, lay in state twenty-four hours while an estimated twenty-five thousand mourners, blacks equaling whites, paid their respects as they passed the open casket where his frail body lay. One person commented, "Alabama was proud to have George Wallace as a son, and Wallace was proud to be an Alabamian."

Former Governor John Patterson and Governor Fob James attended the services in the Memorial Old House Chamber of the Alabama Capitol Building. In paying tribute to Wallace, James touted his achievements. "Wallace raised money to send Bibles to Bangladesh," he said of a little-known fact. Then he called Wallace, "a man with warmth, a historian who understood our own revolution, slavery, and the Civil War. He was born in the Depression, and lived through World War II and the Civil Rights era. He also understood the importance of reconciliation. He took pride in his family, the state and its citizens."

When Wallace was removed to go to the church, almost two hundred thousand people, including state employees and other citizens, respectfully watched as a white hearse led the funeral procession from the Capitol to the First United Methodist Church in ninety-two-degree heat. Part of the state funeral was conducted by retired pastor Charles Carter Shades. Speakers bypassed his career and the attempted assassination and focused on his devotion to his family, his sense of humor and commitment to politics.

Later, the procession formed again for the drive to Greenwood Cemetery. There, Wallace was laid to rest next to his beloved first wife Lurleen in the Circle of Life section.

Perhaps the most impacting comment about George Wallace came from Reverend Franklin Graham, evangelist Billy Graham's son who led the services. He summed up Wallace's change of heart by saying, "I believe if the governor were alive, he would want to be remembered for this," he paused, then offered a variation of Wallace's famous quote: "Jesus Christ today, Jesus Christ tomorrow, Jesus Christ forever."

THE LAST WORD FROM WALLACE

Biographies are elusive portrayals of people. Sometimes they are authentic; other times, they stray from the truth. Although twelve biographies have been written about me, many make harsh judgments, painting a picture of a man who is a bigoted racist with only his own interests at heart.

I hope that man is not me. If history shows me in any favorable light, I hope it will be that I had a sense of fairness, a fairness not based on race, or color, or creed, but on humanity. I hope that it will transcend issues of petty differences and extend to the spirit of the Declaration of Independence, drafted by Thomas Jefferson, that "all men are created equal" and have "unalienable rights" of "Life, Liberty, and the pursuit of Happiness."

My life has been dedicated to such principles. Despite opinions to the contrary, I have tried, in my own way, as a lawyer, legislator, judge, governor, and as a presidential candidate, to appeal to man's best instincts to help those unable, or powerless, to help themselves.

I feel that this biography, by Mary S. Palmer, probably is the most unbiased, objective presentation of my true life story. While it is critical of my deficiencies, it also acknowledges my objectives as a person as well as a politician.

As a human, with faults, I admit inadequacies and inequities, even failures. This book is honest; it neither claims that I am better, or worse, than most leaders. It evaluates me in a fair way, as an imperfect human being with both good and bad qualities.

My successes or failures need not be appraised by man. God is my only true judge. I do hope, nevertheless, that this book does show me to be a creature of God who did whatever possible to make this world a better place because I lived.

George C. Wallace

Wallace Gravesite Marker

THE AUTHOR

Mary S. Palmer is an established author and member of the adjunct faculties at several colleges, where she teaches English, including Faulkner State Community College, Faulkner University and Huntingdon College.

Throughout her writing career, she has published books in a variety of genres—science-fiction, true crime, novels, fantasy and biographies. She has also authored two play productions, award-winning short stories and poetry.

Mary has a BA in English (cum laude) and a minor in French. She also obtained a MA in English with a Concentration in Creative Writing—the first person to receive the degree with the Concentration in Creative Writing at the University of South Alabama.

Mary is an avid traveler who loves adventure. She has visited every state in the U.S. and every continent except Antarctica. Wherever her travels take her, she seeks out people to engage and interact with and loves to hear their stories. Drawing from those experiences, she weaves different elements into her writing.

In between speaking engagements, interviews, book signings and presentations, Mary is currently working on a few new, exciting projects including a mystery thriller, *Fatal Entanglements*, and a novella, *Joe and Jo*, both of which are under consideration by a publisher. Also in the works is *A Clean Slate* coauthored with Loretta Theriot.

PUBLISHED WORKS

- *Time Will Tell* (Second Edition) Release 2016
- *Time Was*—2015

- *Question of Time*—2014
- *Chance for Redemption*—2013
- *Baiting the Hook* coauthored with David Wilton—2012
- *To Catch a Fish* coauthored with David Wilton—2012
- *Time Will Tell*—2012
- *Quest for Forgiveness* coauthored with James McEnery—2004
- *False Gods* coauthored with Elizabeth Coffman—2006
- *The Callings* coauthored with Loretta Theriot—2002
- *MemoraMOBILEia: Alabama Gulf Coast Potpourri* coauthored with Elizabeth Coffman—1993
-

AWARDS AND HONORS

- *Raisin' Cain*, First Place Award for Tourism Writing sponsored by the Southeastern Literary Tourism Initiative and cosponsored with the Alabama Tourism Department. *Raisin' Cain* was mentioned on the floor of the House of Representatives by Congressman Bradley Byrne and became a permanent part of the Congressional Record—2014
- Selected as a member of the Baldwin Writers Group and the Baldwin Five Critique Group—2012 to present
- *Joe and Jo,* Third Place, Screenplay, The Eugene Walter Writer's Fest with the Department of English of the University of South Alabama—2005
- Selected for *Who's Who in America*—2005
- Selected for *Marquis' Who's Who Among America's Teachers*—
- 2002
-

REFERENCES

In addition to the below listed books, an extensive reference list is included on the website:

www.GeorgeWallaceBook.com

PHOTO CREDITS

Alabama State credit: Alabama Department of Archives and History, Montgomery, Alabama

U.S.A. credit: Mary Palmer Collection, The Doy Leale McCall Rare Book and Manuscript Library, University of South Alabama, Mobile, Alabama

BIBLIOGRAPHY

The Advertiser Journal. Montgomery, Alabama. 24 December 1967.

The Atlanta Constitution. Atlanta, Georgia. 14 June 1968.

Buchen, Charlotte. *The Arizona Republic*. Tuscon, Arizona. 28 August 1968.

Cavett, Dick. "The Dick Cavett Show." Interview with George Wallace. Winter, 1975.

Dillin, John. *The Christian Science Monitor*. Summer, 1972.

House, Jack. *Lady of Courage.* Montgomery, Alabama: League Press, 1969.

Jones, Bill. *The Wallace Story.* Northport, Alabama. The American Southern Publishing Company.

Lane, Mark. *Rush to Judgment.* New York: Holt, Rinehart and Winston, 1966.

Meriwether, Louise. *Don't Ride the Bus on Monday: The Rosa Parks Story.* Englewood Cliffs, New Jersey: Prentice-Hall, Inc., 1973.

Medical Advisory Reports from Holy Cross Hospital, Silver Spring, Maryland. 15 May 1972 and 7 July 1972.

The Mobile Press Register. Mobile, Alabama. Issues from 1963-1981.

Parade Magazine. 6 January 1974 and 10 March 1974.

Made in the USA
Charleston, SC
07 August 2016